The U.S. SUPREME COURT and the ELECTORAL PROCESS

Edited by
DAVID K. RYDEN

Foreword
LEE EPSTEIN

GEORGETOWN UNIVERSITY PRESS / WASHINGTON, D.C.

Georgetown University Press, Washington, D.C.
© 2000 by Georgetown University Press. All rights reserved.
Printed in the United States of America

10 9 8 7 6 5 4 3 2 1   2000

This volume is printed on acid-free offset book paper.

Library of Congress Cataloging-in-Publication Data

The U.S. Supreme Court and the electoral process / edited by David K.
    Ryden.
        p. cm
    Includes bibliographical references and index.
      ISBN 0-87840-805-3 (cloth : acid-free paper) —
    ISBN 0-87840-806-1 (paper : acid-free paper)
        1. Election law—United States. 2. Representative government and
    representation—United States. 3. United States. Supreme Court.
    I. Title: US Supreme Court and the electoral process.
    II. Ryden, David K.

KF4886.A5 U17 2000
342.73′07—dc21   00-026366

Contents

III

The Court and Political Reform: Friend or Foe? 165

IV

The Court, the Constitution, and Election Law:
Merging Practice and Theory 243

Contributors

Douglas J. Amy is a professor in the department of politics at Mount Holyoke College. He has written extensively on alternative election systems and brings a special expertise to issues surrounding the American two-party system and multiparty alternatives. He is the author of *Real Choices/New Voices: The Case for Proportional Representation Elections in the United States*, published by Columbia University Press.

Cynthia Grant Bowman received a Ph.D. in political science from Columbia University and a J.D. from Northwestern University School of Law, where she currently is a professor of law. She taught political science at Illinois Institute of Technology and practiced law at Jenner & Block in Chicago from 1983 to 1988, where she participated in the litigation of political patronage cases and was involved in the drafting of Detailed Hiring Provisions to ensure that hiring for the city of Chicago occurred on nonpolitical grounds.

Lee Epstein is professor of political science at Washington University in Saint Louis, Missouri. She received her Ph.D. from Emory University in 1983. She is the author of *Conservatives in Court* (1985), coauthor of *The Supreme Court and Legal Change* (1992), and *Constitutional Law for a Changing America* (1995), and editor of *Contemplating Courts* (1995). Her articles on the Supreme Court, interest groups, and related topics have appeared in political science and law journals, including the *American Political Science Review*, the *American Journal of Political Science*, and the *Journal of Politics*.

Michael Fitts is the Robert G. Fuller Professor of Law at the University of Pennsylvania School of Law. Previously, he served for four years in the Office of Legal Counsel in U.S. Department of Justice, which serves as outside counsel to the president.

Stephen E. Gottlieb is professor of law at Albany Law School, and he has also taught at Cleveland-Marshall School of Law and Marquette University Law School. He has written and edited four books, including

Jurisprudence: Cases and Materials (1993) and *Public Values in Constitutional Law* (1993), and has published articles in the *New York University Law Review, Yale Law and Policy Review, Hasting Law Journal,* and *Boston University Law Review,* among others. A veteran of the legal services program and the Peace Corps, Professor Gottlieb represented a group of political scientists as *amici curiae* before the Supreme Court in *Tashjian v. Republican Party of the State of Connecticut* (1986), a seminal case defining the power of political parties.

Daniel H. Lowenstein is professor of law at the UCLA School of Law. He is the author of *Election Law: Cases and Materials* ((1995), as well as countless articles in the *Harvard Law Review, UCLA Law Review, Harvard Journal of Law & Policy,* the *Journal of Law and Politics,* and others. He authored the California Democratic Party's *amicus curiae* brief in *U.S. Term Limits v. Thornton* (1994), and his extensive practical political background includes legal consultation to private clients regarding election law, active involvement in several California ballot initiatives, service as Special Counsel and Deputy Secretary of the State of California, and consultant in a variety of capacities to federal, state, and local governments.

Nancy Maveety is professor of political science at Tulane University. She authored one of the definitive works on the Supreme Court's representation jurisprudence—*Representation Rights and the Burger Years,* published by Michigan Press (1991)—and also published *Justice Sandra Day O'Connor: Strategist on the Supreme Court* (Rowman & Littlefield, 1996).

Paul R. Petterson is assistant professor of political science at Central Connecticut State University. He has done extensive research and writing on the legal status of political parties before the Supreme Court. He has had articles published in *Polity* and the *Journal of Public Service and Outreach.*

Jeff Polet is associate professor of political science at Malone College in Canton, Ohio. He has been published in *The Social Science Journal* and *Crisis* magazine and has served as a political commentator for several media outlets. He brings a strong theoretical bent to the study of constitutional issues.

David K. Ryden received his Ph.D. at the Catholic University of America and is assistant professor of political science and the Towsley Research Scholar at Hope College in Holland, Michigan. He holds his J.D. from the University of Minnesota Law School and has previously practiced law as a civil litigation attorney in the Minneapolis/St. Paul area. He is the author of *Representation in Crisis: The Constitution, Interest Groups, and Political Parties* (1996).

Howard A. Scarrow is professor of political science at the State University of New York at Stony Brook. He is widely published on the subject of political representation, with articles appearing in a variety of major political science journals. He is the author of *Parties, Elections, and Representation in the State of New York*, and he co-edited *Representation and Districting Issues*.

Bradley A. Smith is associate professor of law at Capital University Law School in Columbus, Ohio. He received his J.D. from Harvard Law School and has had articles appear in numerous academic and popular journals, including the *Yale Law Journal, Georgetown Law Journal, Harvard Journal of Legislation*, and the *Wall Street Journal*. Professor Smith was recently nominated by President Clinton for a seat on the Federal Election Commission. The nomination was awaiting action by the full Senate as this book went to press.

Foreword

Lee Epstein

Let me begin with an experiment readers can easily conduct: Go to a library shelf, pull off a constitutional law casebook, and count the number of Supreme Court cases that involve matters of elections and representation. If your results are anything like mine, dozens will appear on your list—from cases decided well before the turn of the century, such as *United States v. Reese*, 92 U.S. 214 (1876), to Rehnquist Court decisions in *Board of Education of Kiryas Joel Village School District v. Grumet*, 512 U.S. 687 (1994), and *U.S. Term Limits v. Thornton*, 514 U.S. 779 (1994).

Now consider the location of these cases. Again, if your findings are similar to mine, no part of the book is untouched; the cases you find likely involve the president's ability to make appointments,[1] the judiciary's authority to resolve disputes,[2] and Congress's power to enforce amendments,[3] to name just a few—and not even to mention the obvious (such as material on discrimination and voting).

By now I suppose you have discovered the point of this experiment: It is my way of suggesting that the Supreme Court, which we still occasionally deem the "apolitical" branch of government, has played a major role in defining the way our most political of processes works—and has been doing so since its formative years. Yet scholars (and perhaps the justices themselves) rarely piece together the many parts of the election and representational puzzle. Cases involving reapportionment usually end up in the "Voting and Representation" chapter; campaign finance litigation decisions may appear in "Freedom of Speech"; cases about qualifications for membership in the legislature likely fall under "Congressional Powers."

The point that *The U.S. Supreme Court and the Electoral Process* drives home with force is that although these sorts of cases may involve distinct substantive issues, at their core, they implicate fundamental notions of representation in democratic societies. Moreover, when scholars and judges fail to take account of this fact—when they treat these cases in isolation, as they so often do—their writings may be seriously flawed: replete with contradictory assumptions and "solutions" that may be impractical or unwise to implement.

Mere recognition of this fact, on the part of editor David Ryden and his talented contributors, makes this volume worthy of careful consideration. Ryden and company go well beyond simple recognition, however; they attempt to continue where judges and other scholars have left off. They ask the hard questions—ranging from whether it is realistic to expect judges to develop a coherent and integrated theory of representation to the extent to which current doctrine adequately solves contemporary problems regarding the role the Supreme Court should (or should not) be playing in this overarching legal area.

Obviously, no single volume can provide comprehensive responses to all of the relevant questions—but this one comes close. At the very least, because Ryden did not steer his contributors toward particular answers, we readers are treated to a range of plausible responses. Consider the question of whether the Supreme Court should develop a theory or jurisprudence of representation. To Nancy Maveety, the answer is probably yes; in fact, she argues that the Burger Court at least had developed such an approach. To Daniel Lowenstein, however, the answer is probably no. As the title of his chapter ("The Supreme Court Has No Theory of Politics—And Be Thankful for Small Favors") makes clear, he is entirely skeptical of whether the Court can or even should develop a representational jurisprudence.

Ultimately, I am impressed with *The U.S. Supreme Court and the Electoral Process* not simply because I walked away a more informed scholar but also because I believe Ryden and his colleagues have produced a volume that will be useful to the very actors who must decide these cases: our nation's judges and justices. Whether they agree with Maveety, Lowenstein, or scholars whose opinions fall somewhere in between may be less important than the fodder this volume gives them to chew as they confront the difficult, yet critical, questions that electoral disputes raise.

Such issues will be apparent to most readers. What may be less so are the implications *The U.S. Supreme Court and the Electoral Process* has for judges elsewhere. To be sure, American jurists continue to struggle with matters of representation on an annual basis; the decisions in *Buckley v. American Constitutional Law Foundation,* 119 S. Ct. 636 (1999), and *Department of Commerce v. U.S. House of Representatives,*

119 S. Ct. 765 (1999), provide particularly relevant examples. U.S. judges, however, need not make "new law out of whole cloth"[4]—which is exactly the task that confronts many of their counterparts in emerging democracies all over the world, especially in Eastern Europe. A few recent examples suffice to make the point:

- The Constitutional Court in Armenia ruled that it lacked jurisdiction to hear a case involving voting discrepancies in the 1996 presidential election.
- The Azerbaijan Constitutional Court confirmed the reelection of the country's incumbent president amid charges of voting rigging.
- The Bulgarian Constitutional Court, at the request of a governmental prosecutor, may consider the legitimacy of a referendum conducted in 1946 that abolished the monarchy. It has been suggested that the referendum was invalid because the vote was held while the republic was under Soviet occupation.
- The Hungarian Constitutional Court struck down a legislative rule that required political parties to capture at least 15 seats to form a parliamentary faction.
- The Constitutional Court in Russia ruled that President Boris Yeltsin was in his second term of office and thus could not run for reelection in 2000.
- The Slovakian Constitutional Court held that the Minister of the Interior had violated the constitution by interfering with a referendum on direct elections.
- The Constitutional Court of Ukraine decided that certain provisions of an electoral law—challenged as granting parties too many rights and individuals too few—were unconstitutional.

The list is practically endless, but the general point should not be missed: How these courts answer questions pertaining to representation and the electoral process may have important implications for their own credibility and legitimacy, not to mention the ongoing democratization efforts in their nations.

If these courts are looking for guidance, as so many scholars say they are, then *The U.S. Supreme Court and the Electoral Process* is the ideal place to start. It may not provide all the answers, but at the very least it clearly lays out the sorts of disputes they will, in all likelihood, eventually confront and the options available for resolving them.

ENDNOTES

1. *Buckley v. Valeo*, 424 U.S. 1 (1976).
2. *Colgrove v. Green*, 328 U.S. 549 (1946).
3. *South Carolina v. Katzenbach*, 383 U.S. 301 (1966).
4. Walter F. Murphy, *Elements of Judicial Strategy* (Chicago: University of Chicago Press, 1964).

··· 1 ···

The U.S. Supreme Court, the Electoral Process, and the Quest for Representation: An Overview

DAVID K. RYDEN

On January 12, 1999, the U.S. Supreme Court announced its decision in *Buckley v. American Constitutional Law Foundation (ACLF)*, 119 S. Ct. 636 (1999), rejecting efforts by the state of Colorado to rein in the use of ballot initiatives in its state elections. By a 6–3 vote, the Court in *Buckley* struck down a statute that imposed various restraints on the gathering of petitions that sought to put a measure on the ballot for a direct vote by the state's citizens. Those regulations included registration and reporting requirements, as well as requirements that circulators of petitions be registered voters of the state of Colorado and that they wear identification badges. The Court rejected the regulations in their entirety, concluding that they violated the "core political speech" rights of initiative proponents. The majority opined that petition circulation involved "interactive communication concerning political change" that was protected by the First Amendment freedom of speech and held that the Colorado statute was an impermissible interference with this right.

Two weeks later, in *Department of Commerce v. U.S. House of Representatives*, 119 S. Ct. 765 (1999), the Court vetoed the Clinton Administration's plan to implement statistical sampling techniques in the upcoming 2000 census. A narrowly divided Court interpreted the Census Act of 1976 as explicitly prohibiting statistical sampling methods as a more accurate means of counting population for purposes of reapportioning U.S. House of Representative seats among the states.

These two seemingly unrelated cases together provide a convenient introduction to the themes of this book. Both decisions bring home in stark fashion the largely overlooked reality that the decisions of the

1

United States Supreme Court in the realm of elections, politics, and representation have a tangible and formative effect on how the electoral process works and how effectively it satisfies its democratic objectives. These two decisions are profoundly significant less for their particulars than for their general implications and what they reveal about the Court's role in the broad realm of law and politics. These cases are only the most recent illustrations of the underappreciated significance of the Supreme Court as primary shaper of the electoral system. They are a two-pronged reminder of the Court's determinative influence over the practical operation of the political process.

The *Buckley* decision bears on the very nature and extent of representative government itself. The initiative process is the closest approximation of direct democracy. It is being invoked with increasing frequency in states across the country as the public becomes increasingly skeptical of politics, parties, and representative government. The growing popularity of these initiatives is one of the most notable developments in recent American electoral politics. Twenty-four states and the District of Columbia have provisions for putting policy issues directly to their citizens for a vote. During the 1998 election cycle, there were a record number of initiatives nationwide at the local, county, and state levels. In short, resort to initiatives is becoming pervasive.

Nor are the matters decided via the ballot of trifling importance. On the contrary, they constitute some of the most problematic and troublesome issues of our society. In the most recent set of elections, there were ballot initiatives on such highly charged issues as the legal rights of gay men and lesbians, the propriety of affirmative action, and English as an official language. Ballot proposals were used to pass campaign finance reform, establish term limits, reconstitute tax systems, and reshape education programs. Still other initiatives sought to legalize physician-assisted suicide, medical use of marijuana, and gambling within states. Thus, when the Court ventured into the territory of initiatives and referenda, it was taking on an increasingly consequential means of making public policy.

Similarly, the *Department of Commerce* ruling has potentially dramatic ramifications for partisan politics for decades to come. The population numbers from the decennial census are used to set the numbers of lawmakers each state sends to serve in the U.S. House of Representatives. The political implications of the census results, for party politics and the fight for control over the most representative of lawmaking bodies, are obvious. Conventional methods of conducting the census have traditionally resulted in undercounting because millions of low-income minorities and urban dwellers slip through the cracks. Statistical sampling techniques likely would add to the voting rolls large numbers of people who belong to demographic groups that vote Democratic. The anticipated practical effect would be to position Democrats to make substantial gains in the House of Representatives in upcoming elections. Hence, the Court's decision precluding sampling is central to the make-up of the most representative institution of our government.

RATIONALE

A long line of cases decided by the Court have sharply influenced the functioning of electoral politics. The seminal decision in *Buckley v. Valeo*, 424 U.S. 1 (1976), was largely responsible for the system of financing campaigns that has existed since the 1970s. Its consequences—some intended and some not—have produced a system with which few people are pleased. Wealthy candidates spend millions of dollars in furtherance of their own campaigns, interest groups rival parties in their presence and influence on campaigns, and the costs of campaigns have spiraled precipitously upward. It was "deja vu all over again" in *Colorado Republican Federal Campaign Committee v. Federal Elections Commission*, 518 U.S. 604 (1996), which removed certain campaign spending restrictions applicable to political parties. The upshot was an unprecedented deluge of "soft money" (unregulated donations to party committees, ostensibly for strengthening partisan organizations) in the past two election cycles. The consequences of that decision will be felt for years, either in the form of unparalleled spending or as the catalyst that finally leads to an overhaul of the campaign financing system.

In *Baker v. Carr*, 369 U.S. 186 (1962), the Supreme Court cast aside its long-standing practice of avoiding "political questions" and leaped into the thicket of redistricting and reapportionment. Its "one person, one vote" doctrine and vote dilution cases over time led to a highly sophisticated, computer-driven process for drawing electoral districts. Race-based redistricting flourished, contributing substantially to the sharp rise in the numbers of African Americans and Hispanics elected to Congress; those changes were accompanied by the unintended consequence of an overall loss of Democratic seats and may even have played a part in the historic Republican takeover of Congress in 1994. More recent Court decisions narrowing race-conscious redistricting have created difficulties for the politicians responsible for crafting district lines. Once again, the defining characteristics of the current redistricting process, and the controversies surrounding reapportionment, can be traced to the Supreme Court's involvement.

In this decade alone, the Supreme Court has repeatedly found itself in the center of major electoral questions. It found the imposition of term limits on U.S. Senators and House members unconstitutional, effectively nullifying the most popular and widespread grassroots political reform in decades. The Court has essentially outlawed political patronage—the effect of which, many observers would argue, has irreparably damaged partisan organizations' governing and campaign capabilities. At the same time, the Court has upheld state laws making it virtually impossible for minor or new parties to effectively challenge the two-party status quo. It has considered the constitutionality of racial, partisan, and religious redistricting and has barred ballot initiatives limiting civil liberties.

The point is not to criticize or support the merits of any of these decisions, nor to rue or celebrate their consequences. Rather, it is to debunk the Supreme Court's image as politically remote or insulated; it is to press the reality that the Court is extremely influential in molding the nitty-gritty of real-world politics. Indeed, any time Congress or state legislatures effect changes in elections, parties, or other aspects of representative politics, the Court invariably wields the ultimate check. The Court's delineation of the rights, rules, processes, and procedures of election law affects the core aspects of politics. Its judgments determine who influences elections through spending money. It increases or decreases the likelihood that some racial or other group will succeed in electing its preferred candidate. It is the sole refuge for third parties aiming to dent the two-party stranglehold. In the end, any reforms must eventually pass muster with the Supreme Court. In short, the defining attributes of our representative system of elections and government are fashioned to a large degree by judicial opinions relating to elections and politics.

This fact ought not surprise us. Our political system is a product of law and constitution; representative government springs from the legal blueprint of our written Constitution. What is surprising, given the Supreme Court's undeniable sway, is the paucity of integrated or comprehensive studies of the Court's role in molding electoral politics and representative government (see Maveety 1991; Ryden 1996). Decisions on campaign financing, redistricting, voting rights, and other election law issues certainly receive a great deal of attention from lawyers, scholars, and commentators. Yet these cases are almost always studied and analyzed in isolation from each other; they generate a slew of journal and law review articles that invariably neglect the overarching issues, themes, and connections running through election law jurisprudence.

This neglect is not benign. A closer review of election law jurisprudence suggests that the Supreme Court often lacks the requisite theoretical footing in which to anchor its decisions. Its decisions rely on contradictory assumptions about the workings of politics, and they often work at cross-purposes; on occasion, they have serious deleterious consequences for practical politics. It is unrealistic to expect the Court to embrace a neat, integrated, coherent theory of representation that it can apply with perfect consistency. On the other hand, its decisions should not be devoid of theory, disconnected from each other, or isolated from actual real-world politics. Yet those factors often characterize the Court's work.

Consider *Buckley v. ACLF*. The restrictions on petition gathering that the Supreme Court proscribed were relatively insignificant. However, the decision is reflective of how the Court goes about deciding questions bearing on the political system. The decision (which included a majority opinion, a concurring opinion, and two dissenting opinions) left unaddressed the wide-ranging issues that initiatives present for republican governance. Initiatives present a fundamental challenge to the notion of representative democracy contemplated by the Constitution's framers. Yet the Court skirted any meaningful discussion of issues of representation in its resolution of the case. Instead, it decided the case within the narrow confines of individual speech rights. The decision would have benefited from a consideration of important theoretical issues implicated by the case.

Similarly, the Supreme Court decided *Department of Commerce* in a way that assures that statistical sampling will remain a controversy for years to come. The decision was evenly split; four justices thought sampling was an unconstitutional violation of the textual requirement that there be an "actual enumeration" for the census, and four found it constitutionally permissible. The deciding vote, cast by Justice O'Connor, relied purely on statutory grounds. Her avoidance of the constitutional issue ensures that sampling will likely come before the Court again.

The custom of jurisprudential restraint precludes the Supreme Court from engaging in broad speculative dictum that extends beyond the case it is deciding. In both of these examples, the Court confined itself to the facts and circumstances specific to the case before it. In both instances, it bears asking whether the Court was able to make a fully informed, thoughtful, and appropriate decision without weighing broader ramifications for the system as a whole. Its failure to do so reflects a lack of regard for the potential practical repercussions of its decisions.

The Supreme Court will continue to confront disputes that directly implicate the health and well-being of the democratic process. This volume seeks to aid the Court in that task; its objective is to isolate and explore theoretical presuppositions that must be considered if the Court's decisions are to sustain a stronger version of representative democracy. It presents a series of original essays examining recent Supreme Court decisions and their practical/political impact on the workings of the electoral process. This interdisciplinary dialogue—it includes practitioners and students of law and politics—explores the Court's doctrinal approach to questions of voting and elections, representation, and political participation. The hope is that these pages might make some modest theoretical contribution that would edify and inform the Court's work in this important and neglected area.

THEMES

The essays in this volume revolve around five general themes or inquiries pertaining to the Supreme Court's jurisprudence in electoral matters. These themes—culled from the literature of political science and democratic theory—are hardly exclusive or exhaustive, but they resurface repeatedly across the chapters and topics of this book.

Constitutional Law and the Real World

The overarching concern of this book is the extent to which constitutional law and the Supreme Court's decisions adequately mirror the realities and complexities of political representation. The Court inevitably frames the legal arrangements and structures that generate representation. The representative capacity of parties is a function of the Court's decisions on political parties. The nature and quality of representation that flows from electoral districts are affected by the Court's decisions on redistricting. The influences that various financial players bring to bear on elections are the result of the campaign financing decisions. These and other cases require the Court to make certain assumptions about politics and political representation. What are those theoretical assumptions?

Representation can be conceptualized in many ways. It operates through elections, lobbying, legislative outcomes, constituent relationships, and a host of other practices and behaviors. Representation may be descriptive, existing symbolically when we elect a representative who is like us: sharing our race, ethnicity, or religion. It may be policy based, realized when a particular policy comes to fruition. It may reside in the deliberative process itself, through the inclusion of relevant interests in the governing assembly. In short, representation occurs through a slew of actors and activities, in an assortment of shapes and forms. It is a labyrinth of concepts and forms that synthesize an array of activities and participants through institutional and structural means.

Given this complex reality of representation, is it realistic to expect a coherent, integrated judicial articulation of political representation? Such a goal may not be possible or even desirable. Has the Supreme Court at least demonstrated an awareness of the host of processes, practices, and players that produce representation? What are the practical ramifications of the answers to these questions for the electoral process?

Once again, *Buckley v. ACLF* illustrates the importance of these queries. The initiative process strikes at the heart of representative government, as voters opt instead for plebiscitary modes of policymaking. The steep increase in ballot measures confirms Americans' low regard for people who hold public office. Initiatives are the most notable manifestation of a steady movement toward more democracy; they most closely mirror the will and wishes of the people.

This notion runs counter, however, to the Madisonian vision of "refining and enlarging the public view" by channeling it through wise, judicious, elected representatives. Initiatives implicate fundamental questions that occupied the attention of the framers and those who have followed: Simply put, how democratic should our system be? How much democracy can be entrusted to the people? Attitudes regarding the wisdom of this approach to policy making flow directly from one's views of the capabilities of the public itself. Can citizens be relied upon to make enlightened, reasonable policy choices? Or will they be driven by arbitrary whims or momentary passions? Will they be subject to the manipulations of crafty demagogues, as Madison and the other framers feared?

Though these questions relate directly to the basic form representation should take, they completely escaped comment or consideration by the Supreme Court in *Buckley*. Similarly, the *Department of Commerce* case demonstrates how a relatively technical question of statutory interpretation can fundamentally affect representative structures. The Court's decision on sampling is likely to determine the very face of the U.S. House of Representatives.

Individual and Collective Rights

A second theme in this volume is the tension between individual and collective political rights and representational activity. The respective roles of individuals and groups are at the heart of how representative systems are structured and of whom they take note. The individual holds center stage in American liberalism, especially in the rights-conscious constitutional ethos of the modern era. The Supreme Court traditionally has reflected this focus, emphasizing equalization of individual voting, political expression, and participatory rights. But is this enough to ensure effective political representation?

Political theory, in contrast, places great importance on concerted action and group affiliation. Representation and political efficacy in a large-scale democracy demand special attention to group interests. Group theories assert that if political interests are to be acknowledged, they must coalesce in blocs or around associations or collectivities. Political effectiveness requires citizens to pool their voices and resources with others of like mind and interests. In short, meaningful individual participation hinges on the collectivities that exist to represent one's interests. In this context, should not representative structures be cognizant of, and accommodate, a wide variety of group interests in politics?

This tension is present in a great deal of election law jurisprudence. Individualistic concerns have driven the Supreme Court's work in the areas of voting rights, ballot access, and campaign financing. The Court has also recognized a group right to representation in reapportionment questions, at least with respect to racial groups and arguably for partisan organizations as well. Yet its acknowledgment of group politics in the form of parties has been sporadic at best and contradictory at worst. Current controversies likely to ensnare the Court implicate this question; for example, how do group rights affect whether to regulate or restrain political action committees and parties in financing campaigns? How does the answer to that question relate to individual efficacy in campaigns?

How does the Supreme Court answer these questions, if it even considers them? To what degree should constitutional law acknowledge collectivities and their role in the electoral process? How should group rights be balanced against those of the individual? Can individual equality be pursued without addressing organizational inequality and an unlevel group playing field?

These issues are problematic. Some observers have advocated a group-based system of representation as essential to achieving a fair and equitable electoral arena (Young 1990; Grady 1993). Do disparities in resources and clout, however, make a group-based system of representation an absurdity? Can distinctions be made between parties and interest groups, advocacy and for-profit groups, public interest and business groups, or socially designated groups? Is the law capable of ordering and categorizing the plethora of groups for purposes of determining representative status? Significant empirical and theoretical considerations challenge group-based systems of representation and point back to the individual as the only workable empirical unit around which to build representative structures.

Again, the *Buckley* decision provides a useful illustration. It is rife with allusions to the respective rights and influences of group and individual political actors. Initiatives, by reducing political decision making to majority rule, place group and individual influence directly in competition. Initiatives, at least in theory, give individuals equal influence in policy making. They bypass collectivities as the formative influences in politics. Indeed, the objective behind initiatives is precisely that—to preempt party and interest group control of the legislative machinery.

This approach makes sense when it is aimed at special interests such as big business, labor, or the tobacco industry. Is it also appropriate, however, when initiatives are trained on specific individual and minority rights? Ballot measures have become increasingly popular for addressing sensitive, high-profile, areas—gay and lesbian rights, affirmative action programs, government benefits for immigrants, English as an official language. Should Fourteenth Amendment equal protection questions such as these be contingent on the approval of the majority? Should potentially unpopular rights and liberties be imperiled by the rule of the majority?

These objections are amplified when initiatives are not the exercise in pure democracy that they appear to be. More often than not, the placement of a measure on the ballot is driven not by a groundswell of public sentiment or popular opinion but by narrow, well-organized interests. Well-heeled special interests (or wealthy individuals) are usually responsible for funding the petition drive to get a proposal on the ballot, as well as for promoting it during the campaign once it is on the ballot—hence the measures by states such as Colorado to ensure that the process is not exploited by special interests contrary to the public interest.

Political Parties in the Constitutional Context

The third theme of this volume is the constitutional treatment of political parties and party structures. Mention of political parties is conspicuously absent from the Constitution; this fact, however, has not precluded them from residing at the center of our electoral system virtually from the outset. Although the parties are held in low regard by much of the public, they remain integral components of electoral politics, wielding substantial influence in campaigns and elections, as well as in organizing government. How is their ability to perform these functions affected by the legal and constitutional context within which they operate? And how are courts to divine the answers to questions pertaining to parties, given the glaring silence of the Constitution?

These issues are of utmost importance for the effectiveness of representative government. Parties exist in a hostile constitutional framework of limited government that divides power among branches of government, disperses it between levels of government, and overlays upon the branches and levels of government checks and balances and other structural constraints. If government is to function in the face of these obstacles, it requires effective parties. Meanwhile, voluminous state laws further complicate the legal environment for political parties. Hence, the courts have frequent occasion to consider constitutionally the nature, rights, and functions of parties in the operation of American politics. What does the Supreme Court's treatment of parties reveal about its views on representative government? Is its jurisprudence informed by a cognizance of party functions or the multifaceted party dimensions? Does it exhibit a rational, theoretically grounded treatment of parties? Does it matter?

I have asserted elsewhere that the Supreme Court has demonstrated a striking lack of appreciation for the role of parties in democratic politics (Ryden 1996). In cases involving patronage practices, ballot and voter access, and apportionment and redistricting, the Court has failed to appreciate parties' unique structural capacity for meeting the demands of representation. Should parties' constitutional status be predicated on a functional analysis? Should their recognition under the Constitution be contingent on their serving constitutional values and objectives? The Court mirrors the sentiments of the broader political culture, which is largely anti-party. Perhaps the parties ought not look to the courts for something they are unable to earn from the public on their own.

The *Buckley* and *Department of Commerce* cases once again depict how judicial decisions affect parties at the ground level of practical politics. The resort to ballot measures comes at the direct expense of party control over the levers of policy (often with the implicit consent of party politicians wishing to avoid tough policy decisions). Likewise, the dispute over sampling techniques in the census cannot be analyzed outside the context of the partisan fallout. The Supreme Court's decision will affect the relative strength of the two major parties in Congress for years to come. At risk is majority party control of the House, which is the determinative factor shaping the legislation coming out of that institution.

Political Participation and Political Reform

A fourth theme of this volume is the Supreme Court's role in delineating political participation and the limits of political reform. Americans' distaste for parties and politics, and their low estimation of the political process, has intensified reform efforts. Most reforms are aimed at broadening political participation for average Americans. Term limits, campaign finance regulation, open and blanket primary rules, and the initiative process are just some of the measures meant to open the political process. These reform efforts reveal an ongoing engagement of fundamental questions relating to the very efficacy of representative government.

Again, the Supreme Court usually can be found somewhere in the middle of the debate. In some instances, the Court has served as facilitator of reform (for example, in condoning broader rules regarding primary participation and rejecting further restrictions on the initiative process). In other cases, it has loomed as an insurmountable obstacle. With regard to campaign financing, for example, the Court's doctrinal analysis equating money to political speech has hindered reform. The Court has already removed statutory limits on political parties in funding campaigns, despite parties' unpopularity. Its nullification of term limits for U.S. senators and

House members in *U.S. Term Limits v. Thornton*, 514 U.S. 779 (1995), effectively preempted a popular grassroots movement. Its constitutional reinforcement of the two-party system has stymied efforts by minor and new parties to crack the Republicans' and Democrats' lock on electoral politics (see *Timmons v. Twin Cities Area New Party*, 520 U.S. 351 (1997)).

The reforms at stake often reflect the public's willingness to subordinate republican approaches to policy making in favor of direct democracy. The Supreme Court is inevitably drawn into the difficult business of weighing the model of representative government against ever-increasing demands for direct democracy and expanded individual participation. How many answers does the Constitution provide? What is the appropriate function of the Court with respect to political reform? Is it free to rebut, in the name of constitutional principle, the people's will as expressed through the legislative branches? Or does it have an obligation to heed public sentiments with respect to political change?

Politics and Representation

The final question addressed in this volume is the role of the Supreme Court generally in resolving questions of politics and representation. The topics explored in these chapters are inherently political. They raise profound issues regarding the propriety of judicial resolution of these questions, applicable standards of review, and the Court's competency to decide.

Once upon a time, the Supreme Court was far more passive and noninterventionist, leaving the determination of "political questions" to the politically elected branches of government (*Colgrove v. Green*, 328 U.S. 549 (1946)). That attitude changed for good with the Court's leap into the thicket of reapportionment in *Baker v. Carr*, 369 U.S. 186 (1962). Now the courts play an active part in regulating virtually all aspects of the electoral process. Are we better or worse for it? Is there still a question of whether the Court ought even to be involved in disputes bearing on the political process? Is there any going back? If not, how deferential should the Court be toward the elected elements of government? Does the Court have an obligation to aggressively safeguard representative government in the face of self-interested incumbent lawmakers? What sources should it avail itself of in doing so? Should it fall back on political theoretical principles? Should social science data and evidence play a part? These and other unresolved issues confront the Court and its involvement in the business of shaping election law.

APPROACH

This collection of essays explores the themes articulated above through a variety of prisms provided by contemporary cases and controversies. Each chapter confronts a specific issue, subject area, or decision of topical importance. Each author offers an analysis and critique of recent developments in that area and the underlying rationale employed by the Supreme Court. Each chapter is written from a distinct perspective; the authors are students of law and political science, academics and practitioners. These essays are not written from a common position or standpoint. Rather, each chapter has a *view*—the essays are intended to be provocative, to stir debate rather than foreclose it. They are unlikely to resolve the questions definitively; they aim to make a contribution in highlighting the significance of the debate and moving it forward.

The essays are woven together by common threads in the form of three questions regarding the Supreme Court's approach(es) to politics, voting, elections, and representation. First, what does the decision or doctrinal approach in the area under consideration reveal about the Court's attitudes or assumptions respecting political participation and representation? Second, does (or should) the Court have a coherent theory of politics that corresponds with the practical reality of politics, and what are the political and practical ramifications of its theory or rationale for the political/electoral system? Third, how might the Court cultivate or enrich its doctrinal approach to these questions?

The book is divided into four parts, although the themes identified above surface repeatedly throughout the book. Part I examines the Supreme Court's treatment of political representation with regard to a variety of issues. The authors discuss whether the Court has a firm understanding of the complex nature of representation and whether it has taken consistent and adequate steps to protect the political rights not only of individuals but also of groups and collective political organizations.

Part II scrutinizes the Supreme Court's treatment of political parties. The authors probe Court decisions that have affected the overall strength of parties and the two-party system (cases relating to internal party regulations, patronage, and ballot access for minority parties). How has the Court dealt with parties, given the relative lack of constitutional guidance? Is there a consistent theoretical basis behind its rulings, and how have those rulings affected the nature and strength of parties and of the two-party system?

Part III looks at the Supreme Court's responses to recent attempts at political reform, including campaign finance restrictions, the increasingly popular initiative and referendum process, and term limits for Congressional legislators. How have these decisions balanced the push for more democracy against the constitutional tradition of republicanism? Has the Court adequately identified the broader issues at stake?

Finally, we consider whether the Supreme Court has a grand, overarching theory of politics and whether the answer to that question is good or bad jurisprudence. Judicial decisions do not occur in a vacuum; every case has the potential to have a significant effect on the nature of American politics. The *Buckley* and *Department of Commerce* cases are only the latest examples of the Court's power to influence the course and scope of national and state government. The goal of this book is to expose and clarify the central issues regarding the Court's treatment of the electoral process so that we may be more aware of the real-world effects of Court decisions. That awareness alone can improve our judgments, our analyses, and our understanding of the American political system—within and outside the Supreme Court.

··· I ···

The Judicial Search for Electoral Representation

"Your representative owes you, not his industry only, but his judgment; and he betrays instead of serving you if he sacrifices it to your opinion."
—Edmund Burke, *Speech to the Electors of Bristol* (1774)

"In a democratic society like ours, relief must come through an aroused popular conscience that sears the conscience of the people's representatives."
—Justice Felix Frankfurter, *Baker v. Carr* (1962)

Each chapter in this book engages in one way or another the challenges of realizing representative democracy in America and the Supreme Court's part in meeting that challenge. We begin with these overarching questions: What assessments can be rendered regarding the Court's representation jurisprudence? Does the Court have a jurisprudential doctrine that coheres and informs its decision making across specific issues or cases? How do the questions it decides affect representative government, and is the Court cognizant of those connections? What democratic values underpin the decisions? Are they explicit or implicit?

The authors of the essays in this volume answer these questions in widely divergent ways. All agree, however, that the Court should have some grasp of the complexities of political representation. This understanding is no easy task, admittedly, given the multitude of concepts, actors, behaviors, and channels that fashion and form representation. The maze of representative activity includes legislative debate and roll-call voting, ballot behavior on the part of the electorate, campaigning, constituent service, lobbying, and much more. These activities are carried out by an array of actors: individual legislators, parties, interest groups, voters and voting blocs, and the government as a whole. The tangible manifestations of representation are similarly diverse.

Even a starting point—a definition of representation—is difficult to settle upon. Is representation control over a policy-making institution, being entitled to a fair share of influence over the body, or simply having a presence or voice in the elected assembly? Is representation in the electoral arena having an equal vote to cast, equal access to the process, or equal results in electoral outcomes?

In light of the complex weaving of representational forms and faces, one cannot expect from the Supreme Court an integrated jurisprudential theory of representative democratic governance. Nevertheless, the Court should be able to identify dimensions of representation theory that are implicated by particular questions. It should also be competent to craft certain mediating principles that apply consistently across specific issues. The Court should be able, one hopes, to set a doctrinal course that best reflects the complex reality of political representation in a given situation or circumstance. The goal of such a doctrine would be outputs that might better facilitate the efficient operation of our multifaceted representative system.

Part I of this volume (chapters 2–4) addresses overarching representation issues, focusing particularly on the tension between individual and group political actors. Beginning with the general and moving to the more specific, Nancy Maveety's essay serves as the framework for integrating and connecting the chapters that follow under the unifying theme of representation. Her essay provides an overview of how representation rights generally have fared under the current Court, from the perspective of group rights and the constitutional recognition of collective interests.

Maveety parses the Court's work across a broad range of topics from a pluralist point of view. Pluralist notions of representation are based on the central importance of collective political involvement to the realization of individual political goals. Interaction, conflict, and competition among collective interests are at the heart of pluralism. This dynamic implies the need for legal structures that generate, accommodate, and arbitrate group interests and conflicts. Likewise, it compels laws that acknowledge the importance of groups and furnish outlets for the expression of group political behavior.

Although some commentators have argued that the present Court has no intelligible philosophy of political representation—that its pluralism is either ad hoc or theoretically inconsistent (Ryden 1996)—Maveety contends otherwise. Elsewhere, she has credited the Supreme Court during the Burger years with developing a relatively coherent "community of interest" approach to representation issues (Maveety 1991)—identifying interest-balancing and pluralist notions of representation that have guided court policy in the areas of districting, party governance, and electoral competition. Here she offers a critical examination of Rehnquist Court rulings on political representation, voting rights, and racial districting to determine if the Burger Court's group-based format for representation rights survives. She concludes that the Rehnquist Court has retreated from the pluralist policies of its predecessor even while operating within the same conceptual categories.

The subsequent chapters look more closely at the competing pulls of pluralism and liberalism within the respective contexts of electoral arrangements and school districting practices. Their focal point is the central problem of determining what defines people politically for purposes of representation. Is it their individual vote? Or is it the groups with which they identify? Is it economic interests, or perhaps religious ones? Is it their level of education, racial or ethnic identity, class, or perhaps physical location and interests arising out of territory or geography? The answers to these questions determine how voting rights are fixed, how electoral districts will be created, and who is acknowledged when school districts are determined. In the electoral context, they establish in practical terms the value and effectiveness of one's vote. In the school district context, they decide who controls the school district and how the school "represents" the community. In other words, these are formative questions.

Chapters 3 and 4 confront the complicated and interrelated issues of voting rights and redistricting, along with their relation to the larger goal of political representation. Determinations of collective political interests warranting legal recognition (and hence representation) are at the center of the process of line drawing. The exercise of redistricting entails difficult distinctions regarding which identifiable groups of voters should or should not be taken into account.

The most intensely scrutinized area of the Court's redistricting jurisprudence has involved the constitutional propriety of racial gerrymandering. In chapter 3, Howard Scarrow examines the implications of race-based redistricting for political representation and the Supreme Court's largely unsuccessful attempts to define "fair and effective representation." Scarrow attributes the Court's struggles to its difficulty in balancing the import of the individual vote with the necessity of identifying group interests that make up electoral districts. He traces the law from the principles of "one person, one vote" and "vote dilution" through subsequent decisions interpreting the Voting Rights Act (VRA). In the process, the statutory demands of the VRA have increasingly come into conflict with constitutional demands, as a string of decisions have narrowed substantially the constitutionality of the race-based "majority-minority" districts. Ultimately, Scarrow finds individually oriented voting rights increasingly difficult to reconcile with group criteria for representation. He concludes that political parties remain the best way to resolve these tensions.

In chapter 4, Stephen Gottlieb analyzes the nexus between representation and redistricting through the prism of *Board of Education of Kiryas Joel Village School District v. Grumet,* 512 U.S. 687 (1994), in which the Supreme Court denied New York state's efforts to carve out a local school district specifically for a Hasidic community. Gottlieb credits the Supreme Court for its attempts to establish intentional procedural standards for districting questions. *Kiryas Joel* reveals, however, that pure process cannot yield fair representation; it also reveals that the Court has been stymied by an inability to discern substantively what constitutes good or bad districting. Gottlieb concludes from this case that the Supreme Court has no choice but to cultivate a more sophisticated cognizance of districting and the substantive quality of the political representation that flows from it. Otherwise, the coherent treatment of the most important districting issues—electoral, racial, educational, or religious—will continue to elude the Court.

2

Representation Rights and the Rehnquist Years: The Viability of the "Communities of Interest" Approach

Nancy Maveety

"What the Court has done is to convert a particular political philosophy into a constitutional rule."
—Justice Potter Stewart, dissenting in *Lucas v. Colorado 44th General Assembly* (1964)

". . . a comprehensive, all-encompassing constitutional theory of representation has eluded the Court . . ."
—David Ryden, *Representation in Crisis* (1996, 3)

REPRESENTATION AND THE COURT: POLITICAL PLURALISM, PRAGMATISM, OR BOTH?

Is it permissible for the Supreme Court to be "politically correct" but "logically incoherent" on questions of fairness in representation (Peterson 1995, 16)? How should a Court that spurns familiar theories of representation rights be assessed? What about a Court whose vision of representation is "skewed against collective manifestations" and blind to "the communal dimensions of political representation" (Ryden 1996, 34–35)?

Supreme Court justices are accused of being political theorists and castigated for not being theorists. They are not usually praised, however, for being theoretically inconsistent. More often, court commentators attempt to find policy direction within otherwise unenlightened confusion. If law is—as the strategic theorists of judicial behavior would have it—the product of the short-term balancing of competitive interests (*pace*

Epstein and Knight 1997), then the Court's "political philosophy" is pluralist, by definition. Competitive balance among groups is normally a goal of pluralistic political systems, a means to induce fair representation of all interests in the political realm.[1] Presumably, a judicial theory of pluralism would emphasize the importance of groups and group institutions as mechanisms for individual and collective interest representation in the political process. Justices as political theorists, then, would be either sophisticated, simplistic, or reluctant pluralists.

Such variation among judicial theories of political pluralism results from a paradox within American political theory itself: Individuals are the political rights-bearers, but groups are the vehicle for political action. In other words, using a pluralist lens to view the Court's work raises the issue of individual- versus group-based models of representation. This theoretical issue is relevant to jurisprudence because what is "fair" in terms of political representation—what leads to a competitive balance of interests in a pluralistic sense—depends on whether a generic individual's interest or a group's interest is the unit of representation. A particular court policy, such as "one person, one vote," may be individually oriented and, thus, "fair" in terms of individual expression of interests.[2] Conversely, a court's approach to uphold political access rights for groups *qua* groups may be "fair" by virtue of maximizing opportunities for group expressions of interest. Moreover, judicial policy on political representation can be assessed as a framework of representation rights that advances certain group interests, levels the playing field for certain group interests, selectively excludes certain group interests, or misperceives certain group interests.

Does this analysis mean that there are both more coherent and less coherent versions of pluralism on the Court? Yes—particularly in a comparative sense. Current courts are invariably measured in terms of their predecessors. Hence, existing frameworks of representation rights (which sometimes exist only in the minds of the commentators) have a comparative-evaluative dimension within their general explicatory purpose. Thus, the participatory individualism of the Warren Court and the group-oriented balancing of the Burger Court have become the frameworks against which the political representation decisions of today's Rehnquist Court are measured. Whether these particular characterizations of the Rehnquist Court's predecessors are accurate is immaterial to some degree; what matters is that the pluralist philosophies of the Warren and Burger eras are the touchstones against which the Rehnquist record is assayed for consistency, continuity, departure, or alteration.

I begin my scrutiny of the Rehnquist Court record by applying the framework of representation rights that emerged from Court decisions during the Burger years. Although the quality of the Burger Court's pluralist theory and the philosophical merit of its dispensing of group rights is a matter of dispute,[3] most Court commentators would agree that the Burger Court profoundly influenced representation law by refining and, in some cases, establishing the key categories of representation rights claims (Maveety 1991). The Burger Court's community-of-interest approach to representation issues—which was dominated by an interest-balancing, classic pluralist understanding of political representation—guided judicial policy on questions of districting, party governance, and electoral competition. The result was the Court's recognition of certain aggregative institutions as central to the process of political representation. By examining whether the Rehnquist Court views the exercise of representation rights as the protection of these aggregative institutions for different communities of interest, we can ascertain its similarities with its predecessor—and whether such similarities constitute virtue or vice.

Before we can lambaste the current Court for its political philosophy, however, we must confront the assertion that it has none. If we only detect "Court philosophy" by looking for internal, logical coherence—plus some family resemblance to pluralist theory—then straightforward political pragmatism may pass undetected as a theoretically consistent and justified approach (Maltese 1997) to questions of representation rights. Perhaps it should. As we assess the performance of the Rehnquist Court, however, we must face the possibility that it has failed to produce a majority coalition that can consistently agree on any interest or collection of interests as the basis for a theory of representation. If such failure exists, is it evidence of (a) philosophical incoherence or (b) an approach to political representation that does not rely on familiar pluralistic dichotomies, such as individual versus group interests, found in the precedents of its predecessors?[4]

I suggest that the proper response to the foregoing query is (b). The Rehnquist Court's approach does not privilege individual or group interests per se; instead, it scrutinizes the *type* of activity the actor or organization uses to secure the representation of its own or its members' interests: Is the activity—in the Court's eyes—voluntary and uncoordinated/expressive group action,[5] or is it institutionalized group action seeking further institutional protection (as in racial districting cases or party ballot access cases)?

Is this approach a perverse resurrection of the participatory individualism of the Warren years? A recent study of minority representation and race-based redistricting argues that for the past two decades, the Supreme Court has encouraged a division between individualist and group concepts of political identity. Both approaches, moreover, assert the misguided notion that political identity is formed prior to and apart from political action itself (Bybee 1998). This interpretation is persuasive, particularly as a way of understanding the Rehnquist Court as a contemporary participant in an ultimately dysfunctional judicial dialogue. There is one problem, however, with viewing the current Court's work as a resuscitation of an individualist concept of political identity. Because the decisions of the Rehnquist Court seem, at times, so laboriously and studiously pragmatic and fact-based, there is less reason to presume that these justices consider themselves to be generators of a cohesive theoretical system for matters concerning political representation (e.g., Maveety 1996). Indeed, as one commentary observed, it is a methodological rather than a political-ideological fault line that matters most in dividing the justices of the Rehnquist Court (Baugh, Smith, and Hensley 1995, 74).

THE REHNQUIST COURT AND REPRESENTATION: ASKING THE RIGHT QUESTIONS

Thus, we may have to look creatively for answers regarding representation rights and the Rehnquist years. To wit, the following questions would seem to be most relevant:

- How does the Rehnquist Court define fairness in representative structures and processes?
- Is its definition of *fair* legally "correct"—that is, consonant with the pluralist theory of the Burger-era precedents?
- Or is its definition merely politically correct—that is, practical for a pluralist democracy?

To consider the last question first, Peterson (1995) observes—regarding the debate over classifying by race—that "those who first attempt to find a politically satisfactory resolution to racial classification and only then place it within a legal framework are the more likely to have found an ethically satisfying answer" (Peterson 1995, 3). Logical coherence, in other words, may yield politically unsatisfactory and, ultimately, ethically unsatisfying policies as well. (Thus, the politically correct answer in a pluralist democracy is also likely to be ethically correct.) Does Peterson's observation regarding racial classification also apply, however, to issues of fairness in representation?

One complication is that neither politically satisfactory nor ethically satisfying notions of representative fairness are judged by uniformly agreed-upon standards; indeed, "fairness" turns on whether one emphasizes a *descriptive* or *substantive* definition of representation.[6] Guinier (1995) suggests that this difference in goals separates "second-generation" voting rights issues, which focus on minority group members' right to a meaningful vote to elect candidates of choice, from "third-generation" voting rights issues, which concern the marginalization of minority group interests in newly integrated political institutions (Guinier 1995, 31–33). Representative fairness also seems to depend on whether one views pluralism as an equilibrium or a disequilibrium of group interests (Ryden 1996, 3–4), and, if a disequilibrium, whether state or court compulsion of structures that fulfill or enhance the representative equality of groups can be pursued without sacrificing fundamental standards of individual equality (Ryden 1996, 7).

Peterson suggests that because of the practical impossibility of defining fairness with respect to racial interests in a way that is palatable to all *and* theoretically coherent, a tempered hypocrisy with respect to racial group-based classifications is the best policy (Peterson 1995, 16). Analogizing the judicial sleights-of-hand in *Regents of the University of California v. Bakke,* 438 U.S. 265 (1978), and *Shaw v. Reno,* 509 U.S. 630 (1993), Peterson concludes, "Much as Powell had decided in the 1978 *Bakke* case that diversity plans were constitutional because the racial motive could be disguised, so O'Connor argued (in the 1993 case) that racially motivated redistricting is permissible only when the intentions can be masked" (Peterson 1995, 15). Applying this statement to the problem of defining fairness in representation, a practical balancing of political interests and representative objectives would seem to be the politically correct formula for legal policy with respect to representation rights. Balancing, however, entails a certain toleration for inconsistent or messy solutions and for theoretical duplicity.

Moreover, there are some assumptions inherent in Peterson's statement. The first assumption is that the Rehnquist Court—at least in its racial classification and voting decisions—is following the jurisprudential directives of the Burger Court. The second assumption is that some

group-based political rights—chiefly those pertinent to the representation of racial minorities' interests—are beneficial to pluralist democracy
in the U.S. Thus, the Rehnquist Court's political representation decisions
are neither reactionary individualism nor logical incoherence borne of
ineptitude but finely crafted political pragmatism. In terms of our questions, then, for Peterson the law of representation rights during the
Rehnquist years has been legally and politically correct.

If we are to bestow the Solomonic epithet of politically correct on the
work of the current Court, then the first two assumptions must be vali-
dated—that the Rehnquist Court is adhering to the Burger Court's jurisprudential pluralism and that it is doing so by recognizing and protecting
certain aggregative institutions that facilitate group interest representation. Hence, we must explore whether the Rehnquist-era decisions are
"legally correct," that is, consonant with the pluralist philosophy and balancing approach of the Burger precedents.

THE BURGER COURT AND THE "COMMUNITY OF INTERESTS" APPROACH

The Burger Court's jurisprudence of representation rights arguably
mirrored the complexity of political representation by acknowledging the
multiplicity of processes, practices, and players that produce representation. The Burger Court's decisions aggressively pursued a "community of
interest" approach to representation rights questions, protecting the
rights of aggregative institutions that recognized and facilitated political
access by identifiable and legally cognizable communities of interest. The
Burger Court viewed political representation in terms of a pluralist balancing of group interests, and its decisions located the determination of
that balance in the federal judiciary. Some observers would argue that the
Court's very attention to the complexity and balancing of interests inherent in political representation rendered its jurisprudence on "fair representation" messy and conflict ridden, particularly with respect to political
access rights for competing group interests. This criticism is probably fair.
The more pertinent inquiry, however, concerns which group interests the
Burger Court's decisions recognized as legally cognizable—that is, requiring constitutional protection for their aggregative institutions or practices—and whether the Rehnquist Court continued this formula for representation rights.

A 1991 study of the Burger years identified five conceptions of group representation that found varying degrees of doctrinal affirmation in the Court's work on questions of popular control and participation and collective political activity and access (Maveety 1991). These categories reflect important and enduring conceptions of group representation in the American political context, conceptions that are relevant to the institutions and procedures affected by judicial scrutiny since the reapportionment revolution of the Warren era. The five categories are territorial representation, corporatist representation, demographic representation, partisan representation, and litigational representation. Applying this conceptual framework to a selection of Rehnquist Court decisions on political representation provides a measure of those decisions' consistency with Burger Court precedents. This analysis furnishes the standard for judging the legal correctness of the Rehnquist Court's definition of fair representation.

Territorial Representation

Territorial representation figured in the Burger Court's decisions on geographic communities of interest in electoral districting and the legislative authority of local governments. A Burger Court dissenter once identified these decisions as "ceding to geography a talismanic significance" (Justice Brennan, dissenting in *Holt Civic Club v. City of Tuscaloosa*, 439 U.S. 60 (1978)). Fair or unfair, this comment reflects the propensity of most Burger Court justices to protect a geographically defined community, such as a political subdivision, as a political constituency deserving rights to legislative representation and policy-making autonomy. Thus, geographic communities were representable communities of interest for purposes of drawing electoral districts (*Mahan v. Howell*, 410 U.S. 315 (1973)) and political communities of interest for the purpose of legislating on the quality of community life (*Lockport v. Citizens for Community Action*, 430 U.S. 259 (1977)).

The territorial representation cases generally supported the idea that political decentralization is important for democratic participation because the opportunity to influence the conditions of community life furthers citizens' political efficacy. The aggregative institution that enhanced individuals' geographic group interest was the political subdivision, whether that was a state or a municipality. The Burger Court's assumption seemed to be that a geographic community of interest is created by a shared jurisdiction and concomitant governmental powers, though the Court divided frequently over the existence and definition of the "local public interest" (e.g., *Moore v. City of East Cleveland*, 431 U.S. 494 (1977); *Washington v. Seattle School District No. 1*, 458 U.S. 457 (1982)).

Did the Rehnquist Court continue the idea of subdivision integrity for certain policy-making and districting situations? Two decisions suggest that, although a minority bloc that is attentive to geographic communities of interest is active on the current Court, the Rehnquist Court as a whole has weakly repudiated geography as an important basis for pluralist interest representation.

Both *U.S. Term Limits v. Thornton*, 514 U.S. 779 (1995), and *Romer v. Evans*, 517 U.S. 620 (1996), involved the legislative autonomy of states using the initiative and referendum procedure of state constitutions. Both cases involved constitutional challenges to the policies adopted by the people in the states—Congressional term limits for members in Arkansas, and an amendment in Colorado that prohibited laws granting explicit protection against discrimination to homosexuals. In striking down both state initiatives, the Court majorities in the two cases[7] stressed the interests and rights of the national community, as reflected in the mandates of the U.S. Constitution, over the prerogatives and sentiments of state communities. The importance of uniformity in the general law and a commitment to the law's neutrality toward persons superseded, in the words of one justice, "the people of the several states (as) the only true source of power" (Justice Thomas, dissenting in *Thornton*). Clearly, geography is no longer a talisman,[8] at least with respect to the policy-making authority of territorially based interests (*Printz v. U.S.*, 117 S. Ct. 2365 (1997), and the majority-minority districting decisions, discussed below.

Corporatist Representation

Corporatist representation concerns political access for economic interests, and the institutions and procedures that provide such access. The Burger Court's cases dealt with land-based voting schemes in special district elections (*Ball v. James*, 451 U.S. 355 (1981)) and the role of corporate war chests and corporate speech in the political process (*First National Bank of Boston v. Bellotti*, 435 U.S. 765 (1978)). Those issues forced the Court to articulate the balance between individual rights and freedoms in a capitalist economy and individual rights and freedoms in a democratic polity. Arguably, the Court's decisions did not so much strike a balance of group interests in the process of political representation as they promoted the special representational access of certain economic interests.

Perhaps the most important ruling of the Burger Court on the political representation of economically defined group interests was *Buckley v. Valeo*, 424 U.S. 1 (1976). In *Buckley*, representational access was secured through the extension of First Amendment rights to corporate "persons" and their political arms, political action committees (PACs), and through the definition of economic actions such as independent political expenditures as political speech. The Court's sanction of the political use of corporate funds or personal wealth, legally channeled through the membership organization of a PAC, has had far-reaching consequences for the electoral system.

The Rehnquist Court has largely abetted these consequences by further extending First Amendment protection for independent, advocacy-related political expenditures by groups of like-minded individuals. In a way, this doctrine of protection is itself an aggregative institution facilitating participation and representation of interests in the political process.

In furthering the *Buckley* doctrine, the Rehnquist Court has loosened the focus on economically based or corporate interests and the listeners' rights to hear their points of view. That focus had been central to the Burger Court's justification of PAC expenditures as political speech. Instead, the Rehnquist Court seems to be asserting that any special interest group—as long as it is an advocacy-related membership organization and not a political committee coordinated with a candidate campaign—enjoys the First Amendment right to unlimited political expenditures. The most dramatic example of this tendency is the decision in *Colorado Republican Federal Campaign Committee v. FEC*, 518 U.S. 604 (1996), which specifically benefited the uncoordinated expenditures of state party committees. The narrower, more technical ruling in *FEC v. Akins*, 524 U.S. 11 (1998), also suggests, however, that what matters to the Rehnquist justices is the *voluntary* combination of interest-bearing (and dollar-bearing) individuals into corporate form for the purpose of influencing electoral debate—not the particular interest they bear or its legitimacy to a pluralist balance of groups. In *Akins,* the Court remanded the question of whether the American Israel Public Affairs Committee (AIPAC) should be defined as a membership organization whose communications lie outside the Federal Election Campaign Act (FECA) expenditure limitations for political committees.

The Burger Court originally espoused this conceptualization of group representation merely to defend the inclusion of economic-based interests in the formal institutions of the political process. The sad irony is that the Rehnquist Court has expanded this doctrine to mean that financial combinations of individuals and groups are the exemplars of political freedom of association.

Demographic Representation

Demographic representation is the formulation of group political access that the Rehnquist Court has challenged most. The Burger Court first considered the question of race-based districting as a remedial effort to secure fair and effective electoral representation for minority voters in the 1970s. Dilutionary districting, in which otherwise equipopulous electoral districts were gerrymandered to ensure that black voters lacked controlling majorities in most of them, produced situations in which black votes did not "count" in terms of influencing the outcomes of elections. The group interest, reflected in a shared racial identity, lacked adequate representation—measured as the racial group's ability as a bloc of voters to elect candidates of their choice. Thus, certain demographic communities of interest, because of their minority status, required group-conscious districting practices to enjoy competitive fairness *as a group interest* in the single-member district election system. In cases such as *United Jewish Organization v. Carey*, 430 U.S. 144 (1977) (rejecting an equal protection challenge to race-based state redistricting carried out in compliance with section 5 of the Voting Rights Act), *Thornburg v. Gingles*, 478 U.S. 30 (1986) (interpreting the 1982 amendments to section 2 of the Voting Rights Act as prohibiting systematic frustration or exclusion of racial minority groups from electoral competition), and *Davis v. Bandemer*, 478 U.S. 109 (1986) (upholding the justiciability of districting protecting partisan communities of interest), the Burger Court moved toward accepting two key premises: the idea that political competition depends on the demographics of districting and the conception of electoral competition as compensatory majoritarianism (Maveety 1991, 111).

Beginning with *Shaw v. Reno*, the Rehnquist Court evinced a judicial change of heart on these premises regarding the demographic conceptualization of political representation. Writing for a six-judge majority in *Shaw*, Justice O'Connor condemned the segregative impact of race-conscious electoral districting, its tendency to exacerbate racial bloc voting and racial "balkanization," and its stereotyping of voters' *interests* based on their shared racial identity. Applying "the same close scrutiny that we give other state laws that classify citizens by race," Justice O'Connor questioned the representational theory that animated majority-minority districting practices: "A reapportionment plan that includes in one district individuals who belong to the same race, *but who are otherwise widely separated by geographic and political boundaries*, and who may have little in common with one another but the color of their skin, bears an uncomfortable resemblance to political apartheid" (emphasis added) (509 U.S. at 647). In questioning whether demographic groups such as racial minorities could be presumed to share representable interests, *Shaw* established a new cause of action under the Equal Protection Clause: challenging a reapportionment plan for the use of race as an effort to separate voters.[9]

In later decisions—*Miller v. Johnson*, 515 U.S. 900 (1995), and *Bush v. Vera*, 517 U.S. 952 (1996)—narrow majorities repudiated the use of race as the primary factor in electoral districting, although the implications for the constitutionality of particular odd-shaped districts or districting plans pursuant to section 5 preclearance was far from clear (see generally Issacharoff, Karlan, and Pildes 1998). What is clear from a ruling such as that in *Miller* is the Rehnquist Court's view that noncompact districts, drawn merely to secure a particular racial composition and violating other traditional canons of districting (such as respecting subdivision boundaries), cannot constitute tangible communities of interest. For the current Court, demographic districting that relies primarily on race does not further political competition, and the compensatory majoritarianism that it implies does not constitute electoral competition.[10]

Partisan Representation

Partisan representation concerns issues of intra- and interparty democracy and their relationship to the representative function of political parties. Obviously, the political party is a traditionally accepted aggregative institution for group interests. The definition and tradition of responsible party government in the U.S. is inherently dualistic, however, and this dualism was partly responsible for the dualistic legal tradition of party structure and operations that the Burger Court endorsed. The American conception of partisan representation is rooted in the dualism between hierarchical and populist party traditions. The difference between these traditions turns on how party organizations reconcile the representation of the party's collective interests with individual members' and mass voters' participation. Is the party organization an autonomous collectivity, or does the state have the authority to intervene to regulate party affairs and electoral activities? The answer, of course, is both—and the Burger Court's decisions proceeded to balance the rights of party organizations (associational claims of the party "establishment") against the rights of party members (associational and access claims of intraparty factions, independents, PACs, and the general "partisan fringe" of third and minor parties) (Maveety 1991, 6).

In adjudicating cases that raised the question of the interrelationship of the traditional organizational, governmental, and electoral party functions, the Burger Court overtly balanced the hierarchical and populist traditions of the political party, perpetuated the dualistic tradition of partisan representation, and attempted to reconnect questions of party rights to the practical reality of actual party politics. These objectives rendered its decisions a confusing amalgam. It protected the authority of the central party organization on matters of delegate selection and candidate nomination, restricted patronage practices and partisan activities by civil servants, and defended two-party electoral competition while allowing some liberalization in ballot access for independent and third-party challengers. It also protected the political activities of PACs as new electoral intermediaries.[11]

Given the Burger Court's multifaceted doctrinal legacy on partisan representation, it would be hard for the Rehnquist Court to act in a way that is *not* "legally correct." Generally speaking, the Rehnquist Court's decisions have continued the dualistic trend present in the Burger precedents. The Rehnquist Court, however, has sharpened the focus on the hierarchical tradition of parties by defending the decisional autonomy of internal party organizations[12] and limiting ballot access or fusion options for minor parties (*Timmons v. Twin Cities Area New Party*, 520 U.S. 351 (1997)). Two commentators have read the Rehnquist Court's recent party decisions as strengthening state authority in the granting of special privileges to (and imposing special responsibility on) the two major parties (Petterson 1998, 10; Amy 1998, 7–8). One could also read the decision in *Colorado Republican Federal Campaign Committee v. FEC*, in which the Court loosened federal restrictions on independent expenditures by a state party campaign committee, as part of this effort to shore up various institutions of two-party competition. Though the Court was severely divided in *Timmons, Colorado Republican Federal Campaign Committee*, and *Morse v. Virginia Republican Party*, 517 U.S. 186 (1996), political autonomy—rather than any clearly articulated theory of partisan representation—seems to be the value driving the justices in these cases (Petterson 1998, 15).

Litigational Representation

Through litigational representation, the Burger Court addressed standing —the legal right to bring a complaint before a court—as a vehicle for group access to agency proceedings. The litigational representation decisions were about the popular accountability of the administrative branch of government. More generally, these Article III standing cases raised the question of whether group-based litigation functioned as an interest-aggregative institution in certain nonelectoral political settings. Overall, the Burger Court found litigation as representation to be more amenable to special interests than to broad public interests claims, although a majority tended to construe statutory private rights of action fairly narrowly (Maveety 1991, 217–18). The Burger Court's doctrinal legacy was a concern for plaintiff representivity in articulating the group's interest through litigation.

Although a comprehensive review of the Rehnquist Court's decisions on administrative procedures is beyond the scope of this chapter, it is worth noting that several of the Court's political representation decisions clearly assert that a litigant must explicate precisely the context of political activity because context is essential in determining its voluntary character (see discussion below under "An Alternative Pluralism: Representing Activity, Not Interests?"). Thus, the Rehnquist Court identifies certain representational burdens on litigants in bringing rights claims. At the same time, in *FEC v. Akins*, the Court accepted a challenge by a group of voters to the Federal Election Commission's (FEC) decision not to bring an enforcement action against AIPAC, finding that the voters had satisfied statutory standing requirements and the constitutional, injury-in-fact standing threshold. The Court made this finding in spite of the fact that the injury alleged by the group of voters—failure to obtain information on AIPAC contributions that should be publicly disclosed and would affect their assessment of candidates—was a widely shared, though concrete, harm. Because the informational injury was directly related to voting, the most basic of political rights, voters were the appropriate party to bring the grievance.

Without reading too much into *Akins*, the Rehnquist Court has not slammed the courthouse door entirely shut. However, the Court has not been uniformly liberal with its standing doctrine in recent racial gerryman-dering decisions, such as *U.S. v. Hays*, 515 U.S. 737 (1995), and *Shaw v. Hunt*, 116 S. Ct. 1894 (1996), in which the Court limited plaintiff standing to challenge race-based redistricting to voters who reside in the challenged majority-minority districts. In *Hays*, the O'Connor majority rejected the position that "anybody in the state" can state a racial gerrymander claim; plaintiffs must show that they, personally, have been subjected to a racial classification and have suffered personal injury. Moreover, the fact that the state's redistricting plan affects all voters by classifying each of them as a member of a particular congressional district does not mean that every voter has standing to challenge the redistricting as a racial classification. This classification, the *Hays* Court felt, was the description of a generalized grievance. Such a rule not only flies in the face of the *Akins* reasoning, it also seems to contradict the finding in *Shaw v. Reno* regarding the general harm caused by the undue use of race in the electoral districting context. Litigational representation seems to be one area in which it is fair to label the Rehnquist Court as inconsistent—not only with Burger precedents but with its own rulings.

The Court's Retreat from Community of Interests

The conclusion to this case overview is that the Rehnquist Court's rulings are not consonant with the pluralist philosophy and balancing approach of Burger Court precedents. The Rehnquist Court has not advanced the policy of consistently recognizing and protecting the particular aggrega-tive institutions that facilitate interest representation for groups identified by the Burger Court as legally cognizable rights-bearing collectivities. Therefore, despite some views that the Rehnquist Court is continuing the pluralist, pragmatic, and interest-balancing legacy of the Burger Court, a preliminary comparison of key Rehnquist Court rulings with the Burger record on representation rights yields the opposite finding.

Does this conclusion imply that the Rehnquist Court's practical, un-sentimental approach to political representation is without jurisprudential or philosophical foundation? In other words, do these recent decisions reflect hard-edged political pragmatism, stripped of any attention to rep-resentative fairness? Although this Court does not seem particularly solici-tous of communities of interest, it would be premature to conclude that concern for fairness in representative structures and processes is utterly absent from its rulings. Many of the key centrist justices on this Court lack a theoretical or ideological agenda, however, and their opinions—fact-based and narrowly case-specific—reflect this approach. At this point, we can only speculate about the jurisprudence of political representation that will eventually exemplify the Rehnquist era. Based on trends that are already apparent, however, certain tentative conclusions are possible.

AN ALTERNATIVE PLURALISM: REPRESENTING ACTIVITY, NOT INTERESTS?

To some degree, the Rehnquist Court's definition of fairness crosses or defies categories of individual or group-based concepts of representation. Clearly, there is no group interest that a majority coalition can consistently agree on as the basis for a theory of representation—except, perhaps, the interests of states. Even here, however, the Court has been willing to circumscribe local self-rule and interest expression, as in *Norman v. Reed*, 520 U.S. 279 (1992) (state ballot access provisions for new parties invalidated as too restrictive), *Romer v. Evans* (state referendum nullifying special legal protections against discrimination for homosexuals violates the Equal Protection Clause), and *Foster v. Love*, 90 F. 3d 1026 (1997) (state open primary and second ballot system invalid as inconsistent with federal election law).[13] As for individual participation, the Court admits that "reasonably nondiscriminatory restrictions" on the vote are legitimate (*Burdick v. Takushi, Director of Elections in Hawaii*, 504 U.S. 428 (1992)). The Court also tolerates a campaign finance system that privileges financial combinations of interests in electoral dialogue. The individualist versus group approach to representation is simply not helpful in understanding how or whether the Rehnquist Court's decisions effect a competitive balance of interests in a pluralistic sense.

For the current Court, representation rights seem to turn not on group interests per se but on the *type of activity* the group uses to secure the representation of its interests. The Court's decisions appear to distinguish between *voluntary or uncoordinated* (with any institution) group action and *coordinated and institutionally situated* group action. Representative structures and processes should accommodate the former but need not further enhance the latter; indeed, the current Court looks with extreme disfavor upon pleas for rights protections by groups or for political activity already benefiting from institutionalization. This Court rejects what it perceives as "neopluralist equalization" arrangements (Ryden 1996, 105–6) or attempts to modify political procedures to give disadvantaged groups or interests a voice in political debate through *formal legal* mechanisms that equalize group influence—what could be called, in the demographic districting context, "compensatory majoritarianism" (Maveety 1991, 98*ff*). Whether this distinction between voluntary and institutionalized group political activity is tenable either in theory or as applied is irrelevant for the moment; first, we must show that it is a reasonable description of the Rehnquist Court's work.

An interesting case that may shed light on the Court's attitude toward representation as a practice was a campaign finance ruling that addressed the nature of "voluntary" contributions and political action. In *McCormick v. U.S.*, 500 U.S. 257 (1991), the Court overturned a conviction of a West Virginia legislator under the Hobbs Act because of critical ambiguities in jury instructions regarding the statutory definition of *quid pro quo* extortion of funds by public officials. The 6–3 majority opinion was authored by Justice White, a Burger Court holdover who is no longer on the bench. The several opinions in the case suggested, however, that the definition of voluntary political action was important and salient to many members of the court, including Justice Scalia, who filed a concurrence, and Justice Stevens (joined by Justice O'Connor), who filed a dissent. White's decision stressed that "voluntary is what is freely given without expectation of benefit"—even where contributions are given to a representative and legislation beneficial to those contributors is subsequently (or immediately) passed. All of the opinions in the case agreed that anticipation of favorable results from campaign contributions was consistent with federal law—indeed, with pluralist democracy—and that voluntary action could only be judged in a factual context.

McCormick is intriguing because it seems to presage the Court's concerns in a ruling such as that in *Colorado Republican Federal Campaign Committee*, in which the uncoordinated, independent nature of certain party campaign expenditures makes them less regulable and in a sense more volitional and expressive. In the Court's words in *Colorado Republican Federal Campaign Committee*,

> a political party's independent expression not only reflects its members' views about the philosophical and governmental matters that bind them together, it also seeks to convince others to join those members in a practical democratic task, the task of creating a government that voters can instruct and hold responsible for subsequent success or failure. (518 U.S. at 615–16)

Likewise, *McCormick's* fixation on voluntary political action as more authentic seems to be present in Rehnquist Court rulings on majority-minority districting practices and on whether, in districts drawn using race, district residents *"regard themselves as a community"* (*Lawyer v. DOJ*, 117 S. Ct. 2186 (1997); emphasis added). In *Lawyer*, the Court held that a court-ordered districting plan with state consent did not violate the Equal Protection Clause in creating a district with a higher percentage of minority residents than in the counties composing it because race was not a primary factor in its composition. *Lawyer* offered an interesting parry from the more liberal wing of the court on the salience of racial composition in adjudging the constitutionality of a districting plan: "We have never suggested," said Justice Souter's majority opinion,[14] "that the percentage of black residents in a district may not exceed the percentage of black residents in any of the counties from which the district is created, and have never recognized similar racial composition of different political districts as being necessary to avoid an inference of racial gerrymandering in any one of them."

Nevertheless, the presumption of decisions such as *Miller v. Johnson, Shaw v. Hunt,* and *Bush v. Vera* seems to be that a political community created from a policy favoring racial demographics in districting is artificial because it is not the product of voluntary interest expression. To enshrine such a group entity into representation law is to immunize it from the ordinary forces of interest articulation through political competition. Of course, it is interesting to ask how a major party's state campaign committee is less institutionally situated than a group of African American voters. Perhaps the answer lies in the Rehnquist Court's fear that accepting majority-minority districting as requisite under the Voting Rights Act would institutionalize the racial group as an entrenched category of represented interests *and* a collective mechanism for their expression (much as states are institutionalized).

Another point to note is that a strong concurring group of justices (Kennedy, Thomas, Rehnquist, and Scalia) in the *Colorado* case felt that even expenditures by a party committee coordinated with a particular candidate's campaign should not be limited. For these justices, expenditures are the quintessential voluntary political activity because a group interest to be expressed or represented emerges out of the independent actions and affiliative choices of individual contributors. (Not coincidentally, these are some of the same justices who most vociferously object to race-based redistricting efforts.) In contrast, the plurality of contextual centrists/conservatives (Breyer, O'Connor, and Souter) felt that "while the Court is not deprived of jurisdiction to consider this facial challenge by the failure of the parties and the lower courts to focus specifically on the complex issues involved in determining the constitutionality of political parties' coordinated expenditures, that lack of focus provides a prudential reason for the Court not to decide the broader question." Once again, a controlling centrist faction of the Rehnquist Court opted not to theorize beyond the specific factual context of the representation rights claim before them.

Similarly, *Akins* showed the Court's willingness to defer the question of whether an organization falls outside FECA's definition of a political committee because its "major purpose" is not the nomination or election of candidates. The majority remanded the question of whether AIPAC is a political committee engaged in "membership communications" that lie outside of FECA expenditure limitations. It noted that "if the FEC decides that the communications here do not qualify for this exception, then the lower courts can still evaluate the significance of the *communicative context* in which the case arises" (emphasis added).

The concern for protecting a broad conception of voluntary political action does not seem to be present, however, in party ballot access rulings such as that in *Timmons*; indeed, Justice Stevens's dissent in that case accused the Court of not respecting the "expressive purpose of the ballot" for minor parties. *Burdick*, too, is a less-than-solicitous look at the First Amendment associational rights of supporters of write-in candidates. Yet *Morse*—involving the application of section 5 preclearance to a major party's convention registration fees—offers a partial vindication of the "voluntariness" principle. Although Justice Breyer's concurrence concedes the difficulty of First Amendment questions about how far the federal government can regulate the internal working of party conventions (even in pursuit of the Voting Rights Act), he feels the Court "should await a case that squarely presents them." This idea that *the context of political activity is essential in determining its voluntary character* is present in *McCormick*, *Akins*, and *Colorado* (the plurality opinion), as well as in *Morse*. What the various party and PAC decisions, taken together, seem to suggest, however, is that the Rehnquist Court is concerned not with partisan governance or partisan representation per se but with the type or character of group political activity that occurs. This is the Rehnquist Court's take on political representation in a pluralist democracy.

CONCLUDING THOUGHTS ON THE ABSENCE OF THEORY—AT WHAT COST?

In this Tocquevillian celebration of voluntary associations, does the Rehnquist Court provide a satisfactory definition of fair representation? The Court seems to be more concerned with what is unfair—with "unfair" identified as contributing to the institutional entrenchment of an interest (whose expression is not the result of uncoordinated individual actions) that already enjoys representation rights protections. Does the Court apply this standard of representational fairness consistently? Probably not. In identifying communities of interest as the product of voluntary political action and in recognizing (or not recognizing) the aggregative institutions such groups seek to protect, does the Court define the former procedurally, and even formalistically? Possibly. Is the lack of theoretical coherence in the Court's work on representation a matter of pragmatic pluralism and an effort to secure politically satisfactory solutions? This question returns us to the question with which we began, the answer to which must ultimately lie with the decisions' results—which requires empirical analyses of voting, public opinion, the behavior of elected officials, and policy outputs. If the Court is striving for an atheoretical, anti–bright line jurisprudence on political representation, it may have succeeded; yet the political "correctness" of that jurisprudence will depend on political consequences that the Court's nonphilosophical stance on representation rights may precipitate but fail to anticipate.

ENDNOTES

1. Fair representation is a major aspect of voting rights jurisprudence. King, Bruce, and Gelman (1995) speak of six possible standards of racial fairness in electoral redistricting that provide a useful heuristic for other questions of fairness in representation. They identify the six standards as using neutral redistricting criteria, maximizing minority representation, avoiding retrogression in minority representation, maximizing minority representation subject to certain districting constraints, achieving proportional representation, and achieving racial group symmetry (King, Bruce, and Gelman 1995, 90–94).
2. Perversions of this policy of which the Court has been accused—at times, by its own members—include "one acre, one vote"; "one dollar, one vote"; and, most recently, "one man, one minute" (Justice Scalia, dissenting in *Austin v. Michigan Chamber of Commerce*, 494 U.S. 652 (1990)).
3. Although Ryden seems to be including some early Rehnquist Court decisions in his condemnation, his synopsis of the Burger Court record criticizes its

"creation of a group right (to representation) driven more by political considerations than theoretical or philosophical principles . . . (and the) dispensing of
'group representation' rights without a theoretical understanding of the institutional structures that recognize the representative character inherent in all
groups" (Ryden 1996, 6). Maveety (1991, 230) is somewhat more charitable.

4. If the latter, it undercuts much of the existing case law on representation rights,
   facilitating or even promoting cross-cutting judicial coalitions based on judicial
   political theory and on judicial theory regarding precedent.

5. This was the case in *Colorado Republican Federal Campaign Committee v. FEC*
   or the dissent in *U.S. Term Limits v. Thornton*.

6. This dichotomy refers to the familiar distinction between political representation as the representative's reflection of constituents' demographic characteristics and identity and political representation as the functional quality of the
   representative's action on behalf of constituents. For other discussions of formalist versus more substantive definitions of representation, see Pitkin (1967)
   and Rush (1994).

7. The majorities were largely the same—except that in *Romer*, Justice O'Connor
   defected from the dissenting "states' rights" bloc of Chief Justice Rehnquist and
   Justices Scalia and Thomas.

8. Frug (1993) offers an interesting challenge to the idea that residence within the
   geographic territory of local governments is an appropriate basis for assigning
   political rights, as a result of the increasing residential mobility in American
   society.

9. The harm giving rise to this cause of action has been described as a nonindividu-
   alized, expressive harm that results when government gives the appearance of
   endorsing too dominant a role for race in public policy; see Pildes and Niemi
   (1993). See also the discussion of standing in *U.S. v. Hays* and *Shaw v. Hunt*.

10. Justice Kennedy's opinion in *Miller* goes on to say that "our presumptive skep-
    ticism of all racial classifications prohibits us from accepting on its face the
    Justice Department's conclusion that racial districting is necessary under the
    Voting Rights Act." It is important to note, however, that four justices on the
    Rehnquist Court—Stevens, Souter, Ginsburg, and Breyer—remain committed
    to the idea that "ethnicity can tie people together" and that such demographic
    groups therefore merit attention as groups in the districting system of elections
    (Justice Ginsburg, dissenting in *Miller v. Johnson*).

11. See *O'Brien v. Brown*, 409 U.S. 1 (1972); *Democratic Party v. Wisconsin (ex rel
    LaFollette)*, 450 U.S. 107 (1981); *Branti v. Finkel*, 445 U.S. 507 (1980); *Broad-
    rick v. Oklahoma*, 413 U.S. 601 (1973); *Storer v. Brown*, 415 U.S. 724 (1974);
    Anderson v. Celebreeze, 460 U.S. 780 (1983); and *FEC v. National Conservative
    Political Action Committee*, 470 U.S. 480 (1985).

12. Without being terribly careful in answering the question, "Who is the party
    organization?" See *Eu v. San Francisco County Democratic Central Committee*,
    489 U.S. 214 (1989). Also, compare *Morse v. Republican Party of Virginia*, 517
    U.S. 186 (1996), which held that section 5 preclearance under the Voting Rights
    Act applies to internal party nomination practices. To protect the right of
    minority groups to have a full voice in politics, however—as the Supreme Court

has done in minor party presidential ballot access cases such as *Anderson*—the current Court held that a party does not have a fully autonomous voice in its own affairs (Petterson 1998, 10).

13. Given the slim margin of defeat for the states' rights dissenters who defended the state's prerogative to initiate term limits for its congressional delegation in *U.S. Term Limits v. Thornton*, this case cannot be viewed as a clear repudiation of a model of territorial representation.

14. *Lawyer* featured the unusual majority coalition of Justices Souter, Stevens, Ginsburg, and Breyer, plus Chief Justice Rehnquist. Presumably, the state's assent to the plan and the fact that the district in question was not a majority-minority district and was consonant with the state's traditional, nonracial districting considerations, were determinative for Rehnquist. The questions of whether the state had truly consented or whether the district court had acted prematurely animated the dissenters.

··· 3 ···

Vote Dilution, Party Dilution, and the Voting Rights Act: The Search for "Fair and Effective Representation"

HOWARD A. SCARROW

In his celebrated book *Democratic Representation*—published a few years after the Supreme Court's landmark "one person, one vote" decision in *Reynolds v. Sims*, 337 U.S. 533 (1964)—legal scholar Robert Dixon (1968, chapter 11) expressed regret that the Court had failed to acknowledge and confront the complexity of the question of what constitutes "fair and effective representation" in a democracy. Had Dixon lived until the 1990s, he would have seen that the difficult question that the Court failed to confront in 1964 had become the topic of heated debate—by members of the Court and by the scholars who monitor their opinions.

Dixon did not live long enough to observe the event that brought the question of fair representation to center stage—the creation under the Voting Rights Act of so-called "majority-minority" legislative districts. These districts are deliberately designed to contain a majority of black and/or Hispanic voters, to allow members of those minority groups to elect candidates of their choice. The debate became especially noticeable in the wake of the Court's decision in *Shaw v. Reno*, 509 U.S. 630 (1993), a decision that marked the beginning of the Court's retreat from its earlier rulings approving the creation of such districts.

This chapter traces the evolution of the Court's struggle to define "fair and effective representation" (a phrase that first appeared in the *Reynolds* decision). This history illustrates the complexity of that question, especially as reflected in how the Court has dealt with the role played by political parties in the representation process, in the electorate and in the legislature, as well as the question of the rights of *individual*

40

voters versus the rights of *groups* of voters. This history also raises the question of whether the Court is the appropriate institution to resolve such questions.

TWO PERSPECTIVES ON "FAIR AND EFFECTIVE REPRESENTATION"

Vote Dilution

Reynolds v. Sims is remembered as the case in which the Supreme Court ruled that the Equal Protection Clause of the 14th Amendment requires that state legislative districts be made substantially equal in population. As important as the substance of the ruling in the case was the reasoning upon which it was based. Following the approach used in the earlier decision relating to the population size of Congressional districts (e.g., *Wesberry v. Sanders*, 376 U.S. 1 (1964)), Chief Justice Warren's opinion in *Reynolds* held that population disparities in legislative districts violated the equal protection clause of the 14th Amendment because the votes cast within the various districts were not "counted" equally. More specifically, persons living in overpopulated districts had the value, worth, weight, power, effectiveness, or strength of their vote "diluted" or "debased," compared to votes cast in less-populated districts. "Fair and effective representation" meant "one person, one vote." In short, the Court treated legislative apportionment as a simple matter of an individual's *voting rights*, not a matter of citizen representation. The phrase "fair and effective representation" appeared only toward the end of the *Reynolds* decision—and then only as an afterthought, apparently.

In *Fortson v. Dorsey*, 379 U.S. 433 (1965), the Supreme Court extended its emphasis on voter rights and vote dilution by applying the analysis to the dilution of votes cast by *groups* of voters residing within a district. In doing so, the Court left no doubt that when it spoke of the "worth," "value," and so forth, of a vote, it was referring to the ability of a vote to affect the outcome of a district election. The 1965 case was the first involving multimember, at-large legislative districts, in which the several winning candidates are the ones who receive the most votes overall. The Court warned that such districts might be deemed to deny some voters equal protection if those voters could show that those districts operated "to minimize or cancel out the voting strength of racial or political elements of the voting population" (*Fortson v. Dorsey*, 379 U.S.

at 439). Four years later, Chief Justice Warren was more explicit in defining this kind of vote dilution. He noted that at-large systems might deprive racial minorities of the ability "to elect the candidate of their choice" (*Allen v. State Board*, 339 U.S. 544, at 569 (1969)).

The Republican Perspective

Another way of defining fair representation is the republican perspective, following James Madison's distinction between a republic and a democracy in *Federalist 10*. In contrast to the democratic or vote dilution perspective, which focuses on the power of voters to elect candidates of their choice, the republican perspective focuses on representation of citizens in the legislature. According to this view, equal-population districts are required so that citizens are equally represented in the legislative process, thereby increasing the chances that policy decisions will reflect the views of the majority of citizens.

As historian Gordon Wood (1969) has shown, the republican and democratic theories of representation both have firm roots in American history. Indeed, the ratification conflict between the Federalists and the anti-Federalists was in major part an argument over these two competing viewpoints. Speaking for the Federalists, Madison argued that a republican form of government is one in which representatives "refine and enlarge the public views." Madison favored a liberal franchise, but he stressed that the Framers had constructed a republican government, not a voter-directed democracy.

In its early major apportionment decisions, the Supreme Court sometimes seems to have endorsed this republican way of defining fair representation. In *Reynolds v. Sims* and other early cases, the Court found as unacceptable apportionment schemes in which it would be possible for a legislative majority to be composed of legislators elected from districts that together contained only a minority of the state population. One also occasionally finds in these decisions acknowledgment that the goal of equal-population districts is "equal representation for equal numbers of people" (*Wesberry v. Sanders*, 376 U.S. at 18) or that "each representative should cast a vote on behalf of the same number of people" (*Kirkpatrick v. Preisler*, 394 U.S. 526, at 536–37 (1969)). Yet in all of the major apportionment decisions, such acknowledgments by the Court are consistently and overwhelmingly drowned out by the rhetoric of vote dilution and the individualistic view of representation upon which it is premised.

Pluralism and Political Parties

The republican definition of fair representation carries with it the recognition that the electorate is composed of many diverse interests and needs and that legislators from different districts represent this diversity. As Justice Stewart argued in his dissenting opinion in a companion case to *Reynolds v. Sims*, the very fact of geographical districting—rather than statewide, at-large elections—reflects a recognition of a spatially defined diversity of interests; when we speak of representation we are speaking of group interest representation, not representation of "faceless numbers" (*Lucas v. Colorado 44th General Assembly*, 377 U.S. 713 (1964)).

An eminent nineteenth-century jurist made a similar point. Reflecting on the 1842 Congressional act that required states to use districts for the election of their members of the U.S. House of Representatives, Chancellor Kent noted that the act

> was recommended by the wisdom and justice of giving, as far as possible, to the local subdivisions of the people of each state, a due influence in the choice of representatives, so as not to leave the aggregate minority of the people in a state . . . without any voice whatever in the national councils.[1]

The instrument that was expected to give "voice in the national councils" to the people living in these diverse localities was the dominant political party within each of them. The 1842 law was inspired in large part by complaints that statewide elections of Congressional candidates had resulted in a state's single dominant political party winning all of that state's Congressional seats, thereby impairing the ability of political parties in Congress to fulfill their role of representing a large coalition of diverse interests.

American political scientists have long recognized that role as crucial to the achievement of "fair and effective representation" in the United States, with its single-member, plurality-winner, district system of elections (Epstein 1986, chapter 2). Specifically, political parties make it possible for representatives who are elected from a large number of districts, each with distinctive populations and interests, to be responsive to those interests but simultaneously to join together to enact policies that serve the overall public good. Reflective of that tradition is political scientist Gerald Pomper's argument that without the "unifying mechanism" provided by American parties, election campaigns could become "divisive controversies between Catholics and Protestants, blacks and whites, Irish and Italian. When they are functioning well, parties submerge these communal classes in a joint search for electoral victory" (Pomper 1980, 6). After the election, the cross-district electoral coalitions become legislative coalitions whose cooperative behavior takes the form of "horsetrading, logrolling, and backscratching."

Unfortunately, political parties have not always functioned well. Instead of becoming part of a winning coalition, communal groups have been shut out of the political process. Such was the case for many years in parts of the South, where state and local elections have not featured competition between the two major parties. It was to correct that "shutting out" of a communal group—most notably black Americans—that the Supreme Court, through its decisions, and Congress, through its enactments, intervened.

VOTE DILUTION: A EUPHEMISM FOR DEFEAT

The two competing definitions of fair representation were highlighted by the Supreme Court in 1971, when it faced its first major case involving the constitutionality of at-large election districts. The plaintiffs in this case were black voters in the city of Indianapolis who lived in a fifteen-member at-large district for the election of state legislators. The plaintiffs argued that their votes were diluted by the at-large system, and they petitioned the Court to order the dissolution of the single at-large district in favor of many single-member districts.

At first sight, the evidence presented by the plaintiffs appeared to satisfy the Court's evidentiary standard for a vote dilution claim: The votes of a racial minority were being diluted by the overall district majority, and black voters were thus unable to elect candidates of their choice. Yet Justice Byron White, who wrote the majority opinion, denied the plaintiffs' claim. White pointed out that the black plaintiffs were full participants in the political process, that black candidates were regularly nominated by the Democratic party, and that in years when Democrats were successful these black candidates were elected to office. Thus, terms such as "vote dilution" or votes being "canceled out" were simply euphemisms for political defeat. Although proportional voting systems might allow racial groups, religious groups, union groups, Republicans, Democrats, and so forth to be fairly represented, typical American legislative elections are district-oriented, head-on races between candidates of two or more parties. As our system has it one candidate wins, the others lose. Arguably the losing candidates' supporters are without representation.. . . . This is true of both single-member *and* multi-member districts. But we have not yet deemed it a denial of equal protection to deny legislative seats to losing candidates, even in those so-called "safe" districts where the same party wins year after year (*Whitcomb v. Chavis*, 403 U.S. 124, at 153 (1971)).

The following term Justice White again recognized the realities of American politics, especially the role played by political parties. In *Gaffney v. Cummings*, 412 U.S. 735 (1973), the Court approved of, and even praised, a Connecticut single-member districting scheme that was deliberately gerrymandered to produce "political fairness." Under the plan, Republicans and Democrats each were assigned "safe" districts in numbers proportional to their overall support within the state electorate.

What about party supporters who constantly find themselves outvoted in their single-member districts and thus are unable to elect candidates of their choice? Justice White addressed that argument in a case brought by Indiana Democrats against a Republican-engineered gerrymander of the state's legislative districts (*Davis v. Bandemer*, 478 U.S. 109 (1986)). In his plurality opinion, White argued that Democratic voters who were unable to elect a legislator from their district were nevertheless represented by Democratic legislators elected in other districts. Moreover, power to influence the political process is not limited to voting for a winning candidate; district voters who support a losing candidate have as much opportunity to influence the elected candidate as do other district voters.[2] White's ruling was a clear endorsement of the republican perspective on the representative process.

CIRCUMSTANCES SUPPORTING A VOTE DILUTION CLAIM

Despite denying relief to the black plaintiffs in Indianapolis, Justice White acknowledged that the Court might someday rule in favor of an aggrieved racial minority if the plaintiffs could show that they "had less opportunity than did other . . . residents to participate in the political processes and to elect legislators of their choice" (*Whitcomb v. Chavis*, 403 U.S. at 150). Two years later Justice White applied that standard in a case brought by black and Hispanic voters who resided in multimember state legislative districts in Texas (*White v. Register*, 412 U.S. 755 (1973). This time he ruled that the plaintiffs had satisfied his evidentiary standard. In distinguishing this ruling from his ruling in *Whitcomb*, Justice White more fully explained the evidentiary standard required for a successful vote dilution claim. In language that subsequently became part of the Voting Rights Act (see below), Justice White ruled that relief against multimember districts would be granted if racial minorities could show:

> that the political processes leading to nomination and election were not equally open to participation by the group in question—that its members had less opportunity than did other residents in the district to participate in the political process and to elect legislators of their choice (*White v. Register*, 412 U.S. at 766).

To determine whether "the political process" was in fact open to participation by the minority plaintiffs, a court should examine what Justice White termed "the totality of circumstances." White identified circumstances that had come to be associated with attempts in southern localities to keep black voters from exerting political influence: denying black candidates a chance to be nominated by the dominant Democratic party, a history of discriminatory voter registration rules, and election rules that had the effect of favoring white candidates (e.g., majority vote requirements or rules against "slingshot" voting).[3] Where these conditions or other evidence of racial discrimination prevailed, a court would be justified in ordering the creation of single-member districts so that members of a racial minority could elect candidates of their choice—in effect, to allow what political scientists have labeled "descriptive representation" (e.g., black voters being represented by black elected officials).[4]

Thus began what Davidson and Grofman (1994) termed the "quiet revolution"—the transformation throughout the South of multimember, at-large systems into single-member district systems and the resulting election into office of hundreds of black officials.

THE NATIONALIZATION OF THE VOTING RIGHTS ACT AND THE TRIUMPH OF THE VOTE DILUTION STANDARD

While the Supreme Court was cautiously applying the "vote dilution" standard to Fourteenth Amendment claims filed by minority voters in at-large election districts, the Justice Department was dealing with similar questions as enforcer of section 5 of the 1965 Voting Rights Act (VRA). The VRA was designed to protect the voting rights of blacks; it later included linguistic minorities as well. Section 5 of the Act applied only to states and counties that used a literacy test for voter registration and had a record of low voter participation—two factors that together suggested that those jurisdictions might have attempted to reduce black voting participation. In its effect, as with Justice White's "totality of circumstances" test, section 5 applied almost exclusively to jurisdictions in the South.

Section 5 required covered jurisdictions to submit for Justice Department approval all changes they made in voting procedures that might relate to making a vote "effective" (sec. 14). This term was a seemingly clear reference to changes that might result in vote dilution.[5] The types of changes covered by this section came to include all changes relating to legislative districts, including inevitable changes in the design of single-member districts following the decennial census. It was in this role that the Justice Department began in the 1970s the practice of requiring the creation of districts composed of a majority of minority voters—so-called "majority-minority" districts.[6]

Two events led to the expansion of the effective coverage of the VRA to include the entire nation—and with that expansion the creation of majority-minority districts throughout the country. The first development was the amendment of section 2 of the VRA in 1982. Until that time, section 2 was simply a restatement of the 15th Amendment assurance that blacks cannot be denied the right to vote. Thus, section 2 added nothing to the legal argument available to black plaintiffs filing a vote dilution claim. In 1982, however, this section, with its nationwide coverage, was expanded to include Justice White's standard for proving vote dilution in at-large election systems. Repeating White's formulation in his opinion in *Gaffney v. Cummings,* the amended section 2 stated that judicial relief from alleged discriminatory districting will be granted if,

> based on the totality of circumstances, it is shown that the political processes leading to nomination or election in the State or political subdivision are not equally open to participation by (a minority group covered by the Act) in that its members have less opportunity than other members of the electorate to participate in the political process and to elect representatives of their choice.

Leading to this amendment of section 2 was the Supreme Court's decision in *City of Mobile v. Bolden*, 446 U.S. 55 (1980), which raised the evidentiary standard for a 14th Amendment claim to include the requirement that plaintiffs must prove discriminatory *intent* by those who designed the at-large election system. With the passage of the 1982 amendment, plaintiffs could again base their claim on White's less demanding standard. Now, however, that standard was contained in an Act of Congress rather than being inferred from the Fourteenth Amendment as interpreted by a Supreme Court majority.

Yet the 1982 amendment was more than a return to the pre-1980 evidentiary standard for a vote dilution claim. The new section 2 ended with the proviso that in deciding whether "the political processes . . . are equally open to participation by" minorities, a court could take into account the "extent to which members of a protected class have been elected to office." This language clearly suggested that the number of majority-minority districts that would be able to elect a minority official should approximate the group's proportion of the population. The fact that the next sentence stated that protected minority groups do not have a right to proportional representation did little to weaken the clear suggestion of proportionality.[7]

The second major event that led to the expansion of the impact of the VRA was the Supreme Court's interpretation of the revised section 2 in *Thornburg v. Gingles*, 478 U.S. 30 (1986). In that decision, the Court simplified the "totality of circumstances" test to include, in effect, only one circumstance. The single factor that would justify a court overturning an at-large districting scheme (providing that minority voters were sufficiently concentrated to form a single district) was "racially polarized" bloc voting. This term was defined by the Court to mean simply that "black voters and white voters vote differently" (*Thornburg v. Gingles*, 478 U.S. at 53), with the result that the candidates preferred by black voters lost, and the candidates favored by the white voters won. No matter that the explanation for that difference in voting behavior might be something other than race—such as black voters and white voters being motivated by their contrasting political party loyalties. To win a section 2 claim against an at-large election system, plaintiffs need only show a history of contrasting voting patterns by the two groups; the court need not be concerned with the explanation for that difference.[8]

In the context of the dispute then before the Court, the *Gingles* decision was understandable. As with virtually all of the dissolutions of at-large election systems that had been ordered either by the courts or by the Justice Department, *Gingles* involved an election in which candidates were not identified on the ballot by their political party. In *Gingles*, the election was a primary held by the dominant Democratic party. Other cases had involved nonpartisan general elections for local bodies such as city councils or school boards. In either of these types of elections, voters could not distinguish candidates by their party labels; instead, candidates could be identified only by their personal characteristics, such as their race. Thus, rather than a choice between parties, elections presented a choice between races. Rather than a situation in which party labels served as a means of *policy representation*, racial characteristics served as a means of *descriptive representation*. The normal role of political parties in encouraging the "politics of inclusion" in a competitive party system was absent.

The Court's ruling in *Gingles* was also understandable in another sense. Defendants in *Gingles* and in earlier lower court cases had argued that polarized voting patterns could be explained not in terms of race but in terms of income, education, newspaper endorsements, campaign expenditures, incumbency, and so forth. Once these independent variables were controlled in a multivariate regression analysis, a voter's race mattered very little in explaining candidate preference. Confronted with that argument, the Court understandably held that what mattered under the VRA was whether there was a correlation between race and voting preference—not the cause of that relationship.

Finally, the Supreme Court was looking for a simple rule to guide lower courts in deciding vote dilution claims. As in the early apportionment cases in which the Court established percentage standards that defined the extent to which districts could vary in population size, in *Gingles*, too, the Court sought a quantitative measurement provided by election statistics to replace the imprecise "totality of circumstance" test.

THE IMPACT OF THE *GINGLES* RULING

Understandable as it may have been in the context of primary elections or nonpartisan general elections in the South, the simplified evidentiary standard described a voting pattern that existed all over the country, not only in the South. As a lower court judge had noted, by this simple yardstick of "black voters and white voters voting differently," all presidential elections are racially polarized because black voters vote for

Democratic candidates in much higher proportions than do white voters (*Collins v. City of Norfolk*, 605 F. Supp. 377, at 386 (1984)).

Apparently, that wide interpretation of racially polarized voting had not been anticipated by the authors of the 1982 amendment. When the subject of racially polarized voting was discussed in the Senate Judiciary Committee, the Committee majority acknowledged that "with respect to most communities," racial block voting "is not so monolithic, and . . . minority voters do receive substantial support from white voters." Nevertheless, the majority argued in its report, "Unfortunately . . . there still are some communities in our Nation where racial politics do dominate the electoral process" (U.S. Senate, Committee on the Judiciary 1992, 33). As a result of the *Gingles* decision, "some communities" became all communities. Justice White tried to limit the wide application of the new one-circumstance test by urging that it be used only when a black candidate competed against a white candidate, not where candidates of the same race competed in a Democrat versus Republican contest. No majority of justices could reach agreement on this point, however.

The ramifications of the *Gingles* ruling were soon apparent. There were more than 200 cities, in the North and the South, that used at least some multimember, at-large districts for electing their city councils. All of those districts with significant minority populations were now vulnerable to a section 2 challenge. Within a few years, large cities such as Birmingham, Boston, Baltimore, Pittsburgh, and San Diego abandoned at-large systems.

The impact of the *Gingles* ruling grew greater still, however, when lower courts began to apply the *Gingles* test to cases involving single-member districts—an interpretation later ratified by the Supreme Court (*Growe v. Emison*, 507 U.S. 25 (1993)). Consequently, in any area of the country where there was a substantial minority population and where it could be shown that "black voters and white voters vote differently," minority plaintiffs could argue for the creation of as many majority-minority districts as their group's proportion of the population would justify. Accordingly, groups designing Congressional districts in the various states following the 1990 census took no chances; rather than risk expensive litigation under section 2, these cartographers took the initiative and deliberately designed majority-minority districts whenever possible (*Congressional Quarterly* 1991). As a result of these efforts, nineteen additional black and Latino representatives were elected to Congress in 1992 (Lublin 1997, 12).

Designers of state and local legislative districts followed a similar strategy. Thus, the New York State Task Force on Reapportionment reported that it had drawn districts "in strict adherence to the requirements of the Federal Voting Rights Act of 1965, as amended in 1982" (New York State Legislative Task Force on Demographic Research and Reapportionment 1992, 1)." The wide attention given to the numerous newly drawn majority-minority districts is reflected in a story told by Lani Guinier. Among the many requests she received as a result of the notoriety stemming from her failed nomination to head the Civil Rights Division of the Justice Department was a request from a group of dairy farmers in Wisconsin asking for her assistance with their claim that their votes were being diluted (Mansnerus 1993).

In summary, the *Gingles* ruling meant that for minorities covered by the Voting Rights Act—but not dairy farmers—the republican view of representation, and with it the role of voter partisan loyalties, was rejected in favor of the vote dilution/descriptive representation view. This view was not limited to areas where the party system was not working well and where special remedies were required to correct a history of discriminatory practices; it was applied everywhere. It was offered not just to justify dissolution of at-large voting systems but to justify transforming single-member districts into majority-minority districts.

Partisan Impact

The partisan fallout of the revised section 2 was illustrated immediately in a case arising in Ohio—a northern state with a strong tradition of two-party politics. Following the 1990 census, the Ohio reapportionment board—with the apparent approval of the Ohio chapter of the National Association for the Advancement of Colored People (NAACP)—deliberately created eight majority-minority districts. These districts were challenged by a group of Democrats who regarded the plan as a pro-Republican gerrymander and asked the courts to intervene under section 2. The plaintiffs asserted that too many black voters had been "packed" into the eight districts, rather than having some of their number distributed in surrounding districts where they might exercise influence on election outcomes. The Supreme Court denied the claim, refusing to involve itself in deciding whether "influence" districts, as opposed to majority-minority districts, better serve the interests of minority voters (*Voinovich v. Quilter*, 507 U.S. 146 (1993)).

In other states as well, majority-minority districts seem to have benefited Republicans, who stood a better chance of electing their candidates in surrounding districts devoid of many of their black Democratic voters. Those making that argument offered Georgia's experience as evidence. As of 1990, Georgia's Congressional delegation was composed of nine Democrats and one Republican. After the 1994 election, Republicans enjoyed an eight-to-three advantage over Democrats—a reversal attributable at least in part to newly created majority-minority districts.[9]

"BIZARRE" DISTRICTS: RACIAL GERRYMANDERS OR PARTISAN GERRYMANDERS?

The interpretation of the Voting Rights Act took another turn in the mid-1990s, when the Supreme Court began to curtail the creation of majority-minority legislative districts. To justify its retreat from its previous approval of such districts, the Court was forced to distinguish between an acceptable partisan gerrymander and an unacceptable racial gerrymander. In doing so, the Court began to abandon its thirty-year emphasis on defining fair representation in terms of the avoidance of vote dilution.

Following the 1990 census, the Justice Department—now encouraged by the amended section 2—urged states covered by section 5 to include in their newly designed districting maps for Congress and state legislatures the maximum possible number of majority-minority districts. The result was the creation of districts whose shapes became the subject of ridicule; these districts were variously labeled as "bizarre" (*Shaw v. Reno*, 509 U.S. 630 (1993)), resembling a "bug splattering on a windshield" (*Wall Street Journal*, 1992). The first of these districts to attract national attention was a Congressional district in North Carolina that stretched snake-like for 160 miles; at one point, it was so narrow that it embraced little more than the width of an interstate highway.

The Justice Department was not the only actor to encourage this imaginative cartography. Democrat-controlled legislatures in states such as North Carolina, Georgia, and Texas were led by Democrats experienced in the art of partisan, incumbent-protecting gerrymandering; the Justice Department simply encouraged them to put their traditional skills to maximum use. Not surprisingly, therefore, the first judicial challenge to these strangely shaped districts in 1992 was based on the charge that the districts were part of a Democrat-led partisan gerrymander that denied Republican voters their Fourteenth Amendment rights of equal protection. The lower courts rejected this claim. The Supreme Court's refusal to override reflected its 1986 decision that established a very high threshold of proof—yet to be met—before a partisan gerrymander would be declared unconstitutional; the political minority must first demonstrate that the districting system "will consistently degrade a voter's or group of voters' influence on the political process as a whole" (*Davis v. Bandemer,* 478 U.S. at 132).

Their first claim having been rejected, the North Carolina plaintiffs changed tactics. The subsequent lawsuit was premised on the charge that the districting plan was a *racial* gerrymander and that white voters had a Fourteenth Amendment right to participate in a racially neutral election process. In the 1993 path-breaking decision in *Shaw v. Reno*, a majority of the Supreme Court agreed. As elaborated in two later decisions (*Miller v. Johnson*, 515 U.S. 900 (1995); *Bush v. Vera*, 517 U.S. 952 (1996)), the Court adopted the stance that, although race can be taken into account when legislatures draw district lines, race cannot be the "predominant factor" determining a district's design. Districts that are "grotesque" in shape, and thus in sharp variance with "traditional race-neutral districting principles"—compactness, contiguity, and respect for political subdivisions—require that the Court examine closely the motives of those who designed them. (The Court has applied a similar standard with respect to states' affirmative action policies.)

The result of the Court's new approach was illustrated in 1996 when it ruled on the constitutionality of several Congressional districts in Texas (*Bush v. Vera*). Some of these districts—such as the Dallas-based District 30, with its black and Democratic majority—were judged to be unconstitutional because the designers of these districts had used census-derived racial data to guide their efforts. Although evidence showed that 97 percent of blacks in and around Dallas voted Democratic, the cartographers should have used political data to guide them, not racial data. In contrast, other districts equally "grotesque" in shape—such as District 6, with its white Republican majority—were judged acceptable because political factors, such as incumbent protection, were seen by the Court's 5–4 majority as having guided their design. Federal courts have made the same kind of distinction in cases involving state university admission policies; preference for admission can be given to students on the basis of their musical ability or their athletic ability—but not on the basis of their race or ethnicity (*Hopwood v. State of Texas*, 78 F. 3d 932 (1996)).

REVERSALS, CONTRADICTIONS, REACTIONS

The Court's decisions in these majority-minority districting cases marked two substantial retreats from previous holdings. First, by stressing the value of "traditional districting principles," the Court was explicitly acknowledging that "fair and effective representation" cannot be defined exclusively in terms of "vote worth" or its opposite, "vote dilution." The defenders of the bizarre districts likewise advanced arguments based on a comprehensive, republican definition of fair districting. Thus, Georgia defended its districting plan by arguing that the majority-minority Congressional districts were created for the purpose of bringing together "communities of interest" (*Miller v. Johnson,* 515 U.S. at 916). Justice Ginsburg, dissenting from the Court's ruling, agreed, noting that large cities in the United States have often featured districts drawn to reflect the "felt identity" of persons united by a common ethnic bond (e.g., Chinese, Irish, Italian, Jewish, Polish, Russian) (515 U.S. at 944–45). Justice Ginsburg argued that Georgia's districts based on race should be viewed no differently.

In another sense, too, the *Bush v. Vera* decision represented a reversal of the Court's previous reasoning. In *Gingles,* motivations were to be found not worthy of judicial notice: Whatever the motivation of those casting ballots might be, the *fact* of "white voters and black voters voting differently" is enough to support a section 2 claim against a districting scheme. In the Texas case, however, the Court looked behind the *fact* that a district had a "bizarre" shape and inquired into the motivation of those who designed it; having in *Gingles* adopted an empirically verifiable test for a section 2 claim to replace the more subjective "totality of circumstance" test, the Court now introduced the subjective standard of motivation. The ironic result was that minority plaintiffs advancing a section 2 claim would continue to insist that racially polarized voting was reflective of racial voting, not partisan voting (*Goosby v. Town Board,* 956 F. Supp. 326 (1997)), whereas defenders of bizarrely shaped majority-minority districts were now forced to take the opposite tack—arguing that these districts were partisan inspired, not racially inspired.

Apart from these reversals and contradictions, the *Bush v. Vera* ruling, which proved to be the last major voting rights decision of the 1990s, was especially troublesome for critics who monitor the Court's opinions. The Equal Protection Clause of the Fourteenth Amendment seemed to have been turned on its head; rather than being used for its historic purpose of protecting minority interests, it was being used to protect the interests of majorities—the majority party faction (Democrat) in the Texas state legislature and the majority racial faction (white) in the Texas population.

The *Bush v. Vera* decision also was troubling for observers who value the role that political parties can play in the working of American democracy. By approving a one-party gerrymander deliberately designed to protect the party in power against its partisan opponents, the Court stamped its imprimatur on political parties operating at their worst. Gerrymanders designed by one political party, regardless of the data used to construct them, usually are detrimental to the goal of "fair and effective representation"; by ensuring incumbent protection, such gerrymanders weaken the role of elections as instruments of government responsiveness. For voters who are packed into noncompetitive districts, the act of voting itself becomes inconsequential. Most serious, such invidious gerrymanders—in contrast to benign gerrymanders, as illustrated in *Gaffney v. Cummings*—may frustrate the will of the majority. In the first election held under the approved districting plan in Texas, twenty-six of twenty-seven incumbents were reelected. Moreover, Democratic candidates won 70 percent of the Congressional seats despite receiving less than half of the votes overall—the very opposite of what should occur in a responsive party system.

CONCLUSION

As the 2000 census approaches with its new round of reapportionment, the debate over how to achieve fair and effective representation continues. Some critics have urged that the Supreme Court declare most of the Voting Rights Act to be unconstitutional, so that neither the Justice Department nor minority plaintiffs will be able to demand the creation of majority-minority districts. Other critics have urged that the Court follow the lead of Justice Stevens, whose dissent in *Bush v. Vera* argued that partisan gerrymanders, more than racial gerrymanders, must be restrained by the Court.

Perhaps the most provocative suggestions have come from observers who have urged state and national legislatures to enact laws designed to achieve the goal of "fair and effective representation," thus relieving the Court of that burden. Some reformers have pushed for adoption by each state of some form of proportional representation; under such systems, all voters—not just minority voters covered by the Voting Rights Act—are able to elect candidates of their choice by distributing their several preferences (e.g., three preferences in a three-member district) in ways most advantageous to their group or party. Other reformers, especially those who support America's traditional two-party system, prefer a reform that has already been enacted in several states: the creation of an independent, bipartisan commission to design Congressional and state legislative districts. This reform is intended to prevent the one-party gerrymanders of the kind enacted in Texas. One advantage of both proposals is that they allow states themselves to become involved in resolving the difficult questions of fair and effective representation, at least for their own legislatures and local governments.[10] The most appealing feature of the two proposals, however, is that they remove from the judiciary the burden of solving the riddle of how to draw district lines, especially given the United States' racial and ethnic diversity. As this chapter has sought to demonstrate, the judiciary, over a period of nearly forty years, has proved itself unable to deal clearly, logically, and consistently with the kinds of questions raised by that riddle.[11]

ENDNOTES

1. As quoted by Justice Frankfurter in his opinion in *Colgrove v. Green*, 328 U.S. 549, at 553 (1946).

2. One political scientist has referred to such representation as "collective representation" (Weisberg 1978). Justice White had applied the same perspective in an earlier case (*United Jewish Organization v. Carey* 1977)—ruling that white voters in a majority-minority district were represented by white legislators elected from surrounding districts.

3. Because most of these circumstances had been listed systematically by a circuit court decision in the at-large districting case of *Zimmer v. McKeithen*, 485 F. 2d 1297 (1973), they came to be referred to as the "Zimmer factors." It should be noted that the list did not include "racially polarized voting" (see below). A rule against "slingshot" voting—also called "bullet voting"—prevented black voters from targeting their votes in a multicandidate at-large election by voting only for the one or two black candidates on the ballot, rather than for the full quota of choices allowed to each voter.

4. Pitkin (1967) thoroughly discusses descriptive and other forms of "representation."

5. The decision in *Allen v. State Board*, 339 U.S. 544 (1969), interpreted the Voting Rights Act as giving this power to the Justice Department. The most widely cited work of an author who argues that the Voting Rights Act was not intended to be interpreted in this way is Thernstrom (1987).

6. One of the first such districts to be ordered by the Justice Department, following the 1970 census redistricting, was a New York State legislative district in Brooklyn, New York—a county that, to the surprise of many, met the criteria for coverage by section 5. See *United Jewish Organization v. Carey*, 430 U.S. 144 (1977).

7. The impact of the revised section 2 was reflected in the fact that the Justice Department ordered twice as many changes to single-member districts in the three years following the amendment as it had ordered since the enactment of the VRA (McDonald 1992). For a more complete account of the impact of the VRA, see Grofman, Handley, and Niemi (1992).

8. The district court ruling in *Davis v. Bandemer* had ruled the very opposite: that the Indiana Republican gerrymander had resulted in no Fourteenth or Fifteenth Amendment violation because "the voting efficacy of the NAACP plaintiffs was impinged upon because of their politics and not because of their race" (*Davis v. Bandemer,* 478 U.S. at 118).

9. Many of the consequences of majority-minority districts have been of concern even to those who have championed the overall impact of the Voting Rights Act. For example, Lani Guinier has acknowledged that majority-minority districts may result in separating moderate white voters "from blacks who would form coalitions with them but for the subdistricting" (Guinier 1991, 1154).

10. An act of Congress would be necessary before states could elect House members from multimember districts, as required for systems of proportional representation.

11. The Supreme Court's continued difficulty was illustrated in its most recent voting rights decision. On May 17, 1999, the Court approved the concentration of black voters in North Carolina's 12th Congressional District, seeming to retreat from its previous admonition that race-conscious districting was unconstitutional (*Hunt v. Cromartie*, 119 S. Ct. 1545 (1999)).

··· 4 ···

Districting and the Meanings
of Pluralism: The Court's Futile Search
for Standards in Kiryas Joel*

STEPHEN E. GOTTLIEB[1]

THE CASE OF *KIRYAS JOEL*: THE VILLAGE
AND THE DISTRICT

In 1977 the Satmar Hasidic residents of Monroe, New York, seceded from the village to form the Village of Kiryas Joel (Kolbert 1989, A1, B4). The villagers sent most of their children to a private religious school, but they needed the resources of the Monroe-Woodbury public school district to educate their handicapped children. Although the village was

*Editor's Note: This chapter continues the assessment of the Supreme Court's search for quality substantive standards for districting and representation. It offers a more lawyerly analysis than the political science perspectives of the previous chapters. Although the language differs, however, the analysis and conclusions are similar—the Court has failed to offer a substantive definition of representation to guide its decision making. This chapter appraises issues of representation in the context of *Board of Education of Kiryas Joel Village School District v. Grumet,* 512 U.S. 687 (1994), in which the Court rejected an attempt by the New York State Assembly to create a separate school district for a Hasidic community in New York City.

The Court invoked alternative standards to decide the case—examining legislative motives, governmental neutrality, consistency, and delegation of control. It ignored important competing values, however, that underlie our system of representation and are implicated by the case. One set of values is integration and assimilation: How does or should representation approximate or reflect common identity and the interests and good of the whole? Other values point in the opposite direction—toward necessary segregation to allow for the cultivation of a distinct group identity. Whereas Howard Scarrow castigates the Court for its neglect of "fair and effective representation," Stephen Gottlieb concludes that the Court has ducked the real question of what constitutes good or bad districting.

At stake are the central questions of practical pluralism. Who is to be recognized in our system? What interests are to be facilitated, either in creating electoral districts or giving control of schools? Does the system of districting generate representation of the individual, of the group, or of the whole? This analysis requires substantive definitions of good and bad districting—definitions the Court has not offered.

separately incorporated, it remained within the Monroe-Woodbury public school district. The Hasidic parents tried to send their handicapped
children to the public schools for special education, but the children felt
very uncomfortable. Their dress and customs were very different, and,
already vulnerable because of their handicaps, they felt even more uncomfortable in these public schools (*Board of Education of Kiryas Joel
Village School District v. Grumet*, 512 U.S. 687, at 691 (1994)). The
Supreme Court closed off one alternative—having special education
teachers from the public school come to an annex of the religious school
specifically for the purpose of providing special education.[2]

Eventually, the New York state legislature, in response to a request
by the Village of Kiryas Joel, created a separate, secular school district
that included only the Village.[3] The Village used that district solely to
set up a school—with a secular curriculum—for special education for
handicapped children. The New York State School Boards Association
then brought an action against the state Education Department, charg-
ing that the creation of the school district was an unconstitutional establishment of religion.[4] The New York Court of Appeals agreed that
creation of the district violated the First Amendment of the U.S. Constitution.[5]

In *Kiryas Joel*, the Supreme Court was asked to evaluate the district,
created by the New York legislature presumably with the intent to accommodate a group of coreligionists in achieving a secular purpose. On
appeal from the New York Court of Appeals, the Supreme Court agreed
that the district violated the U.S. Constitution.

THE PROBLEM OF REPRESENTATION:
THE RECOGNITION AND TREATMENT OF GROUPS

Kiryas Joel raises competing visions of the recognition of groups in society
and the meaning of equal treatment and, as a result, engages problems
that are at the root of representation. Some of these competing visions
have roots in the Equal Protection Clause of the Fourteenth Amendment
and require integration in some circumstances and blindness toward
group membership in others. Other visions have roots in the religion
clauses of the First Amendment and require respect for self-segregated
groups.

One way to put the relevant question is as follows: How should a
religious minority be treated relative to more dominant faiths, locally and

statewide? In that respect, school district lines pose problems similar to legislative district lines. Should lines be drawn across group boundaries or along them? Drawing lines *across* boundaries produces heterogeneous districts. Legislative districts drawn in this manner are competitive and likely not "safe" for incumbents seeking reelection. Lines drawn that way are also likely, however, to subordinate one group to the whims of another. Whoever is in the majority wins elections. This situation can produce very harsh results; black voters who are a minority in areas polarized over race, for example, have no voice and no influence.

Where heterogeneous populations are incorporated in school districts, members of minority faiths are consigned to public schools in which the curriculum, the cultural practices, the role models, and the symbolism are all set by the dominant group. Which issues, controversial for which groups, will be discussed? Whose songs will be sung? Who will choose the textbooks and the reading lists? Whose children will feel like they are just fine, and whose children will feel disparaged, second class, worthless, and defeated? Where the groups are religious groups, integration can effectively become domination of the minority faith by the majority faith.

For many years, the Supreme Court defended a "wall" between church and state, insisting that there be no involvement of secular authorities in religious matters, no teaching of religion or recital of prayers in the public schools. The wall used to exist as a defense against domination; it was never complete with respect to religion, and it never covered cultural issues that are prominent in Hasidic life. Heterogeneous districting from the Hasidic point of view is not equal or neutral districting—it is decidedly hostile.

Drawing lines *along* group boundaries produces homogeneous districts that are likely to be noncompetitive and safe for incumbents seeking reelection. Competing groups are separated into different districts; larger groups dominate more districts and elect more representatives. This arrangement results in a form of proportional representation in legislatures, whereby each different community is represented in a rough approximation of their strength in the population.

In the school districting context, we can certainly observe differences in the homogeneity of school districts. Many are exclusively Christian, some even more precisely confined to one or a few related Christian sects. Why not the Hasidim? Wouldn't such districting be equal? Wouldn't it treat them just like other groups are treated?

The attempt, on behalf of the Hasidim, to match the conditions in which others go to school may be unacceptable because of the implications for other instances of racial, religious, and ethnic segregation and integration. Historically, *de jure* racial segregation shifted to *de facto* segregation under the guise of local control. School districts' "freedom of choice" plans (in which each family decided, within some limitations, where to send their children) did not satisfy desegregation orders because, after the history of segregation, no one was willing to endure the social ostracism and economic retaliation that would result from sending one's children to the school that "belonged" to the other race. Similarly, residential patterns sometimes reflected prior *de jure* segregation and therefore could not form the basis for desegregated school districts; decisions about the siting of schools and other facilities had to be reviewed to make sure that racial considerations were excluded.

Indeed, the incorporation of school districts, among other decisions that are not explicitly racial, could be undertaken to facilitate segregation precisely as it was undertaken by the Village of Kiryas Joel. To allow some groups to segregate themselves in the religious context can effectively impose segregation on others. Such self-segregation, in turn, conflicts with the desire of many citizens to assimilate into the broader population except for specifically religious activities. In effect, religious self-segregation can imply segregation in other contexts as well. Racial minorities know the pattern too well—hence the problem with individual freedom of choice and with plans that respect group differences by drawing lines between them.

None of the standards the Supreme Court has used to measure the constitutionality of districting in the electoral or educational contexts has solved these difficulties or successfully measured equal treatment. The problems are compounded in the area of the religious diversity of school districts. The Court does not—perhaps cannot—have a standard against which to measure the proper diversity of school districts.

Efforts to resolve such districting problems have included gauging the constitutionality of the districting either in terms of the *motives* of the responsible public officials, *official neutrality* toward the groups involved, the *consistency* of official behavior, whether the state *delegated power* to a religious institution, or whether the district lines *segregated or integrated* school children. This chapter examines each of these approaches.

Motive tests evaluate the constitutionality of legislation on the basis of whether the lawmakers intended to discriminate against a protected group. The problem with a motive test in *Kiryas Joel* is that, regardless of the actions taken, there was no nonreligious motive available; in the legislative districting cases, there is no possible absence of racial motives. The problem of good or bad districting has to be resolved substantively.

Neutrality means that a piece of legislation creates categories that are unrelated to religion (or any other prohibited category). Despite the appeal of this concept, no baseline of neutrality exists; we have no clear understanding of what is unrelated to religion. Moreover, if the concept means that legislation should neither help nor hurt religion unduly, we have no standard from which to reach such conclusions. The same is true of race in electoral districting: We have not defined what districting is good or bad for blacks or whites or what gives them equivalent choices or freedom. The difficulties are amplified in the case of school districting with respect to religious communities. In contrast to situations involving race, there are too many variables and no clear guidelines for which variables to count. Thus, the problems of accounting for religious communities in school districting cannot be solved by neutrality.

The Supreme Court tried to sidestep neutrality in *Kiryas Joel* by substituting *consistency*—what the state had been doing elsewhere. The variations are so large, however, that consistency is hard to define. Moreover, we have no standard for the fairness of what has consistently been done. Thus, consistency is little more helpful than neutrality.

The problem with an analysis based on *control* of a school district by religious institutions is that it sidesteps the elements of homogeneity and size on which it depends. That is, small districts, like charter schools, are likely to be controlled by a small and homogeneous group, perhaps centered in a specific congregation. Yet it is not clear that all small districts are forbidden—just certain ones.

Allowing the Village of Kiryas Joel to secede in this way, however, would threaten to undo the benefits of decades of work to create integrated common schools. The precedent might be hard to contain; if such a privilege were extended to other groups, resegregation of the school population could take place. In the United States, segregation historically has effectively subordinated the minority group. If the Satmar were to remain within the Monroe School District, they would be a small minority dominated by the tastes and beliefs of their non-Satmar neighbors. That situation poses the real difficulty of all districting solutions—the conflict between group autonomy and integration and the potential of both models to produce domination instead of equality.

Equal power may require areas that can be controlled locally by groups that would be subordinated by the larger culture. Indeed, the original premise of the common school movement was that local communities could control their schools without regard to the different cultures of other towns or distant state authorities—although minorities in the local community might have nowhere to turn.

Integration is critical to equality in a different way. It generates equality by mutual acquaintance and contacts, as well as a sharing of resources. When the Supreme Court held in *Brown v. Board of Education*, 347 U.S. 483 (1954), that segregation is "inherently unequal," it had already examined, and rejected, several cases in which states that had practiced segregation had built a new school or roped off an area in an existing university so that black students could get an education without mixing with white students. Getting to know fellow students and professors was part of the preparation of any professional. It enabled them to work together later on terms of mutual trust and respect, as well as to share the experience they would gain in the profession.

Integration also subordinates minorities, however. People get to know each other—but on the terms of the dominant group. Integration creates social pressure that leads to conformity in dress, speech, manners, style, interests, and activities. For the member of the minority who does not learn the majority's social ways or refuses to conform, isolation is followed by loss of referrals and other significant opportunities for personal and professional advancement.

These dynamics reflect two competing visions of equality—through group solidarity and through assimilation. They also reflect two visions of inequality—inability to control one's own life within the community and inability to participate in the external community. These models of equality are incompatible.

If we could fix on a model of equality, the legislative district context allows comparison among districts to see whether the same concept of equality has been extended fairly and consistently. In the school district context, the only comparison is temporal: Is the situation more or less integrated than it might have been if some other decision had been made (subject to judgment about necessary and important competing objectives)? Small districts may be permitted, but segregation is not permissible, even though the implementation of antisegregation principles will inevitably result in considerable unfairness.

THE MOTIVE STANDARD

Motive analysis has been crucial to electoral districting cases and religion cases. Yet it is unsatisfactory in both areas because it leaves totally ambiguous answers about how one should treat the groups involved.

The Motive Test in Establishment Cases

Motive analysis has been central to Establishment Clause analysis since the Supreme Court ruled that to be constitutional, "First, the statute must have a secular legislative purpose; second, its principal or primary effect must be one that neither advances nor inhibits religion; finally, the statute must not foster an excessive government entanglement with religion" (*Lemon v. Kurtzman,* 403 U.S. 602, at 612 (1971)). The Court has largely written the entanglement test out of the law, and it has had great difficulty figuring out what "advances or inhibits religion." Thus, the motive portion of the beleaguered *Lemon* test seems very attractive; as the Court recently wrote, it "continue(s) to ask whether the government acted with the purpose of advancing or inhibiting religion" (*Agostini v. Felton,* 521 U.S. 203, at 222–23 (1997)).

In *Kiryas Joel,* the Supreme Court found the school district unconstitutional on the basis of evidence about the unusual way that the school district was created, the way it followed religious lines, and the way it ran counter to New York's general school districting practices. Justice Souter denied that he was attacking the legislature's motive: "Nor do we impugn the motives of the New York Legislature . . . which no doubt intended to accommodate the Satmar community without violating the Establishment Clause." He focused on its actions:

> [W]e simply refuse to ignore that the method it chose is one that aids a particular religious community, as such, see App. 19-20 (Assembly sponsor thrice describes the Act's beneficiaries as the "Hasidic" children or community), rather than all groups similarly interested in separate schooling (*Kiryas Joel,* 512 U.S. at 708).

At the heart of the inquiry was the "distinction between a government's *purposeful* delegation (of civic authority) on the basis of religion and a delegation on principles neutral to religion. . . ." (*Kiryas Joel,* 512 U.S. at 699). The Court's use of words such as "based," "purpose," "purposeful," and "targeting" show that it was searching for a religious motive.

The Court found a valid underlying secular purpose, using a combination of circumstantial evidence and confessed purpose. The sponsor of the act that created the district described its beneficiaries as "the 'Hasidic' children or community," who were protected from the ridicule of other children. Yet the Court did not invalidate the goal—"to accommodate the Satmar community [within the bounds of] the Establishment Clause" (*Kiryas Joel*, 512 U.S. at 708). Then, however, the Court found "good reasons to treat this district as the reflection of a religious criterion for identifying the recipients of civil authority." The Court also found a religious motive—first in the goal to aid the Satmar, then in finding other alternatives not taken by the legislature. The Court held that the State cannot "deliberately delegate discretionary power to an individual, institution, or community on the ground of religious identity." The Court recognized that the legislature delegated power to the school district, not by express reference to the Satmar's religion, but rather to the residents of the village. Nevertheless, the Court found evidence of legislative intent in the legislature's knowledge of the makeup of the village (and the fact that the new district was drawn along religious lines). Moreover, the new district deviated from the state's trend to enlarge, rather than contract, districts and originated in a special act rather than in a general school district redistricting law. These circumstances revealed the invalid motive of the "delegation of political power to a religious group" (*Kiryas Joel*, 512 U.S. at 699–702, 706–7).

As these remarks indicate, the Court did not clearly distinguish motive analysis from neutrality analysis. The two are related as subjective and objective versions of the same criteria. Justices Souter, Blackmun, Stevens, and Ginsburg used subjective language in concluding that the school district plan was "a purposeful and forbidden 'fusion of governmental and religious functions'" (*Kiryas Joel*, U.S. 512 at 702, citing *Larkin v. Grendel's Den*, 459 U.S. 116, at 126 (1982)). The next portion of the opinion, which spoke for a majority of the Court, similarly questioned whether New York would do the same for other groups (*Kiryas Joel*, 512 U.S. at 702–4). If New York did not exercise its districting "in a religiously neutral way," it would violate the Establishment Clause—and this *ad hoc* legislation made it impossible to verify. Under the circumstances, it was possible that New York took its action because it sought to give the Satmar power over a school district.

The use of a motive test often looks like an easy substitute for the hard analysis of figuring out what the parties actually accomplished—if they meant to do harm, treat them as if they did. In fact, motive analysis is more likely to involve a poorly thought-out intuitive discussion that obscures the issues and avoids the real problems. One of the problems with the motive test derives from questions of proof. Because public bodies usually do not confess invalid motives, courts must often use inferential methods of proof; that is, they must look at the effects. In many areas of law, there is a strong inference that the natural and probable consequences of an action are intended. If several goals can be identified, some of which are legitimate, the inquiry is more difficult; it depends on the standard implicitly required.[6] The standard is implicit because courts have written about motivation as an intuitive entity needing no analysis—a simplistic approach that obscures far more than it reveals. Nevertheless, if the courts treat any legitimate goal as negating the inference of an improper motive, they are implicitly requiring very little—what lawyers call a rational basis or minimal scrutiny test (Gottlieb 1986, 105). If the level of inquiry rises to strict scrutiny, the legitimate goal must be of sufficiently compelling importance to negate the charge that an accompanying illegitimate effect was intended (Gottlieb 1986, 105–6). A middle level of scrutiny would allow a good, rather than compelling, reason to disprove such an intent (Gottlieb 1986, 106).

The motive test, however, conceals all of that analysis and makes the conclusion flexible. The legislature did or did not intend to benefit a group because of its faith depending on how we weigh the evidence. The Court could have found that the Village of Kiryas Joel wanted to separate just like many other groups, and the legislature was motivated to accede to local preferences for ordinary political reasons. The evidence is identical; only the interpretation differs.

The motive test also fudges what ought to be done. To treat a set of behaviors as powerful evidence of a prohibited state of mind or a corrupted political process effectively prohibits the behavior. To prohibit the process or the state of mind without facing squarely the question of what behavior should be encouraged or discouraged muddies the issue. The Court has done that in many of the cases involving racial legislative districting, and it arguably has done that in *Kiryas Joel* as well. The Satmar are just like anyone else—and different. Retreating to motive makes it unclear how they should be treated.

The third problem with the motive test is that (in *Kiryas Joel* as in election districting) motive is unavoidable—both ways. The Court defines discrimination as the motive to treat unequally and employs that definition in its election districting cases—even though, as the Court ultimately recognized, such motive is always present (*Davis v. Bandemer*, 478 U.S. 109, at 128–29 (1986)). Thus, the question is whether the districts were in fact acceptable. The Court has not adopted a substantive standard for proper districting that could answer that question, however. Absent resolution of the substantive question, it is impossible to know whether the motive was to produce a legitimate or illegitimate result. Conversely, resolution of the legitimacy of motive implies a statement about whether the results are considered legitimate or not. The questions are intertwined, and approaching them from the subjective vantage point of motive does not simplify the inquiry.

Despite these objections, the Court now uses motive tests freely. In some religion cases, the Court must decide whether a legislature had a motive to burden the free exercise of religion. In other cases, the Court must decide whether a legislature had a motive to benefit a religion. In *Kiryas Joel*, the legislature was trapped between burdening and benefiting a religion. Motivation with respect to religion was unavoidable; the question is whether what the legislature did was kosher.

Distinguishing bad motives from good is not simply a matter of looking into the hearts of legislators. The problem is whether what they wanted to do is legitimate. In *Walz v. Tax Commission of the City of New York*, 397 U.S. 664 (1970), the Supreme Court upheld a tax exemption for property owned by nonprofit, quasi-public corporations, including churches. The Court found no "legislative purpose" to establish religion. The members of the New York legislature certainly intended to benefit religion, finding religion—along with hospitals, libraries, and like organizations—to be a "beneficial and stabilizing influence in community life. . . ." The effect of the tax exemption certainly was a benefit to religious bodies that owned property. In its motive analysis, however, the Court found the more general motive of benefiting charitable organizations to be sufficient to establish a secular purpose. The Court recognized that "benevolent neutrality toward churches and religious exercise" is "deeply embedded in the fabric of our national life, beginning with pre-Revolutionary colonial times"; therefore, property tax exemptions are permissible for charitable institutions, including churches. The Court characterized neutrality as including benevolence. But benevolent neutrality is not neutral; classifying churches as charitable versus religious but noncharitable is not a neutral decision, but requires judgment. Both motive and the underlying substance are contested and hard to define (*Walz v. Tax Commission of the City of New York*, 397 U.S. at 673–77, 680).

Indeed, the motive test is a sham for other substantive views in cases such as *Kiryas Joel* in which the facts can be characterized in inconsistent ways: Sunday closing is religious and secular, charitable exemptions for churches are neutral in some aspects and preferential in others, and the school district in *Kiryas Joel* was religious and secular. Both types of effect may be reasonable and justifiable, but neutrality and neutral motives explain neither.

Kiryas Joel was a community. Communities often have school boards. As the Court insists, religious organizations are not to be disqualified from doing what others can do. The issue was not the use of the schools to teach the tenets of Hasidic Judaism. It was whether a group of people could incorporate a town and lobby for a school board on equal terms with all others despite their convictions—unless Hasidic Jews are different. There are good reasons to deny them the separate school board, but doing so requires an analysis that deals with the substance of segregation and integration. The motive issue simply creates a problem with no right answer.

Once the uniqueness of the villagers is raised there is no neutral position—only pro and con. The villagers could be accommodated by themselves or they could be submerged and their needs subordinated in the larger surrounding community. *Kiryas Joel* put the Court in the position of choosing to either submerge or separate a religious minority. There is no neutral position.

The Motive Test in Gerrymandering Cases

The problem of merging or submerging the Satmar has a precise parallel in the drawing of electoral district lines. There too, in partisan gerrymandering cases, motive has been a required but moot inquiry. In *Davis v. Bandemer*, the Court first declared partisan gerrymandering cases to be justiciable. To find a districting plan to be a constitutional violation, the Court in *Davis* required a showing of a motive to discriminate against an identifiable political group and a discriminatory effect on that group. The Court further stated, however, that whenever a legislature redistricts, its motive is always to maintain political advantage. The Court ultimately restricted relief to cases in which gerrymandering made turnover virtually impossible for a generation (*Davis v. Bandemer*, 478 U.S. at 127, 129, 132–36).

In contrast to the religious and racial contexts, however, the Court in *Davis* denied any preference for homogeneous or heterogeneous districts. It demonstrated no awareness of how to figure out whether turnover had become impossible. Because partisan motives were an acknowledged part of the process, the Court could not evaluate when the motives were unconstitutional. As in *Kiryas Joel*, motive analysis proved unsatisfying. It does not reveal which motive was primary, what should have been done, or which group is helped or hurt. Motive is totally ambiguous; it is always present, always absent, and always useless.

The Supreme Court has also turned to motive in evaluating racial districting. Although the Court recognizes that a legislature is always aware of race when it draws district lines, that fact by itself is not sufficient to show a racially discriminatory motive (*Shaw v. Reno*, 509 U.S. 630, at 646 (1993)). Such a motive is required, however, to implicate a constitutional claim. A confessed racial classification is presumptively invalid and "can be upheld only upon an extraordinary justification" (*Shaw v. Reno*, 509 U.S. at 643–44, quoting *Personnel Administrator of Massachusetts v. Feeney*, 442 U.S. 256, at 272 (1979)). The Court does not depend on confessed motives, however. If there is a racially discriminatory effect, the Court may infer a discriminatory goal.[7] Where lines follow racial lines, racial segregation may exist even where the district is multiracial.

Such an inference need not be drawn, however. Certain other valid goals, such as maintaining the integrity of political subdivisions, may justify the district (*Shaw v. Reno*, 509 U.S. at 646, citing *Wright v. Rockefeller*, 376 U.S. 52 (1964)). Not every goal is sufficient; the level of review is higher than that of a rational basis. Some motives, however—such as contiguity, compactness, and maintaining political subdivisions—are sufficient to demonstrate that a district has not been "gerrymandered on racial lines."[8] The two inquiries collapse. Failure to follow established lines is evidence of segregation even in multiracial districts. In effect, good-looking districts are probably all right; bad-looking ones are probably discriminatory. Symmetry is not considered. It is not an issue for the Court whether the lines of black-majority districts are as messy as white-majority districts: Whites can have messy districts for all purposes; blacks cannot.

The Problem with the Motive Test

In *Kiryas Joel*, the New York State legislature had to act. The legislature had to decide to draw the line or not draw the line. The Court might have viewed the legislature as acting as a neutral arbiter rather than as a religiously biased initiator. That is one of the circumstances that complicate motive analysis considerably. The situation is very different from that of a state legislature that requires that its public schools display the Ten Commandments.[9] Either decision—to draw a new line or leave the old ones—can be described in religious terms, either to protect or to injure a religious community.

The Court in *Kiryas Joel* alluded to this conflict between benefit and burden by characterizing the legislature's motive as "no doubt . . . to accommodate the Satmar community without violating the Establishment Clause" (*Kiryas Joel,* 512 U.S. at 708). In few other cases has a legislature been faced with such a plain decision between benefiting a religion by acting and burdening that religion by not acting. The Court found that the legislature's creation of the school district was driven by its motive to aid the Satmar. Yet a decision by the legislature to deny the district would have been a failure to accommodate the Satmar's religious beliefs; it would have left the Satmar within the control of people of inconsistent religious views. Thus, motive could be found either way.

The problem with motive tests in these areas is that there is no nonreligious motive available in *Kiryas Joel* and no possible absence of racial motives available in the legislative districting cases. The problem has to be resolved substantively—as good or bad districting.

SUBSTANTIVE STANDARDS FOR GOOD AND BAD DISTRICTING

Partisan Gerrymandering

One obvious place to look for substantive standards about fair and equal districting would be gerrymandering cases. In election districting cases, the Court has understood the uselessness of inquiring into motivation and has therefore confronted the problem of defining gerrymandering.

Although its methods of use vary, the gerrymander has long been used by the politically powerful to gain or maintain advantage when drawing the lines that define school districts, towns and villages, and legislative districts.[10] In 1986, the Supreme Court declared the fairness of legislative districting to be justiciable by the courts. Over Justice O'Connor's objection, the Court declared that there were judicially manageable standards to evaluate legislative districts (*Davis v. Bandemer,* 478 U.S. at

125–26, 147). Nevertheless, the Court's definition was so deferential as to virtually abandon the field it had just taken.[11]

Although the Court has yet to provide standards, scholars have suggested several objective methods of evaluating a legislative districting plan (McDonald and Engstrom 1990, 178–80; Niemi 1990, 171; Niemi and Wolkerson 1990, 256–64). This section examines gerrymandering on the bases of political affiliation and religion, methods that help detect gerrymandering in the political sphere, and why those methods break down when they are applied to religion (because of the difficulty in defining religion).

The Supreme Court in *Kiryas Joel* recognized that creation of the Village of Kiryas Joel School District was "substantially equivalent to defining a political subdivision" (*Kiryas Joel,* 512 U.S. at 702). Traditionally, urban and rural school districts have been subdivisions or cities or counties, respectively, although this pattern is no longer the rule. Whereas the winners of a municipal election get potholes filled and garbage picked up promptly, the majority group that controls a school board can control the ideological message of its schools. Although a public school may not teach religion directly, it can portray a view of history and a view of current affairs shaped by religion through its choices of texts, courses, library books, and teachers. Hence the advantage to be gained by controlling a school board. Gerrymandering can be used to gain this advantage in choosing school districts as easily as it can be used in choosing legislative districts.[12]

Gerrymandering techniques in political districting are limited because of the requirement that districts be equipopulous. Although the Supreme Court eliminated malapportionment as a districting technique through its decisions in *Baker v. Carr,* 389 U.S. 186 (1962), and *Reynolds v. Sims,* 377 U.S. 533 (1964), it has hardly been missed (Gottlieb 1988, 2; Elliott 1974, 213–36, 266). Given control over the legislative map, a minority party can gain or a majority party secure a majority of seats in the legislature by stacking and splitting the opposing party's votes. Indeed, gerrymandering can secure a very lopsided legislative majority and place it far beyond likely legislative reversal.

For example, gerrymandering in New York kept both houses of the state legislature Republican until 1972, despite reapportionment. The legislature has been permanently divided ever since between a Democratic Assembly and a Republican Senate, despite the identity of the electorate. Political dealing between the two bodies preserves this division despite the fact that the public has variously voted Democratic or Republican for statewide offices. Similarly, the Democrats controlled both houses of the U.S. Congress from the late Eisenhower years to the early Clinton years, with minimal turnover of incumbents.

This technique begins with the sacrifice of a few districts by packing them with opposing voters. Although assuring victory for the opponent in these districts, such a plan dilutes the opponent's voting strength in the remaining districts to the point of still greater disadvantage. In most districts, the opponent will lose consistently—and by a large margin. Moreover, gerrymandering increases the safety of incumbents' seats and reduces the voters' control at the polls (McDonald and Engstrom 1990, 178–80; Lowenstein and Steinberg 1985, 6–9; *Davis v. Bandemer*, 478 U.S. at 116–17 and n. 6).

Simply losing, however, is not the ultimate injury. Although a party that consistently gets 45 percent of the votes in a district may lose every election, it can have significant influence on the majority party's candidate, the tenor of the campaign, and, ultimately, on the outcome. The party may not lose every election. Swing votes from majority partisans who break ranks give a minority party hope for a victory. As the minority party's strength is diluted, however, its influence and the effect of swing votes wane as well. This loss of influence in the face of unbridled majority strength is the injury to be avoided (*Davis v. Bandemer*, 478 U.S. at 131–32; Lowenstein and Steinberg 1985, 37–41; Gottlieb 1988, 8–9).

Symmetry is a measure that detects and compares packed and cracked districts. Packing and cracking can be quickly identified through examination of the deviation of party strength within each district from overall party strength. Symmetry calls for equality of deviation among parties. If one party has packed districts, so must the other—and to the same degree. If symmetrical packing is enforced, each district packed by voters supporting one party will be balanced by a district packed by voters of the opposing party, and the remaining districts will more accurately reflect the group percentages that should result when applying formal districting criteria to existing residential patterns (McDonald and Engstrom 1990, 185, 189–90).

Nevertheless, symmetry will not solve the school districting problem. The Supreme Court has not adopted symmetry in the political context, and it has not established a workable definition of gerrymandering. Thus, the Court has no standard in political districting cases to carry over to religious school districting cases. Although inquiries undertaken into motivation and consistency should have raised these questions, the Court made no effort to assess the patterns and comparisons. It would not have had the tools. In effect, the Court's retreat into the language of motivation masks its failure to figure out what is and is not fair.

Moreover, traditional gerrymander-detection schemes break down when they are applied to religion because of the difficulty in defining religion. Do we define the religions as Judaism, Christianity, and Islam? Or do we further subdivide Christians into Catholic and Protestant, or even further into Catholic, Methodist, Baptist, Episcopal, and a variety of other groups? Or is it more realistic to divide religious groups along ideological lines, combining fundamentalist Christians with Orthodox Jews? Absent a definition of religion—a sense of the affiliations that may form among religious groups and a sense of who will be injured by a given gerrymander—setting a baseline by which to detect religious gerrymanders is impossible.

The question still becomes who belongs together and who belongs apart. Communities—defined as municipalities, metropolitan areas, regions, or a variety of compromises—are entitled to their own districts under most (but not all) current law. If those issues are to be handled by means of comparisons, we must figure out what to compare. The Supreme Court did not address whether the home rule denied to the Village of Kiryas Joel was comparable to what their neighbors enjoyed. Such a comparative analysis would bring out the problem of subordination of the Satmar to their neighbors—despite the best of intentions—in the larger school district. That inquiry should be at the heart of the gerrymandering cases, in which homogeneous districts for safe seats and partisan advantage have been treated as acceptable. There the question is sharing the benefits.

Unfortunately, comparative analysis cannot play as large a role for school districts as for electoral districts because other considerations necessarily limit the extremes of homogeneity permissible. A school district completely segregated by race is symmetrical. For each completely packed minority district there exists an equivalent majority district. Nevertheless, the segregation is not permissible. School segregation is invidious; fairness can never be found.

Gerrymandering on a Racial Basis

Legislatures have sometimes been allowed—even compelled—to create legislative districts gerrymandered on the basis of race. The Voting Rights

Act was long interpreted as compelling the creation of majority African American districts in areas in which African American candidates could not get elected by other means. The Equal Protection Clause of the Constitution, which sets forth the concept of equal treatment on the basis of race, has now been interpreted to embody a delicate balance similar to that of the Free Exercise Clause. Equal protection prohibits discrimination and racial distinctions.

In a long series of cases, largely during the Burger era, the Supreme Court interpreted the Voting Rights Act as requiring minority representation. The Act's twin requirements of nondilution and nonretrogression led to the requirement that redistricting plans provide as much minority representation as compact, contiguous minority communities could support (*Thornburg v. Gingles*, 478 U.S. 30 (1986)). In effect, the Court held the Act to require something close to racial proportional representation. If districting provided for as much representation as the minority community justified, it would approximate a proportionate share of the legislative seats. Anything less would be suspect as vote dilution.

These requirements worked as an exception to the Court's rejection of proportional representation in other contexts. They were justified in the racial context to compensate for the history of stratagems used to block and dilute minority voting strength. They were also justified by such strong polarization splits among voters that candidates who show sympathy for one group become *persona non grata* to the other. In most situations, politicians try to assemble winning coalitions. In polarized communities, however, polar groups cannot take part in a coalition or exert political influence. In communities polarized between black and white voters, blacks—when outvoted—were also excluded from influence on the legislature. Absent polarization, there was no reason to impose any requirement of racial representation; indeed, in such situations it would not be clear that there was any particular community of interest nor any reason to suppose that people belonging to a minority might not be better represented by maximizing party fortunes rather than racial fortunes.

The requirement of close to maximum minority representation was also an exception to the Court's unwillingness to choose between homogeneous and heterogeneous districting. The Court had sustained both and declined to find discrimination as an inevitable component of either. In addition to a racial cast, districts might have ethnic, national, immigrant, or religious casts. Nevertheless, the Court has now concluded that maximum racial representation is not a proper statutory goal, based on the requirements of the Equal Protection Clause and its preference for heterogeneous racial districting.

These rules provide no clear guidance for school districts. The Burger Court rules made it easier to identify discrimination. The remedy of separation creates problems under both the Establishment Clause and the Equal Protection Clause, however. The Rehnquist Court rules make it hard to identify discrimination, except for segregation, and make segregation but not other forms of discrimination the objectionable act—for which the approved remedy is integration. Curiously, the Rehnquist Court at the same time is making remedial integration constitutionally objectionable in affirmative action cases and declining to find segregation objectionable in employment discrimination cases. The Rehnquist Court's blurring of the meaning of discrimination in electoral districting makes it difficult to use its electoral districting cases as a model for identifying discrimination in school districting.

Nevertheless, experience with the Voting Rights Act suggests some considerations for school districts. First, as Justice Frankfurter made eloquently clear in his concurrence in *Joseph Burstyn, Inc. v. Wilson*, 343 U.S. 495, at 507–17 (1952), almost everything is sacrilegious to some religious group. Schools cannot avoid taking positions on issues of great moment to some groups. Many groups argue, for example, that the school curriculum encourages "secular humanism." Hence, in some communities, mixing of religious groups can have serious consequences for religious values.

Second, the rules suggest that for polarized communities, separation protects representation. In religiously polarized school districts, the only protection for religious or cultural minorities may be segregation—either by relocating in a more hospitable district or by exiting public schools for private ones. Those options are not always available locally.

Moreover, separating polarized electoral groups into different districts has less relevance for school districts than do the racial schooling cases. Separating electoral districts forces people to take account of each other's views at the legislative level. Separating students in schools results in mutual ignorance.

The Rehnquist Court has changed the rules; in the process, it has brought out the competing policy of equal protection jurisprudence—that of color blindness or legal refusal to embody group distinctions into legal ones. In the Rehnquist Court, the problem is not lack of representation but rather that of singling out minorities for "special" treatment. Thus, the

Rehnquist Court focuses on the ideology of nondistinction. It has concluded in a group of districting cases that it was unconstitutional to make race the primary consideration or "predominant factor" in districting (*Bush v. Vera,* 517 U.S. at 959). For Justices Thomas and Scalia, race could not even be a secondary consideration—so-called majority-minority districts would be proper if and only if they happened purely by accident (*Bush v. Vera,* 517 U.S. at 1001).

In fact, it appears that the Court frequently has gotten its facts wrong. The majority-minority districts drawn were not homogenous. They were not different in kind or shape from districts in which national minorities were not the local majority. Nevertheless, the stated judicial goal in these cases—which the Court applied only to race—was heterogeneity. Minority representation would be out and integration in, regardless of consequences.

If a state is racially polarized, such districting is not neutral. Rather, it systematically subordinates racial and religious minorities. Thus, it reads equal representation out of the Equal Protection Clause and out of the Representative Government Clause as incorporated into the Fourteenth Amendment. To apply that policy to the Establishment Clause as well could read equality out of whatever religious neutrality the First Amendment may provide.

Regardless of the vagaries of the Rehnquist Court's approach, the policy behind it suggests the importance of integration. Americans have used integration as a tool to deal with everything from class differences to Americanization of immigrants to gender differences to international relations. Indeed, the religion clauses of the First Amendment are mute evidence of the American belief in integration. These policies have relevance in the educational context: The common school was designed precisely to overcome the differences of Americans and create a *common* place for Americans of all kinds. The purpose of the common school, however, was overwhelmed by urbanization, which created areas and populations too large to allow full mixing. As neighborhoods took shape and suburbanization took place, the failure of the common school to provide a meeting place for Americans of different backgrounds, in either urban or rural America, became obvious. For people committed to the ideology of the common school—namely, integration—that development was very troubling.

Behind both policies and the Court's swing between them, however, lies the lack of definition. It is not clear to the Court what gerrymandering is. The Court has set no standard in Voting Rights Act cases for a district that is too homogeneous and no standard for a district that is too hetero-geneous. If a district changes over time and becomes homogeneous or heterogeneous, it is a perfectly acceptable district. If the same district is created by those responsible for districting, not one of the Warren, Bur-ger, or Rehnquist Courts can give clear answers about whether the dis-tricts are improperly drawn.

In racial as in other districting contexts, sometimes we allow singling out and sometimes we do not, to some changing and indeterminate degree.

The Religion Cases and Neutrality

The Supreme Court insists on neutrality at least among faiths if not generally with respect to religion. Yet neutrality is largely incoherent as an idea, partly because of the identity between the people and their faiths and partly because accommodation and favoritism are often indistin-guishable. The problem of neutrality is exacerbated by issues that are prominent in the interpretation of the religion clauses.

The Satmar Hasidic communities of Williamsburg, Brooklyn, and Kiryas Joel constitute a culture strongly linked to their Jewish faith (*Kiryas Joel,* 512 U.S. at 690–91, 738). Indeed, the culture and religion of these communities are inseparable. Much like the self-sufficient Amish commu-nities of Wisconsin, these Hasidic communities isolate themselves from the modern world (*Wisconsin v. Yoder,* 406 U.S. 205, at 210 (1972); *Kiryas Joel,* 512 U.S. at 690–91). In such a community, it is unclear whether an act of a legislature is accommodating the community because of its separatist culture or because of its religion. In *Wisconsin v. Yoder,* 406 U.S. at 209–10, the Amish stressed the link between culture and religion to show that a compulsory education law burdened their religious beliefs rather than their cultural beliefs. In *Kiryas Joel,* Justice Scalia tried to minimize the connection, arguing that the school district was created for a secular purpose to benefit a village.[13] In both cases, the Supreme Court recog-nized the link and treated culture as merging into religion, thus triggering an inquiry under the Religion Clauses of the First Amendment.[14] The problem of devising neutral standards is made more chimerical by the merging of the group with its faith.

The Court's description of neutral standards for religious groups is more unsatisfactory because accommodation and favoritism, equality and discrimination, are often indistinguishable. Initially the Court held that accommodation should be made unless there were strong reasons otherwise (*Sherbert v. Verner*, 374 U.S. 398 (1963)). Nevertheless, the Court seldom has required accommodation and has provided only minimal scrutiny for actions that were extremely destructive of minority faiths. This trend culminated in *Employment Division, Department of Human Resources v. Smith*, 494 U.S. 872 (1990). The Court in *Smith* held that only formal neutrality was required—defining neutrality circularly as "generally applicable, religion-neutral laws." The Court noted "that leaving accommodation to the political process will place at a relative disadvantage those religious practices that are not widely engaged in" (*Employment Division v. Smith*, 494 U.S. at 890). Legislation that impinges on religion without singling out religion in general or any specific faith was enforceable regardless of the impact on the practice of religion. Indeed, it is impossible to determine in *Smith* whether the treatment of Native American use of peyote was equal treatment (because such "drugs" are different from those that are legal) or unequal (because Judeo-Christian faiths are permitted to use wine).

The Court has treated preference for one faith over another as mostly strongly prohibited by the First Amendment; it also has held that religious institutions should be treated on equal terms with secular ones. Nevertheless, the Court has sustained tax exemptions for churches (*Walz v. Tax Commission of the City of New York*, 397 U.S. 664 (1970)). Again, it is impossible to determine whether the tax exemption is an example of equal treatment for churches—because it treats churches the same as (other) charities—or whether it is an instance of favoritism because religion is singled out. Once again, the baseline of neutrality turns out to be elusive and contested.[15]

Without a baseline, it is never clear whether a practice is protected free exercise, protected equal access, or prohibited establishment. In the context of partisan gerrymandering, the Supreme Court has not used the symmetry concept or insisted on neutrality. In the religious context, it insists on neutrality, interpreted in a way that permits substantial real inequality. The Court continues to ignore symmetry, which is a measure of real equality; if it did turn to symmetry, however, it would find that concept difficult to apply in this area.

In the case of the Satmar villagers, it is not clear what practice to compare them against. Many towns and school districts are religiously homogeneous. Yet integration is the ideological expectation. Thus, giving the Satmar a school board outside the Christian community may be equal access or religious establishment—or both. Both policies, perhaps with equal justice, appear to be both neutral treatment and discriminatory.

The Court has not been able to define what districting is good or bad for blacks or whites or what gives them equivalent choices or freedom. Such definitions are even more difficult in the case of school districting with respect to religious communities. In contrast to situations that involve race, there are too many variables and no clear guidelines for which variables to count.

Thus, the problems of accounting for religious communities in school districting cannot be solved by neutrality. This problem is particularly serious because, absent a viable concept of neutrality, it is not clear that the problem can be solved at all. We simply have no standard that would allow us to describe whether the Satmar were being treated just like everyone else or what treatment without respect to religion would be.

Consistency

In *Kiryas Joel*, the Supreme Court tried to support neutrality with consistency—what the state had been doing elsewhere. Justice Souter wrote:

> Because the district's creation ran uniquely counter to state practice, following the lines of a religious community where the customary and neutral principles would not have dictated the same result, we have good reasons to treat this district as the reflection of a religious criterion for identifying the recipients of civil authority. (*Kiryas Joel*, 512 U.S. at 702)

In fact, "the trend in New York is not toward dividing school districts but toward consolidating them" to create "districts large enough to provide a comprehensive education at affordable cost (*Kiryas Joel*, 512 U.S. at 700). The court noted that "[t]he origin of the district in a special act of the legislature, rather than the State's general laws governing school district reorganization, is likewise anomalous" (*Kiryas Joel*, 512 U.S. at 700–701).

Consistency and neutrality are closely related: Consistency generalizes neutrality as equal treatment of comparable groups over a series of decisions. Therefore, in the districting context, consistency, like neutrality and equality, can be interpreted as symmetry.

Consistency might be understood as a process standard, comparing decision making on this school district to other recently handled districts. For example, we might ask whether New York has been consolidating or dividing districts—and whether it can change its mind. Alternatively, consistency might be understood as a substantive standard, comparing the way representation or community control is effectuated in different districts. We might ask whether identifiable religious groups control other districts and who is subordinated to that control.

Either approach is sabotaged by the problem of defining religious groups. Should we group competing denominations of the same broad religion together, even though the denominations have vied and fought bitterly with one another in the past? Is the integration of Christian sects in innumerable school districts comparable to the integration of Christians, Hasidim, and non-Hasidic Jews in Monroe Township? Is the absence of non-Christians from most districts comparable to the segregation of Hasidim in the Village of Kiryas Joel? The variations are so many and so large that consistency is hard to define. Moreover, we have no standard by which to assess the fairness of what has consistently been done.

In the legislative districting context, one can take a statewide view and balance types of districts without excluding people from communities or disrupting their lives. In the school district context, districting is physical segregation. The cure of balancing control by one majority in some places but instituting control by some minorities in other places may be worse than the disease: It institutionalizes segregation. The unavailability of remedies available in legislative districting, however, makes the problem of fairness still more difficult in school districting.

The Supreme Court's approach to *de facto* segregation has been to ask about reasons (objectively) or motives (subjectively). Neither analysis is neutral or embodies a neutral standard; they both depend on subjective assessments of the significance of competing considerations and a judicial determination of the appropriate level of scrutiny. Both approaches raise questions about whether the same standards are applied to different groups—though in situations of infinite variety. Thus, both versions cover considerable risks of inequality. Doing this fairly in the religious context is even more difficult than in the electoral context, given the difficulties of identifying appropriate discrete faiths. Have the Hasidim been treated like all others? It would be difficult to know even if we could explain what that might mean.

Thus, consistency is little more helpful than neutrality and largely conceals underlying standards and choices.

Delegation

Motive, neutrality, and consistency do not resolve the problem of districting schools among families of different faiths. The Court in *Kiryas Joel* turned to a different idea—that by drawing the lines as it did, New York put control of the new school district into religious hands. The Court wrote that the New York statute violated the Constitution "by delegating the State's discretionary authority over public schools to a group defined by its character as a religious community, in a legal and historical context that gives no assurance that governmental power has been or will be exercised neutrally" (*Kiryas Joel*, 512 U.S. at 696). The Court held that "the State's manipulation of the franchise for this district limited it to Satmars, giving the sect exclusive control of the political subdivision" (*Kiryas Joel*, 512 U.S. at 698).

The Court's language deliberately refused to distinguish the population of the sect from the corporate organization of the sect. Based on that factual conclusion, it held that a state may not "deliberately delegate discretionary power to an individual, institution, or community on the ground of religious identity" (*Kiryas Joel*, 512 U.S. at 698–99). The Court then assimilated the delegation idea into the neutrality idea, holding that "[w]here 'fusion' (of governmental and religious functions) is an issue, the difference lies in the distinction between a government's purposeful delegation on the basis of religion and a delegation on principles neutral to religion." (*Kiryas Joel*, 512 U.S. at 699).

One problem with invalidating a school district on the grounds that it is controlled by the same people who control religious institutions, however, is that no religious tests for office are permitted by the Constitution.[16] The mere presence of religious officials on a school board cannot invalidate the district.

A second problem is that this test sidesteps the elements of homogeneity and size on which it depends. Small school districts are much more likely to be homogeneous with regard to factors such as religion, race, and national origin. Thus, the Court may implicitly be condemning small local school boards for the partisanship of which James Madison complained in *Federalist 10*. That problem is not solved, however, by extending the boundaries to the somewhat larger but still small Monroe-Woodbury School District. To insist that the Hasidim go to school with their neighbors is to insist that they be educated in accord with the dominant culture. It is a matter of subjugation by submersion in a larger group, just as gerrymandering is aimed at subjugation by "stacking" some voters (in segregated areas) and "cracking" others (in areas dominated by the competing party or culture).

If we focus on that crucial implicit issue, however, we are brought back to the questions of representation, fairness, and equality that the Court has not solved in any of the areas before it. These problems cannot be successfully resolved by a still-nonexistent standard of fair districting. If the attack on delegation conceals an attack on small, homogeneous districts, the issue is whether such districts violate a policy of integration and whether, if they do, it is justifiable.

Segregation and Integration—The Requirement of Undifferentiated Treatment

Although there have been a variety of forms of discrimination on grounds other than race and gender—and "tracking" programs may accomplish considerable segregation of students within schools—systematic segregation of students in schools does not appear to have been widespread with respect to religion or national origin. Nevertheless, the illegality of segregation is implicit in the law. Indeed, the Supreme Court has applied the same principles of nondiscrimination to religious persuasion and national origin[17] as it has to race and gender—with the possible exception of affirmative action. Indeed, much of the opposition to affirmative action developed because of the now-discredited practice of applying quotas to religious minorities, especially Jews and especially in the pre-World War II period. The Court has actually treated Jews as a racial minority (*Shaare Tefila Congregation v. Cobb*, 481 U.S. 615 (1987)). Hence, there is good reason to believe that the Equal Protection Clause bars segregation on religious grounds just as it bars segregation on racial grounds (Choper 1982, 581–83). Moreover, the history of the Fourteenth Amendment is replete with discussion of a variety of minorities, and there is nothing in the history of the Amendment to suggest that religious minorities would be treated with any less concern.[18]

The risks of inequality to individuals involved are heightened by segregation, and history suggests that the risks are extreme. It should be clear, however, that there are corresponding losses. Indeed, religious districting is still contested ground. Religiously neutral districting can be characterized as diversity, assimilation, or integration. Diversity and integration sound quite positive, but assimilation clarifies the stakes and the competing values. Religiously sensitive districting can be characterized as homogeneity, autonomy, or segregation. Segregation poses clear dangers, but autonomy is valued. Thus, even to the extent that integration can be defined and required, it imposes responsibilities as well.

In a religiously integrated system, fair treatment of students on ethnic, racial, religious, and ideological grounds should be defined transactionally by what is done and taught. Yet those very standards are themselves the root of what are known as the culture wars. Fair substantive standards conflict with the tradition of community control. There also is no judicial resolution of what it means to be fair. Under a Supreme Court that defines indoctrination as the purpose of education, minorities can complain with great justification (*Ambach v. Norwick*, 441 U.S. 68, at 76–80 (1979); Gottlieb 1987).

One aspect of the traditional resolution of this dilemma has been to allow minorities to opt out by paying the cost of private education—which the Hasidim had done for most of their children. The alternative is to permit segregated public institutions but to distinguish segregation enforced by the majority from separatism requested by the minority. This approach is comparable to the one-direction principle of affirmative action. Given the current status of affirmative action, however, that solution does not seem to be feasible, regardless of whether it would be wise or foolish.

CONCLUSION

Board of Education of Kiryas Joel Village School District v. Grumet was not an easy case to begin with, as indicated by the flurry of opinions in the New York Court of Appeals and in the U.S. Supreme Court. Concepts that would work in the context of districting, such as symmetry, will not work as easily in the context of school boards. The absence of a central notion of what makes districting good or bad in any context, however, undermines the effort to define what might be good or bad districting for schools. We are guessing.

At stake is a much larger issue: the meaning of pluralism. If we try to respect groups and their identities and practices, such respect may come at the cost of integration, as well as defeat for people committed to a cosmopolitan viewpoint. Indeed, this respect may come at the cost of the common school movement itself. If we try to define equal treatment as treatment without regard to religion—as we are trying to define it with respect to race—then it will come at the cost of separatism, of the ability to build group identity without paying the extra costs of separate facilities. These alternatives define what being American means. They also open chasms in some of the thorniest areas of American life—areas in which the resolutions are anything but consistent, in the courts or elsewhere. Sometimes we integrate, and sometimes we segregate. Sometimes we equalize; sometimes we privilege.

My own inclination is to take a cue from Justices Cardozo and Black. Cardozo asked what was essential to "ordered liberty" and "the indispensable condition of nearly every other form of freedom" (*Palko v. Connecticut*, 302 U.S. 319 (1937)). Justice Hugo Black and his academic namesake Charles Black argued that the provisions for democratic government in Article I, section 2, of the Constitution implied other necessary freedoms.

Much of our history has been based on the conclusion that integration rather than segregation is necessary to the process of ordered liberty; integration creates the sense of common community that is essential to maintain a free society against the inclination to make major battles over all differences (thereby distinguishing the United States from Yugoslavia). If that is so, *Kiryas Joel* may have been rightly decided—but for the wrong reasons. If integration were applied as a constitutional policy to *Kiryas Joel,* it would also have repercussions in much Establishment Clause and equal protection jurisprudence. In effect, the concept of representation is the consequence of a more fundamental concept of what we are as a people. The issue cannot be punted via a concept of symmetry in the religious context; we have to take a stand. The traditional stand has been public support for integrated institutions and private support for segregated ones. The Supreme Court has been breaching that line—except for the Satmar Hasidim.

On the other hand, consistency may be overstated (Phillips 1997, 59–62). We might be able to accommodate minority faiths such as the Amish in *Yoder* without threatening the general rules of the Establishment Clause or the Equal Protection Clause. The Supreme Court has rejected the possibility of an exception for affirmative action in the context of race (*Adarand Constructors, Inc. v. Pena*, 515 U.S. 200 (1995)).

The Hasidim have hardly been the favorite of the laws: The Court insisted on splitting the Hasidic community in Williamsburg (*United Jewish Organization v. Carey*, 430 U.S. 144 (1977)) and subordinating it in Monroe-Woodbury. Yet the comparison to the Amish is substantial: Both are old German sects unwilling to change from their habits or even from the apparel they adopted in premodern Europe. Nevertheless, exceptions also invite unfairness. Is there less unfairness in compassion toward such quaint minorities or in choosing who gets the benefit of such exceptions? Is there greater danger in recognizing such differences or in subordinating them in a Madisonian vision of the liberal state?

Endnotes

1. The author wishes to acknowledge a special debt to Joseph G. Arsenault, J.D., Albany Law School, 1995. Mr. Arsenault, who had been my assistant, and I originally undertook to write this chapter together. I laid out several propositions based on concepts I had developed in prior articles on gerrymandering and on motive analysis. Mr. Arsenault drafted several sections developing those ideas but also adding important insights of his own. Unfortunately, a career change made it impossible for him to continue. Obviously, I take full responsibility for the chapter, though I owe Mr. Arsenault a considerable debt for the work he did that is reflected here. In addition, Jennifer Ploetz diligently checked and edited the draft.
2. *Aguilar v. Felton*, 473 U.S. 402 (1985).
3. 1989 N.Y. Laws 748. Governor Mario Cuomo, signing the bill on July 24, 1989, anticipated the constitutional challenge that was to follow but called the bill "a good faith effort to solve this unique problem" (*Public Papers of Governor Cuomo* 1989, 251–52).
4. *Grumet v. N.Y.S. Educ. Dep't*, 579 N.Y.S.2d 1004 (Sup. Ct. Albany County, 1992) (finding that creation of the district violated the U.S. and New York constitutions), *aff'd*, 592 N.Y.S.2d 123 (3d Dep't 1992), *modified and aff'd*, 618 N.E.2d 94 (N.Y. 1993), *aff'd*, 512 U.S. 687 (1994).
5. *Grumet v. Board of Educ. of Kiryas Joel Village Sch. Dist.*, 618 N.E.2d 94, 101 (N.Y. 1993), *aff'd*, 512 U.S. 687 (1994).
6. See *McCulloch v. Maryland*, 17 U.S. (4 Wheat.) 316, at 423 (1819): "Should congress . . . adopt measures which are prohibited by the constitution; or should congress under the pretext of executing its powers, pass laws for the accomplishment of objects not intrusted to the government; it would become the painful duty of this tribunal, . . . to say, that such an act was not the law of the land."

    See also *Bailey v. Drexel Furniture Co.*, 259 U.S. 20, at 38 (1922):

    > Although Congress does not . . . expressly declare that the employment within the mentioned ages is illegal, it does exhibit its intent practically to achieve the . . . result. . . . Taxes are occasionally imposed

... on proper subjects with the primary motive of obtaining revenue from them and with the incidental motive of discouraging them by making their continuance onerous. They do not lose their character as taxes because of the incidental motive. But there comes a time in the extension of the penalizing features of the so-called tax when it loses its character as such and becomes a mere penalty with the characteristics of regulation and punishment. Such is the case in the law before us.

7. Motive will be inferred if a statute that is race-neutral on its face is "unexplainable on grounds other than race." *Shaw v. Reno*, 509 U.S. at 643 (quoting *Arlington Heights v. Metropolitan Housing Dev. Corp.*, 429 U.S. 252, at 266 (1977)). The same principle applies to a statute that is "ostensibly neutral but is an obvious pretext for racial discrimination." *Shaw v Reno*, at 643 (citing *Yick Wo v. Hopkins*, 118 U.S. 356 (1886)).

8. *Shaw v. Reno*, 509 U.S. at 647: "We emphasize that [compactness, contiguity, and respect for political subdivisions] are important not because they are constitutionally required—they are not—but because they are objective factors that may serve to defeat a claim that a district has been gerrymandered on racial lines" (construing *Gaffney v. Cummings*, 412 U.S. 735, at 752 n. 18 (1973); *Karcher v. Daggett*, 462 U.S. 725, at 775 (1983)) (Stephens, J. concurring).

9. See *Stone v. Graham*, 449 U.S. 39 (1980) (finding a Kentucky statute requiring posting of the Ten Commandments in public school rooms unconstitutional because it had no secular purpose).

10. *Washington v. Seattle School District No. 1*, 458 U.S. 457 (1982); *Brown v. Board of Education of Topeka*, 347 U.S. 483 (1954); *Gomillion v. Lightfoot*, 364 U.S. 339 (1960) (striking down a plan by which boundaries of city of Tuskegee, Alabama, were redrawn as a 28-sided figure to exclude all but four or five black residents, yet not a single white resident); *Davis v. Bandemer*, 478 U.S. 109 (1986).

11. "...[U]nconstitutional discrimination occurs only when the electoral system is arranged in a manner that will consistently degrade a voter's or a group of voters' influence on the political process as a whole" (*Davis v. Bandemer*, 478 U.S. at 132).

12. See Cassidy (1995, B3) (conservative, Christian candidates for Central Dauphin, Pennsylvania, school board accused by moderates of being controlled by the Christian right); Trachtenberg (1995, C1) (Apple, the computer manufacturer, distributed to schools a CD-ROM version of an American history text that referred to birth control, abortion, and homosexuality; Apple was forced to stop distribution of the CD-ROM to grade schools because of complaints about the subject matter); Bailey (1995, 41); Impoco (1995, 30) (voters in Vista, California, replaced religious-right trustees with moderates after the former proposed replacing the sex education curriculum with a course called "Sex Respect" that did not discuss safe sex, gender bias, or birth control but rather railed at abortion and homosexuality); Neuberger (1995, B1) (magazine removed from school library shelves because of discussions of abortion and homosexuality); *Rowland*

    v. Mad River Local School District, 730 F.2d 444 (6th Cir. 1984), *cert. denied*, 470 U.S. 1009 (1985) (guidance counselor fired because she was bisexual).

13. *Kiryas Joel*, 512 U.S. at 738 (Scalia, J., dissenting), and see *id*. at 708.
14. *Kiryas Joel*, 512 U.S. at 710; *id*. at 699 (plurality opinion); *Wisconsin v. Yoder*, 406 U.S. at 216–17.
15. McConnell (1992, 120–27), for example, objects to the anti-Catholic bias of the Court's "wall of separation" as understood by the Warren and Burger Courts— and, one should add, the Vinson Court, which announced the wall.
16. U.S. Constitution, art. 6, paragraph 3.
17. *Shaare Tefila Congregation v. Cobb*, 481 U.S. 615 (1987) (applying 42 U.S.C. 1981 and 1982 to ethnic origin); *Saint Francis College v. Al-Khazraji*, 481 U.S. 604 (1987) (ethnic origin).
18. President Andrew Johnson vetoed the Civil Rights Bill because it made citizens of Indians, Chinese, and Gypsies as well as Blacks (*Congressional Globe* 1866, 1679). Members of Congress made plain, however, that they meant to include all persons without regard to such distinctions, (see, e.g., *Congressional Globe* 1866, 2892).

··· II ···

Political Parties: The Key to—or the Scourge of—Representation?

"Let me now . . . warn you in the most solemn manner against the baneful effects of the spirit of party."
—George Washington, *Farewell Address* (1796)

"Democracy is unthinkable save in terms of parties."
—E. E. Schattschneider, *Party Government* (1942)

Each of the chapters in Part I ultimately concluded by questioning the Supreme Court's ability to adequately capture the nature of representation in its election law cases. For Nancy Maveety, the Court under Chief Justice Rehnquist has been so pragmatic, fact specific, and narrow in its decision making that it cannot or will not foster a more cohesive philosophical framework for matters respecting political representation. Likewise, Howard Scarrow asserts that the Court's decade-long search for "fair and effective representation" in electoral arrangements conclusively established only one thing—that the Court is incapable of handling districting issues in a theoretically coherent way or in a way that captures the many faces and facets of representation. Its failure to clearly demarcate the interests that deserve representation in the districting context has undermined the goals of stability, fairness, and representativeness. Its treatment of questions at the heart of representation has lacked clarity or consistency. Finally, Stephen Gottlieb criticizes the Court in its articulation of a variety of districting standards, asserting that it misses the crucial question of what constitutes good or bad substantive redistricting.

In short, the Court has not provided a sound definition of positive representation, either theoretically or substantively; nor has it been able to isolate an encompassing set of legal processes, procedures, or standards for generating political representation in the law. How might these shortcomings be rectified? One potential answer is suggested by Howard Scarrow's party-centered prescriptions for the conundrum of racial redistricting.

Political party subsystems have long been considered by one school of political scientists as crucial institutional representational linkages. Parties relieve the tensions of representation theory and are an indispensable means of meshing and melding individuals, groups, and states into a representative pluralist democracy. Political parties simultaneously enhance group influence, diffuse factions, and balance majority rule and minority rights. They have a unique capacity to pursue multiple democratic aims such as aggregation, consensus, compromise, and civic education. According to this view, only political parties are constituted so as to consolidate and accommodate the competing strands of representation; by acknowledging the host of channels through which representation operates, party structures engender a richer, more effective system of representation (Ryden 1996, 115–22).

This school of thought points to an elevated legal standing for political parties as the answer to the Court's struggles in the realm of election law. Significant obstacles and objections surround a party-conscious jurisprudence, however; these challenges are the focus of Part II of this volume. The relationship between political parties, the Constitution, and the Court has historically been one of ambiguity and ambivalence. The framers distrusted political parties and omitted them from the Constitution. Indeed, a primary motive in their government building was to control party factions, which they regarded as a considerable threat to liberty. Nevertheless, political parties quickly sprang up out of necessity. They have proven to be an integral and irreplaceable component of American politics, particularly in campaigns and elections. Despite the low esteem in which political parties are held in many corners, it is difficult to imagine an electoral system without them.

The evolution of party systems and traditions developed outside the constitutional framework, however. That constitutional design was based on the ideal of limited government; principles of federalism, separation of powers, and bicameralism were intended to make it more difficult for the government to produce results. Political parties, as a means of overcoming that institutional fragmentation, pull in an opposite theoretical direction than the Constitution. At the same time, the Constitution is not overtly hostile to political parties. Parties may seek refuge in First Amendment rights of expression, assembly, and association. Moreover, some observers would argue that they are essential to the realization of fundamental constitutional values such as democratic responsiveness, consent, and accountability. Without political parties, democratic governance might well be unattainable; hence the argument for a constitutional order that makes room for parties, notwithstanding their absence from the text.

The lack of clarity in the parties' constitutional standing has complicated the job of the Supreme Court. It has deprived the Court of the means necessary to treat them in a doctrinally consistent manner. Political parties' hazy constitutional status means that "the party institution is unlikely to conform very neatly to lawyerly doctrinal categories" (Maveety 1991, 187). The Court must not only confront the framers' antipathy toward political parties and the absence of textual guidance, it also faces the absence of a clearly accepted, normative understanding of parties and their roles and functions. No consensus exists within the legal or political science communities for a constitutionally grounded responsible party government that might inform the Court's consideration of political parties.

These difficulties have not prevented the Court from undertaking to define political parties' constitutional status; the parties' historical prominence in electoral politics has inevitably left the Court with no choice. In recent years the Court has encountered parties often, and in a variety of contexts: It has examined the propriety of party patronage and partisan primaries, considered parties' role in the drawing of district lines and financing campaigns, and evaluated ballot access regulations. As a result, the Court has contributed to the legal environment within which political parties must operate. In the process it has been influential in determining how well or how poorly political parties fulfill their functions as channels of representative government.

Meanwhile, the steady decline of political parties has been well documented. A host of factors have fed that decline—from candidate-centered politics and the television/mass communications era to the rise of rivals in the form of interest groups and the loss of patronage as a tool for building party organizations. What part, if any, has the Supreme Court played in these developments? One assessment has laid at least partial blame on a jurisprudence largely indifferent toward parties (Ryden 1996). The Court has been castigated for blurring obvious distinctions between independent candidacies and party organizations in ballot and voter access cases. It has subordinated political parties to other collectivities in creating a group right to representation in gerrymandering disputes, and until recently excluded parties from the discussion in campaign finance altogether. In severely circumscribing patronage, the Court has refused to acknowledge either political parties as governing agents or the time-honored role of patronage in building partisan organizations. The Court has mostly affirmed progressive reforms that badly weakened political parties in their electoral, organizational, and governing capacities. In this view, the Court has reinforced a larger political culture that is increasingly hostile to political parties and their control of elections and government. It has been complicit in undermining party influence in favor of an individualistic, unmediated, participatory form of politics, making more difficult the parties' task of reversing their fortunes.

Part II (chapters 5–8) explores these contentions from alternative perspectives. Michael Fitts's comprehensive assessment of the Court's treatment of political parties generally is followed by chapters exploring the parties' constitutional status in three specific contexts: party control over the process of nominating candidates, partisan patronage practices, and the relative standing and rights of minor parties in a two-party system.

In chapter 5, Fitts offers a more charitable view than that outlined above, asserting that the Court has done as well as could reasonably be expected. He asserts that tensions and inconsistencies in the Court's treatment of political parties are an unavoidable and even necessary ambiguity in our constitutional definition of majority rule. Political parties resolve basic philosophical conflicts *outside* the purview of explicit constitutional and judicial direction. This situation suggests the need for less comprehensive, rather than more comprehensive, judicial attention to political parties. At the same time, rapidly evolving party structures have certainly complicated the constitutional resolution of these issues and may warrant reexamination of the judicial stance toward parties.

Chapter 6 confronts a recurring issue surrounding the legal/constitutional status of political parties: how to reconcile parties' associational rights and organizational autonomy with the state's authority to regulate parties. What rights do political parties have in defining the boundaries of their association? Can they limit participation to ensure greater commitment to party ideology, policy, and program? When and how can the state curb party freedom in the interests of an efficient electoral system or expanded individual participatory rights? Paul Petterson considers these questions through the prism of *Morse v. Virginia Republican Party,* 517 U.S. 186 (1996), in which the Court struck down the Virginia Republican Party's imposition of a $45 registration fee for participation in the state convention. Petterson defends the encroachment on party autonomy as necessary to ensure higher principles of equal rights in the electoral process.

Petterson places the *Morse* decision within the broader framework of political parties' constitutional status, isolating two competing schools of thought in the Court's delineation of the associational rights of parties. The "natural order" view reflects a preference for widespread party competition and frowns on state intervention in party business. The "constructed order" view places greater value on stable party systems requiring active, aggressive regulatory intervention by the state. Petterson interprets the narrowly divided decision in *Morse* as clear indication that the tension between party freedom and state power is unlikely to be judicially resolved any time soon.

Chapter 7 analyzes the constitutional propriety of patronage—the practice of dispensing the spoils of electoral victory to supporters. The tools of patronage—granting of government employment, promotions, public contracts, and the like—were means by which political parties traditionally bolstered their organizational and governing abilities. Over the past two decades, the Supreme Court has narrowed substantially the constitutionally permissible uses of patronage; in the process, it has revealed a great deal about its understanding of political parties and their role in the electoral process. Cynthia Grant Bowman employs an empirical analysis of the suitability of patronage, while also examining fundamental theoretical questions regarding the American political system. For example, does patronage tend to establish and maintain one-party politics? Does the absence of patronage, and the loss of the benefits of party discipline and accountability that go with it, present greater dangers of splintering and factional politics? Bowman concludes that the assumptions undergirding patronage practices are largely unfounded. She regards the prohibition of patronage as compelled by considerations of good government and as necessary to eliminate governmental corruption and inefficiency.

Timmons v. Twin Cities Area New Party, 520 U.S. 351 (1997)—the focus of chapter 8—provides further insight into the Supreme Court's thinking about the representational aspects of the party system and our electoral structures. The Court in *Timmons* upheld a Minnesota ban on fusion—a practice whereby a minor party offers as its candidate the candidate of one of the major parties. In so doing, the Court offered a strong defense of the two-party system and the electoral rules that support it. Doug Amy roundly criticizes the decision. He views the muffling of minor party rights as undermining more accurate representation through a multiparty system. Amy cites a large body of empirical and theoretical political science literature that favors multiparty systems and cuts against constitutional protection for two-party electoral arrangements. He views *Timmons* as an illustration of how *not* to use political theory as a prop for judicial decisions; in his view, the Court in *Timmons* mouths platitudes with little explanation or empirical support. The pivotal importance of party competition warrants a more serious judicial effort to furnish a theoretical and empirical foundation for the decision. In this instance, the inherent self-interest of state legislators in perpetuating their power requires that the Court seriously examine the purported "state's interest" justifying the two-party legal bias.

··· 5 ···

Back to the Future: The Enduring Dilemmas Revealed in the Supreme Court's Treatment of Political Parties

MICHAEL A. FITTS

The U.S. Constitution safeguards a host of individual political rights. As other chapters in this volume repeatedly underscore, however, it never outlines with any clarity how those rights should blend together to define group decision making (Ackerman 1991). To inform this debate, legal scholars have sought to explicate on countless occasions the legitimacy and ability of nonelected courts to define the domain and appropriate exceptions to democratic rule (Ackerman 1991; Bickel 1962; Ely 1980; Tribe 1980). This issue, which is often referred to as "the countermajoritarian difficulty," is the greatest conceptual dilemma of modern constitutional law; it has consumed as much intellectual firepower over the years as any region of Supreme Court jurisprudence.

Given the centrality of this debate, it seems odd that political parties have not been a more important subject in legal scholarship or Supreme Court doctrine. As many commentators have noted, lawyers and political scientists approach the topic of political parties from very different perspectives. To many political scientists, parties are central to government decision making; this attitude is revealed in E. E. Schattschneider's famous observation that "political parties created democracy and that modern democracy is unthinkable save in terms of the parties" (Schattschneider 1977, 1). Most lawyers begin at a very different starting point; the language of the Constitution and the *Federalist Papers*, which are the legal foundation of our democracy, nowhere even mention parties. Few lawyers, except the "usual suspects," ever write about political parties.

When they do, it is only when the subject of political parties is directly raised by the legal doctrine and cannot be avoided. Indeed, many political scientists maintain that when the courts do take account of political parties in their decisions, the analysis appears to be incoherent and the results not sufficiently supportive of a strong party system (see, e.g., Rush 1994).

The purpose of this chapter is to explain this difference in perspective, which I suggest is quite predictable, even defensible. In the process, I offer a rough justification for the seeming incoherence of at least some of the Supreme Court doctrine in this area. My fundamental point is that the constitutional debate over the countermajoritarian difficulty seeks to resolve an exceedingly intractable normative issue—the reconciliation of individual and group political rights. The structure of political parties, on the other hand, is a means by which this central dilemma of constitutional law can sometimes be resolved informally and productively without the political and normative difficulties of *explicit* legal intervention. The structure of our party system also enables such resolutions to be updated more easily as our political culture evolves. From this perspective, one can see that the very qualities that make political parties effective in performing the functions Schattschneider attributes to them also make it conceptually difficult for courts to integrate them explicitly into traditional legal doctrine. The functional virtue of political parties is their doctrinal vice.

The first section of this chapter describes the underlying purposes of political parties and why they offer such value for our political order while simultaneously creating fundamental problems for legal analysis. The second section then illustrates this dilemma in two of the most important cases recently decided by the Supreme Court on political parties: *Timmons v. Twin Cities Area New Party*, 520 U.S. 351 (1997), and *Colorado Republican Federal Campaign Committee v. FEC*, 518 U.S. 604 (1997). Finally, the third section extends this analysis more generally to the current debate on the transformation of political parties and campaign finance reform. As political scientists well know, the nature and performance of political parties have changed in recent years; some scholars doubt their normative value or even future existence. Exploring this debate from the perspective of the underlying functions of political parties, however, reveals the conceptual value of parties and problems with more explicit legal regulation.

THE FUNCTIONS OF PARTIES

The Theory of Party-Centered Politics

What are political parties, and why don't the courts do a better job of analyzing and supporting them? In their ideal form, American political parties are organizations directed to the mobilization and aggregation of citizens to secure political control of government. From a lawyer's point of view, what is critical is that political parties are neither purely public nor private entities; they serve as a bridge—in some sense the most important bridge—between government and the private world.

Ideally (with special emphasis on the aspirational quality of that term), the mission and structure of American political parties should lead them to perform four critical functions that the government and courts find difficult to undertake directly. First, they should be in the business of *mobilizing* as much of the public as possible—that is, trying to overcome all of the collective action problems that hamper individuals from participating in and creating a full democracy. What is crucial here is the necessary size of political parties and their collective identity; because they seek to control government, they should have an organizational interest in attracting as many people as possible to their cause without being too beholden to narrow constituencies. Second, to be successful, political parties also need to *channel public debate*. Although lawyers like to think of the First Amendment as promoting free and open debate, a successful political campaign does not operate that way. As part of the process of building support among members and identifying the collective goals for the government, issues need to be prioritized and narrowed.

The third, and related, function of political parties is to *promote compromise* (that is, make hard tradeoffs in policy) among supporters. Given the prevalence of and high cost of strategic behavior, any successful political system must have a means for reconciling losers to the ultimate outcome. Political parties have a structural incentive to fulfill this mediating role as part of their effort to bring divergent groups together and mobilize the population on their behalf. The private, informal nature of political parties also facilitates this process; the moral and group sanctions of parties can sometimes be a more effective means of reducing internal strategic behavior and promoting agreement among members than the open and formal mechanisms of government itself (see Posner 1996). In this sense, the standard line, "Republicans don't attack Republicans," promotes societal goals far beyond the strategic self-interest of the party itself. A similar claim has been made on behalf of private economic markets and political pluralism—that resolving value conflicts informally can have advantages for ameliorating political conflict and increasing political legitimacy (see Becker 1983; Epstein 1995).

The fourth role of political parties, which is implicit in all of the foregoing, is to *define what is meant by democratic or majority rule.* Despite a perpetual debate in legal circles over the meaning of "We The People," the Constitution nowhere clarifies what majority rule and the nature of the vote really means, other than formally. How our political parties function serves to transform a legal system focused on the individual voter and individual rights into a collective decision-making process.

For the most part, political parties perform these roles without direct judicial or governmental intervention. Schattschneider (1977, 60) implied this attitude in his classic statement, "Democracy is not to be found in the parties, but between the parties." To the extent this statement is true, strong parties result from the competition of private political forces. Political parties—like other private organizations—should be able to run their internal structures however they want because the public check on their performance should be provided by competition from other parties. This process is similar to the proverbial "invisible hand" resolution of the public/private tension in economic markets, to which legal academia has devoted considerable attention over the years (Epstein 1995). In this case, however, instead of private markets that promote the public economic good through the invisible hand, the private political market of political parties should help pursue the public political good of government policy.

The Limits of Party Theory

Of course, this analysis represents the ideal. The reality is more complicated. Just as the invisible hand of the private economic market fails to magically implement public policy, party competition is imperfect at best. This imperfection first became evident in the so-called White Primary cases, which started with *Nixon v. Herndon*, 273 U.S. 536 (1927), and ended with *Terry v. Adams*, 345 U.S. 461 (1953). In these cases, the Supreme Court confronted the exclusion of African Americans from the primaries and conventions of strong southern state Democratic parties. In the absence of serious two-party competition, there was no political check on the exclusionary behavior; oligopoly was found to exist in political, as well as in economic, markets. The decision in *Morse v. Virginia Republican Party*, 517 U.S. 186 (1996)—which applied section 5 preclearance under the Voting Rights Act to filing fees in party conventions—is a present-day reflection of that concern.

Contrary to Schattschneider's claim, it also is not clear what sort of party competition will provide the appropriate check—two, three, or more parties—and in what form. Such structural decisions raise fundamental questions about the meaning of majority rule. Finally, to complicate matters even further, we are not clear who should speak for, and thereby control, the party: the formal party organization or its elected representatives in government (Lowenstein 1993)? In classic law and economics vernacular, one needs a pre-existing property rights system—that is, a definition of who controls the party—before one can hope to have an idea about what a functioning private competitive system should look like. Unfortunately, our theory of party competition is not as complete or as normatively developed as our theories of private markets.

Given these ambiguities, the government and the courts are obligated to decide indirectly, by how they structure party competition, some of the issues we might prefer the parties to magically decide through the invisible hand: What are the appropriate limits of compromise? When will democracy be furthered between parties, rather than within them? More generally, where is the appropriate locus and extent of agenda control?

As an example of these problems, consider the need to channel public debate (described above). This function is a necessary consequence of our electoral system; indeed, it has led First Amendment scholars such as Ed Baker and Ronald Dworkin to argue that the First Amendment shouldn't even apply to elections, at least not in the way we ordinarily think (see Baker 1998; Dworkin 1996). This perspective, however, is not something the legal system likes to admit—as evidenced by the fact that the point of Baker's work is to show how the courts have tried to conceal this fact. Deals, forced compromises, and agenda control can also cause problems for courts and academics. Although such activities may be necessary to motivate popular participation and forge agreements in the real world, they don't comport with many lawyers' ideal of legitimate government activities, especially when viewed through a First Amendment lens. As noted above, an informal, private system of inducing compromise can have many benefits over a formal public process.

Finally—and perhaps most important—the Constitution does not define, except in formal terms, the meaning of democratic majority rule. Whether courts are or should be in the business of (in the famous words of Justice Frankfurter) "choosing among competing theories of political philosophy" (*Baker v. Carr*, 369 U.S. 186, at 300 (1962), clearly they have serious problems in performing that task with any precision. This project has led to some of the most creative theorizing in legal academia—from arguments for a judicially mandated "equally effective vote" to a claim that all groups should "take turns at setting the substance of government policy" (Guinier 1991).

In light of these functions, it should be clear why the courts have difficulty assimilating these traditional functions of political parties explicitly into legal doctrine, even though we need these duties to be performed successfully. To put it bluntly: A nondemocratic court prefers to avoid these types of frank judgments by deferring to private political process—or at least analyzing through the lens of an allegedly neutral standard, such as procedural due process, consent theory, or fundamental principle. Many of the great debates in constitutional law concerning the appropriate standard of judicial review of legislative decisions have attempted to confront similar issues by postulating the neutrality of various decision rules—ultimately, and not surprisingly, with limited success (see Tribe 1980; Brest 1981; Klarman 1991). Regulation of political parties presents similar problems, as the Court confronts analogous issues through the procedural lens of political regulation.

THE SUPREME COURT'S DOCTRINAL TREATMENT OF PARTIES

Parties and Voting Rights

Given the lack of normative consensus, we should not be surprised that Supreme Court decisions regulating parties try to avoid these issues directly or confront them only indirectly through discussion of process—and never draw clear, predictable, coherent lines. This tension is most obvious, and has been the subject of the greatest discussion, when voting rights were directly at issue—namely, in recent cases interpreting section 2 of the Voting Rights Act and the old gerrymandering cases, beginning with *Baker v. Carr*, 369 U.S. 186 (1962), and ending with *Davis v. Bandemer*, 478 U.S. 109 (1986). In *Davis*, by deciding on permissible limits on party redistricting, the Court was faced with defining the limits—and thereby the goals—of party rule. This latest foray into the subject resulted in the constitutional rule that no redistricting system should result in the "continued frustration of the will of the majority." Not surprisingly, a standard based on "frustration" can be interpreted quite disparately: Some observers have regarded it as imposing a requirement of proportional representation, whereas others have viewed it as nothing more than a "smell test" (see Shuck 1987). The lower courts seem to have backed away—as they probably had to.

A similar dilemma has been revealed in racial redistricting cases, in which the Court originally championed a type of proportional representation test to determine whether redistricting adequately protected the voting rights of African Americans under section 2 of the Voting Rights Act (see *Thornburgh v. Gingles*, 478 U.S. 30 (1986)). Unfortunately for the proponents of the 1982 amendments to section 2, the protection of African American representative seats has not uniformly advanced the substantive policy agenda of black citizens because of section 2's indirect effect on the electoral prospects of the Democratic party. Concentrating African Americans in districts served to dilute white Democratic voters, thereby reducing the number of Democratic representatives (Pildes 1995). Unless the Court is willing to look into the internal mechanics of Congress and the legislatures and develop a standard for evaluating the substantive effectiveness of the vote, direct judicial intervention is unlikely to be expanded here as well (see *Miller v. Johnson*, 515 U.S. 900 (1995)). In today's political climate, this is an increasingly remote prospect, especially in view of the normative problems described above.

Timmons and the Two-Party System

The most recent cases on political parties present the same dilemmas, although the Court has wisely not attempted to intervene with as broad an intellectual brush. In *Timmons*, the Court upheld a Minnesota ban on fusion candidates; that is, it upheld the prohibition against third parties nominating the candidate of a major party on the general ballot. The Court reasoned that the ban furthered the state's interest in party stability and ballot coherence while not substantially infringing the interests of third parties.

Putting aside, for the moment, the underlying purposes of a party system, many of the Court's arguments seem nonsensical under a conventional First Amendment analysis. If First Amendment rights for parties mean anything, they would seem to protect a party's right to nominate whomever it wants—assuming, as was true in *Timmons*, that person is an otherwise eligible candidate. Contrary to the Court's assertion that forcing the party to go to its second choice is only a "slight" imposition on party interests, the choice of a candidate often defines the collective identity of the group. Imagine the Republicans without Ronald Reagan, or the Democrats without Franklin Roosevelt. Because of this prohibition, minor parties are forced either to nominate a loser or to be submerged under the anonymous umbrella of a major party banner. The impact on party strength can be substantial, as the historical evidence submitted to the Court on the consequences of fusion bans confirmed. The fact that in *Timmons* both the major and minor party organizations agreed to the joint nomination adds to the concern.

A similar criticism can be made of Justice Rehnquist's claim in *Timmons* that ballots are not "fora for political expression." This statement was a definitional attempt to avoid First Amendment scrutiny. The ability to identify a candidate as connected to the party—that is, to give her a party identity and hence to solidify party identification within the public—would seem to lie at the heart of First Amendment party rights.

The ban is far more defensible, however, when it is understood in terms of the stark underlying purposes of political parties, however difficult they may be to incorporate into traditional First Amendment analysis. First, fusion tickets raise concerns that are best described by analogy to copyright terms. Parties nominate and invest in individuals as their standard-bearers. With fusion candidacies, minor parties derive some of that benefit by hitching their wagon to the majority party candidate-star. The Court may have been alluding to this dynamic with its reference in the decision to the need to combat "voter confusion." Confusion, however, like candidate copyright concerns, is not ordinarily a justification for such stark interventions in the First Amendment context.

The other obvious objective of the fusion ban is to give the majority parties some degree of agenda control against potential opposition. With the ban, members of the public are not permitted to pledge allegiance to a minor party and vote for a majority party nominee at the same time. Nominees also have to choose which party they will serve as a nominee. In other words, the bald purposes and effects of the ban are to support major parties, hurt third parties, and force compromise—moving nominees and party voters to the two major parties, reducing the leverage of third parties, and presumably supporting the middle.

Obviously, these stark value judgments are not embedded in the language or history of the Constitution—nor are they openly defended in the Court's opinion. In my view, a strong two-party system probably *is* beneficial for all of these reasons. Party control of the institutions of government in general facilitates greater political accountability to the public for government action, at least over the long run (Fitts 1988, 1990, 1996). I freely admit, however, that all of these classic arguments are based on a series of contestable empirical and normative assumptions— that third parties will push to the extremes, rather than the centers (see chapter 8 of this volume). They also assume that our political system would not be sufficiently enriched and political participation increased by a still wider diversity at the wings in political representation (Hasen 1998).

Because one person's "silent majority" or "underrepresented minority" is another's "special interest group" or "obstructionist outlier," courts like to avoid making these types of explicit agenda control judgments, at least directly. The fact dependency of the judgments only underscores the problem. As a result, it should not be surprising—nor necessarily bad— that the Court's statements supporting the two-party system here and elsewhere in the party regulation cases have been couched in narrow language and obscured in unpredictable balancing tests.

Colorado Republican Federal Campaign Committee v. FEC: Parties in Campaign Financing Law

The other recent major party case was *Colorado Republican Federal Campaign Committee v. FEC*. In that decision, the Supreme Court, in a series of split opinions, held unconstitutional the Federal Elections Commission's (FEC) regulatory limitation on uncoordinated party campaign expenditures. Applying the *Buckley* standard that independent campaign expenditures are protected by the First Amendment, the Court concluded that spending by parties that was not coordinated with a particular campaign could not be regulated. At the same time, it deferred reaching the question of whether coordinated campaign expenditures fell within the *Buckley* criterion and would also receive full-blown First Amendment protection. In so doing, various members of the Court speculated on the types of pressure a party may legitimately impose on a candidate through party spending. The case raised fundamental issues about the proper role of political parties, albeit framed in terms of the widely criticized framework of *Buckley*.

Needless to say, campaign contribution cases raise some of the same conceptual problems as voting cases; once we move away from a formalistic rights analysis—that money is speech and a vote is a vote—drawing lines becomes quite difficult. The authors of *Buckley* hoped they were avoiding a slippery slope by drawing a contribution-versus-expenditure distinction. That approach protected independent political expenditures under the First Amendment but assumed that contributions raised a higher probability of impermissible corruption and could be regulated in a manner consistent with First Amendment speech rights.

Unfortunately, even under this formalistic framework, the Colorado case raised for *Buckley* adherents the classic unanticipated hypothetical situation—coordinated expenditures by a party for a candidate. Were candidate-related party expenditures more like political action committee (PAC) *contributions* to candidates and subject to FEC limitations? Or were they closer to candidates expending their own money and protected by the First Amendment? Although *Buckley* critics who would support limits on all campaign contributions and expenditures need not worry about the conceptual distinction, for those attempting to maintain the *Buckley* divide, the treatment of party-coordinated expenditures requires a subtle analysis. On the one side, in an attempt to fit into the *Buckley* framework, Justice Thomas argued that there is an identity between parties and candidates, thereby making party contributions like the candidates' own expenditures. This proposition, admittedly, was somewhat odd, given Thomas's claim that parties are a source of positive pressure on candidates. Recognizing the dilemma, Thomas went on argue that, to the extent that political parties are subject to private pressure, they "diffuse" those interests. Assuming that parties performed that affirmative role well, one could then conclude, as Justice Thomas did, that parties "can't corrupt candidates" and thus cannot be regulated under *Buckley's* application of the First Amendment.

The plurality opinion by Justice Breyer, which agreed that party contributions were "less likely to corrupt," ultimately refused to reach the coordinated expenditure issue, noting that party contributions "share relevant features with PACs"—a concern highlighted by recent scandals in Washington. Justice Stevens went one step further in his dissent, arguing for a presumption of abuse. Maintaining that the party/candidate relationship "created a special danger that the party—or the persons who control the party—will abuse the influence it has over the candidate by virtue of its power to spend," Stevens concluded that the Court should defer to the FEC's judgment that the contributions were covered.

Various legal academics have echoed the concern that political parties are no more than an aggregation of special interests (see Macey 1990; Lowi 1997). To the extent that metaphor is true, presumably no loophole should exist. All contributions pervert the process. If political parties perform the ideal typical role described above, however—of which Justice Thomas's description of "diffusion" is a part—the loophole of coordinated party spending, under Thomas's analysis, would presumably constitute an exercise of core First Amendment activity, at least under the *Buckley* framework. There should be no improper influence or bias.

Was the Court right to delay resolution of the latter issue? It is hard to conceive of a more fundamental discussion by the Court on the value of political parties—albeit through the twisted lens of the *Buckley* doctrine. Resolution of the issue is complicated by technical questions beyond the scope of the present analysis. For example, would striking down limits on party campaign expenditures serve ultimately to invalidate other restrictions, such as limits on contributions to parties or party spending in presidential campaigns—and how would those changes in turn affect the system?

At the same time, the case required the Court to confront a series of difficult factual and normative questions about the role of political parties—questions that lie at the heart of the Thomas/Stevens exchange and the problems raised in this chapter. As noted above, there is a serious empirical debate about whether political parties are getting stronger or weaker. During the past few years, the level of party voting in Congress, the strength of the national party organizations, and the amount of party funding have all increased, while party identification and party-line voting by the public continue to decline (see, e.g., Aldrich 1995). How these complicated cross-cutting trends affect the strength of parties and the incentives of parties to check or diffuse narrower interests—the issue in *Colorado Republican Federal Campaign Committee v. FEC*—is not clear, and may not be for some time.

Predictions are further complicated by the legal equivalent of a Heisenberg uncertainty problem: Whatever rule the courts adopt here and in other cases may affect how the parties perform their role and how the political process responds to these changes, such as with limits on "soft money" contributions. Ultimately, judgments may also simply depend on one's baseline: Political parties do a more effective job than an atomistic system of freestanding candidates in withstanding narrower constituencies—though not as well as if party identification remained strong or perhaps if some ideal alternative regulatory system, such as public funding, were implemented. Wise judicial intervention will thus require a complicated, "second-best" analysis.

THE COURT AND FINANCE REFORM: WHAT ROLE FOR PARTIES?

This factual conflict reveals a more fundamental conceptual problem implicit in all campaign regulation debates, which the opinions and commentary on *Colorado Republican Federal Campaign Committee v. FEC* hint at. Justice Stevens' dissenting opinion not only expresses concern about political parties acting as conduits for private special-interest contributions, it also challenges the pressure put on candidates on the party's behalf, which jeopardizes candidates' independence. A *Harvard Law Review* commentary on the case echoes these concerns, suggesting that any party influence may constitute improper pressure, whether diffused or not, as an intrusion on the civic republican independence of candidates (*Harvard Law Review* 1997). This analysis is a direct rejection of the mediative role of parties outlined in this chapter. Opponents of *Buckley* who believe all "inequality" in campaign spending is wrong may agree with this analysis, but they are then faced with answering the $64,000 question that has perplexed many commentators who have written on *Buckley*: What type of "political pressure" is then permissible and protected by the First Amendment? Although some observers argue that Congress should make these decisions through campaign finance reform legislation, at some point the courts will need a framework for judicial review of Congressional action. In other words, some institution must perform the functions undertaken by political parties and described above.

This debate underscores the conceptual minefield present in the more general debate over the reform of campaign finance and political parties. Virtually all legal scholars condemn the influence of money in politics on the grounds of political inequality. This widespread consensus on the problem tends to break down, however, when one attempts to construct an acceptable alternative system of government or judicial campaign regulation. There are two different types of problems.

The first problem is in deciding what type of influence is appropriate if *Buckley* should be overruled. Needless to say, every regulatory system will produce—or at least implicitly accept—inequalities in media access, volunteer support, public recognition, candidate recruitment, campaign finance, or even public acceptability (Cain 1995; Smith 1998). Not all differences can be eliminated. Once legislatures and the courts are faced with resolving the appropriate equality of distribution across a variety of political resources, however, a host of complex factual and normative questions are presented because the definition of equality is inherently normative (Westen 1990).

To offer one illustrative example: Some prominent advocates of heightened judicial review argue that a form of false consciousness produced by our current social structure undermines political debate, regardless of the distribution of current resources, and must be combated through government intervention (Fiss 1996; Sunstein 1995). In other words, real equality demands affirmative compensation. In this sense, defining what the appropriate distribution of campaign and electoral resources should be, like defining what group rights or democratic decision rules should be, ultimately raises fundamental and substantive questions about democratic policy.

Beyond our difficulty in reaching explicit agreement on such questions, a second problem must be confronted: the political and institutional legitimacy of the government and courts making these decisions directly and explicitly. To the extent that a strong party system exists, such decisions are made indirectly through party competition. This process may seem more popularly legitimate and, as the political culture changes, facilitate evolution of the standards over time. Legal academics have made a similar argument on behalf of private economic markets and pluralism as a means of resolving conflict informally (see Becker 1983; Dahl 1956). To the extent that courts make these judgments, however, the tradeoffs in values will necessarily be more explicit, are more likely to be frozen over time, and will be promulgated by what at least some observers view as an undemocratic institution. Although legislative regulation may avoid some concerns regarding democratic legitimacy, it invariably raises different problems of self-dealing and capture by those who will be regulated. For example, at what point should a court decide—or allow Congress to decide—what the distribution of volunteer support and issue ads should be in American society? Each academic who confronts the question of what the distribution of campaign resources should be in a post-*Buckley* world must resolve this normative quagmire (Foley 1994; Hasen 1993; Smith 1996). As Archibald Cox once observed, "Once loosed, the idea of equality is not easily cabined" (Cox 1966).

Of course, these institutional concerns do not mean that the Supreme Court should retain *Buckley* or that Congress should not pursue significant campaign finance reform. Just as proponents of private economic markets have had to concede the systemic failures of private economic markets, party enthusiasts have had to recognize the drawbacks to parties, beginning with the White Primary cases. As a factual matter, political parties have been less successful at withstanding—or "diffusing"—narrow interest groups than their proponents have claimed. They also have successfully frozen out many groups—in the middle as well as at the extremes—that most observers would argue deserve greater attention. This discussion is not intended as a normative defense of political parties as they now function.

At the same time, the analysis does help explain the problems the Court faces and the seeming inconsistencies in its case analysis. If the Court overrules *Buckley* and starts down the road of major campaign finance reform and regulation, we will be faced with an alternative system constructed by a real Congress and Court making explicit decisions about appropriate representation. No one can be *sure* they will be up to the task—either as a political matter or as a normative matter.

CONCLUSION: AS GOOD AS CAN BE EXPECTED

In light of this factual and normative ambiguity, it is not surprising that the Court delayed resolution of the party issue in *Colorado Republican Federal Campaign Committee v. FEC*. In my view, it would have been a mistake for the Court to have written a long legal treatise on parties and campaign expenditures in its decision on the case. This area warrants humility and deference to private political forces—at least initially.

To be sure, technical issues in the case may determine the ultimate resolution. Depending on how these and other issues are resolved, the Court ultimately might uphold the FEC limits on coordinated party expenditures—even though it might believe (as I do) that parties, as the best institutional vehicle for overcoming many forms of inequality, should be strengthened. Given the current system, a party exemption could well unravel the current regulatory framework, as well as create a serious appearance problem that might hurt political parties in the public eye even more.

These judgments, however, require subtle factual predictions, as well as a certain normative consensus—exactly what is lacking in this context. Ultimately, that is my point: For an institution interpreting a document that never mentions parties—and with a doctrinal library that is formalistic, individualistic, and potentially hostile to parties—the Court seems to be doing as well as can or should be expected, however muddled its approach may seem to an outsider. That is the nature of the enterprise.

··· 6 ···

Partisan Autonomy or State Regulatory Authority? The Court as Mediator

PAUL R. PETTERSON

During the twentieth century, one of the most challenging and divisive issues for the Supreme Court has been the legal status of political parties. Are they an arm of the state—a part of the government even though the Constitution omitted them from its architecture of politics? Or are they free political associations, entitled to conduct their affairs as they choose? To the layperson's eye, the answers the Court has reached have been contradictory. In some situations—particularly those involving racial discrimination in the electoral process—party activities have often been found to be "state action," and thus subject to the reach of Fourteenth and Fifteenth Amendment protections of citizenship and voting rights. In an alternative jurisprudence that began to develop in the late 1950s, many party activities have been protected under a "freedom of association" located in the First Amendment.

The case of *Morse v. Virginia Republican Party*, 517 U.S. 186 (1996) —involving the Virginia Republican Party and its 1994 U.S. Senate nomination process—reveals that these contradictions in the Court's jurisprudence persist to this day. Specifically, questions of racial bias and fair access to the political process continue to collide with assertions by political parties that they should be able to order their affairs as they see fit. This conflict is not a clash of wrong and right but of two sets of constitutional rights and political claims sharing the same territory. The problem for the Court is that its recent members have not reached consensus on how to balance these two rights or on a shared understanding of political parties.

An examination of *Morse* and the Court's overall record on party freedom of association reveals duality and division within its jurisprudence, but not of the meaningless kind. In fact, the Court has been engaged in an ongoing debate between justices who value maximum protection against racial bias by the state and those who believe that political parties should have the benefit of the doubt in these disputes. There is a related debate, within the freedom of association stream of jurisprudence, between a vision of parties as part of a "natural order" of politics and a vision of parties as entities in a "created order" of elections structured by state law.

This chapter explores the meaning of *Morse*: where it fits in these debates and what it means for the Court's future jurisprudence in this area. The chapter begins with a review of the "white primary cases," which established the legal relationship between party activities and state authority; it then examines the freedom of association decisions (to place *Morse* in its appropriate context). The chapter proceeds to analyze *Morse* to determine whether the Court has been consistent with its earlier rulings and their meaning for practical party politics and the practice of democracy. In the context of the Court's overall jurisprudence, *Morse* reflects dualities that are likely to persist, at least in the near term. Although these "contradictions" create continuing uncertainties for parties, governments, and citizens in the areas of participation and representation, they should not be regarded as the failings of an incompetent Court. Rather, they reflect deep questions about representation and other aspects of democracy with which our entire political order continues to struggle. The Court has been no more divided, and no less sensible, on these dilemmas than the American polity as a whole. Although one might wish that it had found or provided more conclusive answers in *Morse*, we should not be shocked or dismayed that it did not.

THE CONTEXT OF MORSE: WHITE PRIMARIES AND FREEDOM OF ASSOCIATION

The heart of the jurisprudence underlying *Morse* is ultimately rooted in the politics of late-nineteenth-century America. This era, known for the start of Populist and Progressive democratic reform efforts, also had a darker side. Many of the reforms were used to restrict, rather than enlarge, the scope of participation and party activity. In particular, southern states disenfranchised African American males through a variety of restrictions on voting, including poll taxes and literacy tests. The most blatant collusion of the political parties in this disenfranchisement was the use of "white primaries," which restricted voting in primary elections (often the key electoral contest in the southern states) to white persons only. For decades, these primaries went unchallenged. Then, from 1927 to 1953, the U.S. Supreme Court took up the issue of white primaries. In the process, it redefined the ability of the Constitution and governments to protect the participation and representation rights of African Americans and other racial minorities.

Although an earlier decision (*U.S. v. Newberry*, 256 U.S. 232 (1921)) had found primary elections to be outside the scope of state action, the Court revisited this question in its first white primary case, *Nixon v. Herndon*, 286 U.S. 73 (1927). Texas had passed a law barring African Americans from voting in Democratic Party primaries; the Court struck down this law as state action infringing on the equal protection clause of the Fourteenth Amendment (Claude 1970, chapter 4). The Court affirmed and expanded this reasoning in *Nixon v. Condon*, 286 U.S. 73 (1932), finding that transferring the power of disenfranchisement from the state legislature to the Executive Committee of the Texas Democratic Party did not privatize the discrimination; it was still state action subject to the Fourteenth Amendment. The Court had thus established its authority to protect participation rights (Claude 1970).

The Court muddied the waters briefly with its decision in *Grovey v. Townsend*, 295 U.S. 45 (1935), in which an informal resolution of the Texas Democratic Party was found to be a private associational action, shielded from the *Nixon* precedents. Six years later, in *U.S. v. Classic*, 313 U.S. 299 (1941), the Court laid the seeds for reversing *Grovey* by establishing that primaries in general were "an integral part" of the electoral process subject to the Fourteenth Amendment. *Grovey* was overturned in *Smith v. Allwright*, 321 U.S. 649 (1944), when the Court held that the electoral process as a whole is essentially a state function under the Fourteenth and Fifteenth Amendments and that Texas (again the defendant in this case) was complicit in any effort by its political parties to bar African American voting. This principle was reconfirmed (and stands to this day) in *Terry v. Adams*, 345 U.S. 461 (1953). In *Terry*, the Texas Jaybird Association argued that its private primary was not state action, but the Court found that its actions usually determined the Democratic Party nominee and were thus governed by the *Smith* precedent (Claude 1970, chapter 4). Thus, by 1953 the Court had decisively established the constitutional protection of African American political participation in the nomination and election of candidates.

These white primary cases laid the legal foundation for the Voting Rights Act (VRA) of 1965. The VRA was enacted to enable the voting ability supposedly protected by *Smith* and *Terry*. One of the most important portions of the Act is section 5, which provides for "preclearance" of any changes in voting or election procedures in states with a history of racial discrimination in the electoral process. The purpose of this requirement was to shift the burden of proof from affected voters (who had to go to court repeatedly to fight the white primaries) to the states and parties contemplating changes. In this way, discriminatory practices would be blocked before implementation, rather than being redressed after the fact (Grofman and Davidson 1992, part 1).

The importance of the white primary cases lies in the precedent and powers they established for constitutional intervention in the electoral process. The ability of citizens of all races to participate and have their votes counted in elections (including the nomination machinery) is a constitutional guarantee that outweighs any private associational rights used to justify discriminatory practices. The section 5 preclearance requirement of the VRA strengthens this protection by demanding that states with a history of discrimination demonstrate that an electoral change will *not* result in new discrimination. Thus, the modern Court and Congress have provided substantial and ongoing support for a democratic election system that ensures fair representation for all.

Smith does not represent the complete picture of the constitutional rights of political parties, however. Although the Court has acknowledged that political parties are integral to the state's electoral machinery, it also has found that many partisan activities enjoy the protection of the First Amendment and therefore are beyond the reach of government regulation. The concept of freedom of association—first clearly enunciated in the context of a political interest group in *NAACP v. Alabama*, 357 U.S. 449 (1958)—has been applied to political parties since the late 1960s. It represents a separate "track" of constitutional precedents from those cases directly implicating voter rights and discrimination. Despite *Morse's* relatively narrow factual basis, it is noteworthy in the context of understanding the Court's philosophy in this area. *Morse* represents a clear intersection of these two lines of precedent, forcing the Court to weigh its dualistic thinking and balance these two areas of representational and democratic jurisprudence.

The first direct linking of freedom of association to political parties was *Williams v. Rhodes*, 393 U.S. 23 (1968). George Wallace's independent campaign for the presidency brought suit against Ohio's ballot access laws, claiming that the early filing requirements and organizational requirements imposed on minor parties violated the freedom of association of his supporters. The Court majority, employing a "strict scrutiny" standard of review, agreed. The justices found that Ohio's laws infringed on freedom of association and were not justified by a sufficiently compelling state interest. They made particular note of the *advantage* that Ohio's laws gave to the two major parties. (Ironically, the case involved Wallace's American Independent Party—whose platform questioned much of the civil rights and voting rights movement.)

In 1975, the justices faced the question of whether Illinois could compel the national Democratic Party to seat delegates at its 1972 convention who were chosen by procedures established by Illinois law rather than those of national party rules. In *Cousins v. Wigoda*, 419 U.S. 477 (1975), the Court ruled that the national Democratic Party had the right to decide how the delegates to its own convention are chosen, including the right not to seat delegates selected by Illinois law. Once again employing strict scrutiny, the justices expanded the rights of political parties to control their nomination processes. (In this case, a slate of alternative delegates led by Jesse Jackson was the legal beneficiary of the Court's action.)

This pro-party doctrine was strengthened by the Court's ruling in *Democratic Party of the United States v. Wisconsin ex rel Lafollette*, 450 U.S. 107 (1981). The national Democratic Party brought suit against Wisconsin's open primary law to enforce a party rule mandating that all bound delegates to the Democratic National Convention be chosen only by Democratic voters. The Court agreed, holding that the state cannot restrict the national party's freedom of association in the absence of a compelling state interest. Unlike *Morse*, however, this case did not involve issues of preclearance or racial discrimination.

The Supreme Court revisited the issue of ballot access for third-party presidential candidates in *Anderson v. Celebrezze*, 460 U.S. 780 (1983). In that case, independent presidential candidate John Anderson contested Ohio's early filing deadline on the same freedom of association grounds that Wallace had used in 1968. Employing strict scrutiny and a three-part balancing test the Court invalidated the Ohio law and again protected minor party access to the ballot in presidential contests.

The freedom of political parties to control their nominating procedures was reaffirmed in *Tashjian v. Republican Party of Connecticut*, 479 U.S. 208 (1986). The Connecticut Republican Party's 1984 effort to open its primary contests to unaffiliated voters conflicted with Connecticut state law mandating that all primaries be open only to registered party members. The Court overruled this state law as infringing on the freedom of association of Connecticut Republicans.

This cursory review reveals a general trend in the Court's decisions toward expanding the ability of political parties to structure their own affairs, especially nominating procedures, as well as toward expanding the access of minor party presidential candidates to the ballot. There has also been a consistent strain of dissents in these cases, however, relying largely on issues of federalism and the contention that parties are not simply occurrences of a "natural order of politics." Instead, according to this view, they are part of a "constructed political order" (and, as state creations, properly within the purview of state law and regulatory authority). This alternative viewpoint has prevailed in some cases, leading to many 5–4 Supreme Court decisions. The end product is a jurisprudence that has defended freedom of association but is also engaged in an ongoing internal debate over the parameters of that freedom.

How does freedom of association relate to the voting rights cases and *Morse*? Both lines of jurisprudence involve questions of representation and democracy: who can participate in the political process and what forms that participation may take. The question that unites them is, participation for whom? The voting rights cases seek to ensure that all citizens, regardless of race, have the freedom to participate fully in voting and in the electoral process. This effort at expansion has occurred in the face of arguments (on and off the Court) that states have legitimate powers to make their own choices about the structure of the electoral process, unless clear discrimination is demonstrated.

The freedom of association cases have also addressed the question of participation, although with somewhat different concerns. Although the Court has strongly defended expanded participation by third-party presidential candidates in the ballot access cases, its larger concern has been with the freedom of political parties to control their own affairs, including who participates in their decision making. As *Lafollette* and *Tashjian* indicate, this analysis can mean either contraction or expansion of who has a voice in party matters. This jurisprudence, as in the voting rights cases, has confronted a dissenting voice that believes state governments should exercise broad authority over these matters. The Court has also clearly distinguished those cases involving race discrimination issues from its general freedom of association rulings, however.

In this context, *Morse* represents the intersection of these two divergent answers to the question of the proper scope of political representation and participation rights. Virginia was covered by the preclearance provisions of section 5 of the Voting Rights Act. The justices thus had to weigh the interests of protecting voter rights against the rights of the Virginia Republican Party to structure its own nominating procedures, as well as the rights of Virginia (as a state) to make its own choices regarding election procedures. Given the precedents reviewed above, it is no surprise that *Morse* engendered much debate and could muster only a plurality opinion from the Court.

THE MORSE CASE

Morse v. Virginia Republican Party grew out of the highly contentious and nationally visible 1994 U.S. Senate race in Virginia between Democrat Charles Robb and Republican Oliver North. North parlayed his fame as a conservative icon from the Reagan era to make a run for the Senate. Republican moderates unhappy with the prospect of North as their candidate sought to challenge him at the Republican nominating convention. As part of this effort, a participation fee of $35–$45 was imposed on Republicans who wished to attend and vote (*Morse v. Virginia Republican Party*, 517 U.S. at 190). Prospective delegates challenged the fee under the Voting Rights Act, eventually forcing the Court to confront head-on the tension between protecting all voters and protecting party autonomy in decision making.

A plurality of the badly divided Court sided with the challenge to the participation fee and against the Virginia Republican Party. Relying on the Voting Rights Act, the plurality held that section 5's preclearance requirement legally outweighed any rights of the party to structure its nomination procedures (*Morse*, 517 U.S. at 186–89).

Justice Stevens's plurality opinion (in which only Justice Ginsburg joined) relied heavily on the history and text of the Voting Rights Act. He noted that Virginia clearly fell under the jurisdiction of section 5 and was therefore under an obligation to preclear electoral changes that fundamentally affect voting rights (including the right to a voice in nominating whom one can vote for). Even if the party were a purely private organization (with full freedom of association), Stevens asserted that its actions were still covered by section 5 because the state's guarantee of automatic ballot placement for major party nominees gives their nomination the stamp of state authority (*Morse*, 517 U.S. at 193, 197).

Stevens regarded the white primary cases as placing primaries (and by extension, other nomination procedures) under the aegis of the Fourteenth and Fifteenth Amendments, which the Voting Rights Act was designed to complement and enforce. He quoted extensively from the debates surrounding the passage of the VRA to establish the authors' intent to reach into all parts of the voting process, to ensure that the intent of the law was not evaded by legal loopholes (*Morse*, 517 U.S. at 199–200, 208–209).

Stevens also dismissed two arguments raised successfully by the Virginia Republican Party at the trial court level. He asserted that a Justice Department regulation excluding party activity outside primaries from section 5 coverage was outweighed by the intent of the VRA itself, as well as the fact that the Justice Department had previously demanded preclearance of some convention procedures. Stevens also found the Virginia Republican Party's reliance on *Williams v. Democratic Party of Georgia*, 409 U.S. 809 (1972) unconvincing. Although the Court in *Williams* had ruled that section 5 did not cover convention delegates, Stevens found that the facts of that case did not involve as clear an exclusion from nomination procedures as was at issue in Virginia. According to Stevens, the legislative history of the Voting Rights Act, particularly section 5, clearly indicated that its authors intended it to apply to the full process of candidate nomination, even if this was not made perfectly explicit (*Morse*, 517 U.S. at 201–5). In other words, Congress had decided to place significant boundaries around party freedom of association when a "higher" value—protecting against racial discrimination in the voting process—was involved. One freedom had to be balanced against another in these circumstances.

Why not let such instances be handled and proved in court on a case-by-case basis, rather than requiring preclearance? Stevens asserted that one of the main purposes of the Voting Rights Act was to eliminate this case-by-case burden on those defending voting rights. That burden was exemplified by the white primary cases, which spanned nearly thirty years (with heavy expense and energy)—in part because of the absence of a conclusive prohibition and preclearance structure. Under the VRA, the burden shifts permanently to those proposing change in states covered by the Act (*Morse*, 517 U.S. at 213). In these states, party freedom is restrained by the need to redress a past history of discrimination and prevent its recurrence.

In addition to relying on section 5 of the VRA, Stevens also argued that the party's action is linked to state authority by virtue of the state's grant of special privileges to the two major parties. The granting of automatic ballot placement for Republican and Democratic nominees is the state's stamp of special approval to these nominees that gives them a strategic edge over minor parties (*Morse*, 517 U.S. at 195). This concern is consistent with Stevens's opinions in the Court's freedom of association cases (e.g., *Anderson*). There, as in *Morse*, Stevens argued that states should not be allowed to unfairly advantage certain parties because such procedures would reduce the ability of voters to associate with the party or candidate of their choice. As in *Morse*, the minor party presidential ballot access cases seek to protect the right of minor groups (either racial or political) to have a full voice in politics. In *Morse*, however, this analysis meant that to protect the rights of minor groups, a party must sacrifice some autonomy in its affairs. The key for Stevens was the *history* of abuse by the political process in Virginia; in such instances, redress of past discrimination had been found by Congress to outweigh a party's right to full autonomy.

Although Justices Breyer, O'Connor, and Souter concurred with Stevens's general verdict, they reached that conclusion on narrower grounds. Relying on the contextual history of the VRA and its passage, they concluded that the party's actions clearly fell within the purview of section 5 and thus required preclearance (*Morse*, 517 U.S. at 235). What distinguished Breyer's concurrence was that he and his colleagues did not take on the character of the party's action itself, as Stevens clearly did. They preferred to leave such judgments to enforcement officials at the Justice Department. In an overall context, however, they were persuaded that section 5 was applicable to the case at issue, and they came down on the side of strict enforcement of voting rights protections and against broad freedom of association guarantees.

Four justices (Justices Scalia, Kennedy, and Thomas and Chief Justice Rehnquist) were not convinced by either line of reasoning; they issued three separate dissenting opinions totaling almost fifty pages (*Morse*, 517 U.S. at 241–91). They tended to view this type of internal party decision as beyond the reach of the Voting Rights Act. They argued that the Court's plurality unwisely and improperly restricted the party's freedom of association. They concluded that the majority doctrine in *Morse* is likely to leave political parties confused about the scope of government authority to supervise party affairs. Kennedy's dissent, for example, relied heavily on the *Lafollette* decision, repeating its central assertion that a key freedom for political parties is the right to determine the boundaries of the association, to say who can and cannot participate

in party affairs. If that important associational principle were to be upheld, Virginia Republicans were entitled to impose an attendance fee or
otherwise restrict convention participation (*Morse*, 517 U.S. at 248–51).

Taken as a whole, the opinions in *Morse* revealed a Court divided on
the issue of how to proceed when voting rights and party freedom of
association guarantees are in legal conflict. The plurality camp (five justices) were persuaded by history, precedent (the white primary cases),
and legislative intent that the interests of the mass of Virginia voters
legally outweighed those of the Virginia Republican Party in this instance.
A minority of these justices (Stevens and Ginsburg) also saw a connection
between the participation/voter association rights protected in *Anderson*
and those at stake in *Morse*. This analysis was largely congruent with the
behavior of these justices in past cases, where they have been suspicious
of state actions restricting the voices of minor groups (political or racial).

The dissenting camp in *Morse* (four justices) tended to side with
party freedom of association, and the 5–4 division of this case mirrored
the close division that has characterized this entire line of jurisprudence.
The dissenters viewed the legal and historical case for this intrusion into
party affairs as insufficient, rejecting the notion that the major parties are
acting undemocratically or gaining unfair advantage by imposing the fee.
They pointed to previous Court decisions that gave internal party affairs
strong First Amendment protection, especially against the weak seed of
legislative intent relied upon by the plurality.

Of course, the dissenting justices in *Morse* are not concerned solely
with freedom of association. Their opinions and positions in past freedom
of association cases have not been entirely consistent with their positions
in *Morse*. Their concerns over time have had just as much to do with
federalism as with political parties. Chief Justice Rehnquist, in particular,
has been a staunch proponent of state interests against the intrusion of
national forces (dissenting in favor of Wisconsin in *Lafollette*), whether
they are the national Democratic Party or, as in *Morse*, the federal government. Thus, even though Rehnquist in *Morse* joined in a dissent that
relied on the very case he disagreed with, his concern for the overall
balance of federalism was the real center of the dissent.

CONCLUSION: WHAT IS THE MEANING OF MORSE?

Morse v. Virginia Republican Party is neither a watershed case nor a
major departure (positive or negative) from the Court's previous lines of

jurisprudence. It is significant, however, in revealing the fault lines that have existed for some time on the Court. The particular dilemma at issue—between voting rights protections and party freedom of association—ultimately is a question of representation, a tension between the representation of political parties and the representation of African Americans and other victims of discrimination. The meaning of *Morse* lies in its clear conflict between these two types of representation and what it tells us about the Court's current (and possibly future) thinking on this conflict. Whose representation should take precedence? Under what circumstances? Why?

The main concerns in addressing this tension involve issues of political understanding and theoretical grounding. Do the members of the Court understand the complexity of representation and how it develops? Such an understanding certainly is not readily apparent from *Morse*, in view of the focus on precedents and interpretation of relevant statutory law. This focus frustrates observers who are looking for a clear "theory of parties" in *Morse* and other Court opinions. The opinions of the Court are not always as politically savvy or as grounded in scholarly reasoning as some politicians or scholars might like. The Court lacks fixed definitions for critical concepts such as *political party* or *voting*, not to mention *democracy*. Hence, it often comes across as insufficiently cognizant of practical political conditions surrounding a particular dispute.

This frustration over the absence of political analysis and theoretical clarity in the Court's opinions, however, though valid to a point, misperceives the nature and the role of the Court in this area. First and foremost, the Court is a legal body. It is confined to the specific dispute before it, and it must decide that dispute based on statutes and common law, not abstract ideology. Despite the fact that the Court can use legal interpretation and current scholarship in various fields to broaden and expand the law, it is still a judicial body, not a think tank. It lacks the capacity to seek out problems, the time or venues to engage in full scholarly analysis, and the authority to simply pronounce on questions as it sees fit. What the Court can accomplish in enunciating a discernible theory of parties, representation, and politics must be judged in the context of the nature and scope of its authority and the practical constraints under which its members function.

One *can* discern from *Morse* a clearer resolution of the issue of balance between party freedom and voting rights and the tension between collective and individual political rights. Although the Court's previous opinions on freedom of association conferred significant protection to political parties, they never clearly protected a *group* freedom of association. Rather, the Court has understood freedom of association as an individual right with collective consequences. As a result, when the interests of individuals who have collectively suffered voting and representational discrimination are at odds with the representational interests of a party and its members, a majority of the Court has often come down—as it did in *Morse*—on the side of the first group. (One sees here again the ironic parallel with the cases involving minor party presidential candidates such as George Wallace.) Its purpose is not to vitiate the party members' representational interests but simply to recognize that they must be sensitive (and occasionally subordinated) to the representational needs of other particular citizens. The Court's calibrating of the representational balance in this fashion is grounded in Congressional statute (the Voting Rights Act) and judicial precedent (the white primary cases).

The *Morse* opinions speak to the meaning of representation, though not with tremendous clarity. Although the reasoning is grounded in statute and precedent, the implicit bias of the majority opinions is toward maximizing the participation of all citizens in all aspects of the electoral process. This bias is particularly true for Justices Stevens and Ginsburg. In essence, *Morse* would appear to favor more direct forms of democratic participation, as opposed to a "responsible party" approach that emphasizes the role of mediating institutions such as political parties in implementing representative democracy. Remember, however, that *Morse* was a narrow 5–4 decision, with a vocal minority favoring a pro-party vision of participation and representation.

The *Morse* opinions also speak to the question of which governmental authority should properly decide questions of representation. On this issue, *Morse* reflects an ongoing debate within the Court about the nature and scope of American federalism. The majority in *Morse* favored a federalism slanted toward federal authority and, on issues of representation, grounded in federal protections to maximize the participatory ability of all Americans. The four-justice minority favors an approach to federalism that is much more sensitive to state lawmakers (as democratic representatives of their citizenry) and the decisions they make. Thus, with the change of a single vote, the Court would have taken a much more deferential stance toward the actions of the Virginia Republicans in the *Morse* case.

The decision in *Morse* should also be considered within the broader context of power in American politics. Although the Court is now a much more active force in politics—reflective of an era of "politics by other means"—it still is only one force among many. As the debates in *Morse* and earlier cases reflect, the Court must wrestle with the intent and objectives of the other federal branches (i.e., Congressional legislation such as the Voting Rights Act), the powers and agendas of the fifty states (federalism), and the protections guaranteed by the Constitution (freedom of association); it then must balance all of these factors to the relative satisfaction of the overall political system. It must confront highly contentious issues in real political time, and because the Supreme Court has no real power beyond that of judgment, it surely is aware of the political winds and the election returns. To expect the Court to be philosophically clear and practically unambiguous is expecting a great deal of a functioning, fully engaged political institution.

What does *Morse* tell us about the future of political party and representation jurisprudence on the Court? The answer is twofold. First, the differences between those who want to maximize party freedom and those who view political parties as part of a more "constructed," legally established order of politics have not abated—and are not likely to. Second, cases such as *Morse* add racial fairness issues into the mix of deciding who should govern party activities—an ingredient that makes these issues even more contentious and divisive. *Morse*'s five written opinions confirm that assertion. If *Morse* is any indication, anyone who desires a clear and unambiguous philosophy of parties and political participation from the Court is likely to have a long wait. For those who can view the Court more realistically within its larger political and historical context, *Morse* is yet another example of a healthy, thoughtful, and vigorous judicial debate over questions of democracy, participation, and freedom.

If the justices are so divided and ambiguous, why examine the views of the Court on these questions in any great detail? Can they teach us anything useful about the electoral process? Or are the justices simply engaged in a confused and meaningless ideological quarrel? The answer is that the opinions of the Court are meaningful and instructive, both ideologically and practically.

Understanding the debates within the Court on questions of party freedom and voting rights is significant in good measure because of the growing role and authority of the Court in this area of law (and in

American politics in general). Although the Court either returns authority to the parties or (as in *Morse*) upholds governmental authority, the Court itself has taken on new authority and involvement. The Court has become a third active force in shaping our political parties and electoral process, and scholars must continue to better understand how the justices of the Court think about these issues.

··· 7 ···

The Supreme Court's Patronage Decisions and the Theory and Practice of Politics

CYNTHIA GRANT BOWMAN

Primary election day 1998—St. Patrick's Day—in Chicago: Precinct captains stand in the cold rain, the required number of feet from polling places, greeting arriving voters and handing out literature for candidates of the "Organization"—the Democratic Party machine of Cook County. The party and electoral system over which the machine had presided for many years (roughly 1931–1976) was substantially defunct, however. Some observers would say the Cook County Democratic organization fell victim to the Supreme Court's prohibition of patronage (specifically, the awarding of city jobs to political supporters). Others attribute its demise to the entry into politics of a large mass of African American voters, whose needs the machine had ignored (Grimshaw 1992, 91–166; Kleppner 1985, 8, 41–90, 137–49). Whatever the cause, election day 1998 looked different from elections twenty years before. Not a single precinct worker came to my door. Instead, floods of glossy material came through the mail slot—expensive, colorful flyers delivered in repetitive mass mailings. For the "important" statewide races, radio and television advertising supplanted the face-to-face contacts of yesteryear.

If the demise of the machine were not clear from the way the 1998 primary was carried out, the results of the day's polling provided ample proof. In the era of the machine, the Democratic organization virtually monopolized primary elections (Allswang 1986, 55). By contrast, in the eight years after the death of the first Mayor Daley (the current Mayor Daley, Richard M., is the son of legendary party boss Richard J. Daley), there were as many contested primary elections in Chicago as there had been in the previous 43 years (Green 1984, 20). Primary election day 1998 was no exception. The gubernatorial primary was hotly contested by four candidates, largely because white liberal and African American voters failed to agree on a single candidate. Mayor Daley did not endorse any candidate, and the one widely believed to be his favorite was defeated decisively. Meanwhile, the party candidate for Lieutenant Governor squeaked by with only a 1,000-vote margin. The Democratic machine was clearly dead in Chicago.

In its heyday, the Cook County Democratic organization controlled 35,000 patronage jobs (Wolfinger 1972, 373). It used these jobs to reward its army of precinct workers for turning out the vote for organization candidates and to punish them when they failed to do so. Of course, most patronage employees were also required to contribute to party coffers on a regular basis (Knauss 1972, 97–100; Royko 1971, 61).[1] In a 1977 court document, local government employers testified that preference in hiring for more than 20,000 positions was given to persons sponsored by the machine, that such sponsorship was given in return for performing precinct work, and that the political work done by these patronage workers "help[ed] elect candidates supported by the various members of the Democratic County Central Committee" (*Shakman v. Democratic Organization of Cook County*, 481 F. Supp. 1315, at 1325 (N.D. Ill.1979)).

In a series of decisions issued between 1976 and 1990, the Supreme Court prohibited these patronage practices, holding that they impermissibly interfered with the exercise of the First Amendment rights of current and potential public employees; in 1996, the Court extended the ban to the awarding of government contracts on political grounds as well (*Elrod v. Burns*, 427 U.S. 347 (1976); *Branti v. Finkel*, 445 U.S. 507 (1980); *Rutan v. Republican Party of Illinois*, 497 U.S. 62 (1990); *O'Hare Truck Service v. City of Northlake*, 518 U.S. 712 (1996); *Board of County Commissioners of Wabaunsee County v. Umbehr*, 518 U.S. 668 (1996)). Until the most recent decisions, these cases were decided by narrow margins, with the dissenting justices publishing lengthy opinions decrying the effects of the Court's action on political parties, elections, and participation in American local government. These exchanges provide a fascinating look at the Court's attitudes and assumptions regarding the operation of politics in the United States. They present another intriguing theme as well—dissenting Justice Powell's charge that the Court was ignoring "a highly practical and rather fundamental element of our political system [for] the theoretical abstractions of a political science seminar" (*Elrod v. Burns*, 427 U.S. at 382). Justice Scalia renewed the theme fourteen years later in his more strident discussion of the opposition between tradition and abstract logic (*Rutan v. Republican Party of Illinois*, 497 U.S. at 95–6; *Board of County Commissioners of Wabaunsee County v. Umbehr*, 518 U.S. at 686). This debate poses a key question: Has the Court been ignoring history-based reality in the development of its patronage jurisprudence?

In this chapter, I explore the Court's internal dialogue concerning the relationship of patronage to the political process. In the first part of the chapter, I review the cases from *Elrod v. Burns* to the patronage contracting cases in 1996. In the second part of the chapter, I analyze in greater depth what the majority and minority opinions in each case reveal about the Court's thinking about political parties, elections, and participation. I then consider whether the attitudes and assumptions of the various justices amount to coherent theories of politics and whether these theories—such as they are—reflect the reality of the political process. In closing, I offer some evaluative remarks about the Court's performance in deciding these cases.

THE SUPREME COURT'S EXPANDING PROHIBITION ON PATRONAGE

Elrod v. Burns: The Ban on Patronage Dismissals

The Supreme Court's first patronage case emerged from the thicket of Chicago politics. When Richard Elrod, a Democrat, was elected sheriff in 1970, he followed time-honored tradition by firing all of the Republican non-civil-service employees in the sheriff's office and replacing them with members of his own party. Rather than accepting their fate, several of the fired employees went to court to prevent their discharge, arguing that firing them constituted a violation of their First Amendment rights of association and political affiliation. The Supreme Court agreed, holding that to make the continuation of an employee's government job depend on his or her support of the party in power was coercion of belief and association. Because the employees' First Amendment rights were at stake, the challenged practice—patronage dismissals—was required to meet a very high standard (often called strict scrutiny) to be judged constitutionally permissible; under this standard, the defendant must show that the practice furthers a vital governmental interest and does so by the least restrictive means. The Court determined that the practice of patronage firing failed this standard and therefore was unconstitutional.

In *Elrod* and the Court's next patronage decision, *Branti v. Finkel*,[2] Justice Powell dissented and was joined by two other justices. Although Powell conceded the effect of patronage on the First Amendment rights of governmental employees, he concluded that it was nonetheless necessary to vital governmental interests (*Elrod v. Burns*, 427 U.S. at 381–87; *Branti v. Finkel*, 445 U.S. at 527–32). In particular, Justice Powell emphasized the historic role of patronage in democratizing the political process (because urban machines had registered immigrant voters), stimulating political activity (because patronage workers performed tasks necessary to electoral campaigns), and contributing to the maintenance of strong and accountable parties (because patronage was available to discipline party members). Justice Powell doubted that either voluntary funding or voluntary participation would suffice to fuel the necessary work of parties on the local level, in "unimportant" elections, or between elections if candidates could not reward their supporters with government jobs (*Elrod v. Burns*, 427 U.S. at 384–85).

Not only was patronage essential to the continued operation of political organizations, Justice Powell argued, it was also necessary to build party loyalty and avoid "splintering" and "unrestrained factionalism" (*Branti v. Finkel*, 445 U.S. at 528). By contrast, strong political parties allowed candidates to present their views to the electorate, recruited and mobilized voters, and helped elected officials carry out policies endorsed by the electorate. In Powell's opinion, political parties could not perform these functions unless they had the means to ensure party discipline via patronage, both by hiring employees loyal to the party and by enabling an elected executive to gain the cooperation of members of the legislative branch (*Branti v. Finkel*, 445 U.S. at 529–31). Powell predicted dire consequences for the American political party system as a result of the majority's decision prohibiting patronage dismissals of public employees.

Rutan v. Republican Party of Illinois: Goodbye to Patronage Hiring

Although patronage firing was prohibited as a result of the Supreme Court's decision in *Elrod*, the status of hiring on political grounds remained an open question until 1990, when the Court decided *Rutan v. Republican Party of Illinois*. In *Rutan*, the Court held, by a vote of 5–4, that patronage hiring and other personnel decisions taken on political grounds unconstitutionally pressured individuals to ally with a party not of their preference, to work for candidates they did not support, and to contribute money to promote policies with which they did not agree. This practice amounted to coercion of belief in violation of the First Amendment (*Rutan v. Republican Part of Illinois*, 497 U.S. at 62).

Justice Scalia's vehement dissent in *Rutan* is longer than the majority opinion. Scalia argued that the majority was sacrificing an age-old American political tradition in the name of "some abstract principle of First Amendment adjudication devised by this Court" (*Rutan v. Republican Party of Illinois*, 497 U.S. at 96). Justice Scalia's method of approaching this question was quite different from that of Justice Powell, however. Whereas Powell agreed generally with the First Amendment analysis employed by the Court but disagreed with its conclusions when evaluating the governmental interests served by patronage, Scalia rejected the very act of submitting the institution of patronage to constitutional adjudication at all. This position is understandable only in the context of Scalia's "originalist" theory of constitutional interpretation, which holds that the Constitution should be interpreted in light of the understandings and traditions at the time of its enactment. For Justice Scalia, a right that did not clearly exist at the time of the drafting of the Constitution or its amendments should not be read into the document by judges interpreting it today. Consequently, a practice such as patronage, which is not expressly prohibited by the Bill of Rights and has existed throughout American history, is presumptively constitutional. Indeed, for Justice Scalia the pedigree of patronage employment—from Washington and Jefferson through Jackson to Mayor Daley—ends the constitutional question; it *cannot* be unconstitutional because it has a long history of acceptance and use.

The question of whether patronage is good practice and should be maintained is another issue entirely, which Scalia believed should be left to the legislative branch. If the people's representatives want to replace patronage with a civil service system, or some mix of patronage and merit, they could do so. In other words, the disagreement between the *Rutan* majority and Justice Scalia involved not only matters of constitutional interpretation but also Scalia's opposition to what he perceived as judicial activism. Nonetheless, Justice Scalia went on to describe the historical benefits of patronage, its link to party discipline, its fostering of a broad-based two-party system, and its role in the social and political integration of excluded groups (*Rutan v. Republican Part of Illinois*, 497 U.S. at 104–8). Scalia was convinced that the *Elrod* and *Branti* decisions contributed to the decline of party strength, feeding the growth of interest-group politics during the 1980s (*Rutan v. Republican Party of Illinois*, 497 U.S. at 107) and giving rise to splintering and factionalism that bode ill for the body politic. Although Justice Scalia acknowledged the negative side effects of patronage—corruption and inefficiency in government, as well as some constraint upon individual views (*Rutan v. Republican Party of Illinois*, 497 U.S. at 108–9)—he argued that it has played a largely positive, perhaps even essential, role in maintaining a pragmatic, non-ideological, stable two-party system in the United States.

The 1996 Decisions: The Death of Patronage Contracting?

Given the narrow majority in *Rutan*, one can hardly blame Justice Scalia for being astonished when the next two patronage decisions were decided by 7–2 majorities voting to prohibit patronage contracting. *O'Hare Truck Service v. City of Northlake*, which arose in the Chicago suburbs, involved the owner of a trucking company that from 1965 to 1993 had provided towing services for the city of Northlake. In 1993, the mayor of Northlake—who had pronounced himself pleased with O'Hare's services after his election four years earlier—asked John Gratzianna, the owner of O'Hare, for a contribution to his reelection campaign. Not only did Gratzianna refuse to contribute; he also supported the mayor's opponent and displayed that candidate's campaign poster at O'Hare's place of business. Soon afterward, O'Hare was removed from the rotation list of towing contractors. Justice Kennedy, writing on behalf of the majority, saw this case as a relatively straightforward example of the conduct forbidden by the Court in *Elrod*; the government contract was terminated in retaliation for refusing to comply with a demand for political support, in violation of the contractor's rights of political association (*O'Hare Truck Service v. City of Northlake*, 714–18).

The companion case of *Board of County Commissioners of Wabaunsee County v. Umbehr* presented a slightly different set of facts. Mr. Umbehr had held an exclusive trash-hauling contract with Wabaunsee County, Kansas, for ten years, during which time he repeatedly criticized the county board at public meetings and in the newspaper. In 1991, the Board terminated Umbehr's contract, arguing that it was free to do so because an independent contractor such as Umbehr was not entitled to the same First Amendment protections as a government employee.

Because Umbehr's conduct was speech, however, rather than affiliation or association with a political party, the Supreme Court held that it was not covered by the strict scrutiny test of *Elrod* (*Board of County Commissioners of Wabaunsee County v. Umbehr*, at 678) but by the balancing test applied to cases involving speech by public employees; this test requires the Court to weigh the government's interests as an employer against the employee's interests in free speech (*Pickering v. Board of Education*, 391 U.S. 563, at 568 (1968)). If the government's interest in promoting the efficiency of public service through workplace discipline and solidarity outweighs the employee's interest in commenting upon matters of public concern, the individual may be fired despite the effect on First Amendment rights.

The majority's decisions in *O'Hare Truck Service* and *Umbehr* included little discussion of the political effect of extending the prohibition against patronage to government contracts. The only pragmatic considerations raised by the majority were those pertinent to the government's need to ensure that public services are delivered efficiently and in a manner true to the public policy the administration promised to implement. These goals could be served, according to the Court, by the ability to terminate a contract for unsatisfactory performance or, in a case in which the contractor's speech genuinely interfered with the efficient provision of the services, to defend termination under the *Pickering* balancing test (*Board of County Commissioners of Wabaunsee County v. Umbehr*, at 674–76).

Justice Scalia, supported only by Justice Thomas, filed a single dissent to the decisions in *O'Hare Truck Service* and *Umbehr*. Justice Scalia's main focus, again, was the long-standing American tradition of rewarding one's friends with contracts and withholding them from one's political enemies; hence, the practice could not be unconstitutional under Scalia's interpretive scheme (*Umbehr*, at 688–89). Justice Scalia also noted that state and federal legislatures have enacted numerous laws governing public contracts, arguing that the judiciary should leave this task to those legislative bodies better equipped to draw the fine distinctions required (*Umbehr*, at 690–95). Finally, he stressed the difficulty that courts and litigants would have in discerning situations in which a contractor (or employee, for that matter) has simply exercised his or her right of political affiliation versus when he or she has gone beyond that right to engage in an exercise of speech. Thus, it would be difficult to determine which of the two lines of cases—*Elrod/O'Hare Truck Service* or *Pickering/Um-behr*—governs a particular case (*Umbehr*, at 706–08).

WHAT THE PATRONAGE CASES REVEAL ABOUT THE COURT'S THINKING ABOUT POLITICAL PARTIES, ELECTIONS, AND POLITICAL PARTICIPATION

In this section I discuss the justices' attitudes and assumptions about political parties, elections, and political participation as revealed in the patronage cases and explore whether these assumptions reflect the realities of the political process. For obvious reasons, none of the justices' viewpoints amounts to a coherent theory of politics—nor should they. Developing a political theory is not the task of judges deciding constitutional cases. Rather, they are called upon to decide the issues presented by the specific conflict before them, to do so as narrowly as possible in a constitutional case, and to elaborate a rationale that will attract the five votes necessary to a majority. Nonetheless, there are startling differences of political perspective among the justices—most especially between Justice Scalia and the majorities in the recent patronage cases. At the same time, there is substantial agreement among the justices about the value of maintaining a broadly based two-party system in the United States, although they disagree about the primary threats to this system and about the appropriate modes of ensuring its continuance.

Elrod and *Branti*: Individual Rights and the Democratic Process

Justice Scalia accused the *Elrod* majority of sacrificing a valuable traditional institution—patronage—in the name of "some abstract principle of First Amendment adjudication devised by this Court" (*Rutan v. Republican Party of Illinois*, 497 U.S. at 95–96). He disparaged the Court for disposing of the issue "like some textbook exercise in logic" (*Board of County Commissioners of Wabaunsee County v. Umbehr*, at 701). In other words, Justice Scalia argued, the *Elrod* plurality simply derived its prohibition of patronage by abstract logical deduction from the First Amendment, without any consideration of the effect of that interpretation on the workings of the American political system.

In fact, however, the majority opinions in *Elrod* and *Branti* treat the First Amendment as integrally related to the workings of the democratic political process. Free speech is regarded as essential to this process—especially to the operation of our party and electoral systems. The First Amendment not only performs a "checking" function on the government, it also increases the total amount of information available to the electorate (Schneider 1992, 522–25). By contrast, patronage impairs the free functioning of the electoral process by its power to deter political opposition, discouraging open criticism of the government and reducing the electoral chances of opposition candidates. It tips the process in favor of the incumbent party, which can reward or punish through its control over government employment (*Elrod v. Burns*, 427 U.S. at 356). Indeed, as one commentator points out, patronage may effectively insulate government from criticism by removing from the debate the individuals who could most effectively expose abuses of power—current public employees (Schneider 1992, 526).

Another way of approaching this question is to focus on the value of the two-party system itself. What is a two-party system good *for*? Certainly part of the answer would be that a two-party system prevents a monopoly of power and opinion by one group, which could then suppress the rights of other groups; it also works to organize and aggregate opinion and power into groups that are broader than those dedicated to single interests. Two (or a small number of) parties thus function to give the electorate a realistic choice among a manageable set of alternative policies. Moreover, while one party is in power, a two-party system can organize support for and criticism of those policies, each of which is essential to an effective democratic polity—and to the protection of individual rights.

Neither the justices in the majority nor the dissenters in *Elrod* and *Branti* would quarrel, I believe, with this description of the value of a two-party system. The majorities in those cases kept firmly in mind, however, that the two-party system is essentially a means to an end. Maintenance of a representative system of government is the fundamental value, but this goal may not always be identical with the perpetuation of any particular party system (*Elrod v. Burns*, 427 U.S. at 368–69). Moreover, the *Elrod* and *Branti* majorities saw patronage's tendency to create a one-party system as a more serious threat to democratic government than the possibility of third parties or the multiplication of interest groups.

Powell's Dissent and the Fear of Faction

In his dissent, Justice Powell viewed the political world somewhat differently. The greater threat to the American party system, in Powell's view, is presented by factionalism and a politics of special interest groups. A strong, disciplined, and accountable two-party system is necessary as a remedy for these evils—and patronage was essential to the maintenance of that party system. Strong parties allow the executive branch to implement its programs by working with legislators from the same party. This cooperation was possible, Powell thought, only if the executive could use patronage as a means of discipline (*Branti v. Finkel*, 445 U.S. at 530). This system was threatened by the Court's prohibition against firing patronage employees.

There are substantial problems with Justice Powell's image of the American party system and its relationship to patronage. It assumed, first, that the power to hire and fire is necessary to ensure that the personnel in the bureaucracy are solidly behind the administration's programs. The power to appoint policymakers at the top of the hierarchy on political grounds and the capacity to dismiss, for cause, employees responsible for implementing their decisions are adequate to this task, however. Second, Justice Powell assumed that patronage somehow enables the executive to gain the cooperation of legislators as well. How is this to happen? Presumably, one way is that patronage allows the executive to further the reelection of legislators through the efforts of armies of patronage workers. Material incentives such as hiring or awarding contracts to friends of the legislators in return for their votes on bills before the legislature, however, present serious potential for corruption, inefficiency, and unduly costly government.

Moreover, Justice Powell's image of a disciplined and accountable two-party system does not reflect the reality of the American political system, however unfortunate that system may be. Disciplined parties have never been a feature of the American political landscape; they are characteristic of a system such as that in Great Britain, however, where a unitary government is based on notions of parliamentary sovereignty. In England, a party is genuinely in power when its members are elected to a majority of the seats in Parliament. It not only controls the majority in the legislature, it also forms the executive and thus has the power to put its policies into effect. The party in power can be held accountable by the electorate if it does not follow through with its program (indeed, the government may fall if it loses a major vote in the legislature).

This type of party system is far removed from that in the United States. Here the Constitution has intentionally dispersed power among three branches of government that check and balance one another; the executive and legislative branches may be in different hands, and parties often operate independently on the different levels of national, state, county, and municipal government. Here, unlike in Britain, individuals vote independently of parties; a candidate, once elected, has a loose connection to the party organization with which she or he is affiliated and tends instead to relate directly (or perhaps via public opinion polls) to the electorate. Many observers believe that our political system would be better with stronger parties, and perhaps that is true. History, however, shows that patronage is not an effective or acceptable route to that goal.

As Robert Merton once noted, patronage did function in many areas to centralize power where power was formally dispersed (Merton 1949, 71–81). Thus, the first Mayor Daley was able to turn Chicago's City Council into a rubber stamp and pass whatever policies the machine wanted. The price, however, was enormous—in terms of inefficiency, corruption, and unresponsiveness to the interests of substantial minorities, such as the growing African American population of Chicago (Bowman 1991, 65–67, 78). It is also legally and ethically questionable whether patronage should be used as an end run around structures designed by a constitutional document intended to separate and disperse power.

If patronage-fed political parties had in fact produced a considered assessment of the issues and effected a genuine brokering of the interests of the majority of the citizens, perhaps I would reach a different conclusion about the value of patronage. The relationship between patronage parties and political participation touted in Powell's and Scalia's dissenting opinions is vastly overdrawn, however. Once government jobs have been distributed as rewards, they cannot constantly be redistributed (Wilson 1961, 376–78). For this reason, patronage does not function well as an incentive; it tends instead to be awarded retrospectively, to reward individuals and groups that have been helpful in the past. The goals of the party organization then become those of the groups that already form its core—not a majority of all voters or a fair cross-section thereof, but a minimal winning coalition based on what has worked in the past (Bowman 1991, 78). Thus, in Chicago the machine continued to favor policies beneficial to the older white ethnic wards and simply ignored the demands of more recently arrived black and Hispanic residents. In short,

Justice Powell's assessment of the numerous benefits conferred by patronage parties on the American political system was sadly mistaken.

Rutan: The Majority

The First Amendment remains the centerpiece of Justice Brennan's majority opinion in *Rutan*. The amendment is regarded as inextricably tied to the proper functioning of the American political system, which depends upon each citizen being free to make his or her own judgment about matters of political concern (*Rutan v. Republican Party of Illinois*, 497 U.S. at 75). In addition, Justice Stevens notes in his concurring opinion that history is devoid of evidence that patronage has ever fostered a *two*-party system, rather than perpetuating control over government in one group (*Rutan v. Republican Party of Illinois*, 497 U.S. at 88, n. 4).

Before turning to Justice Scalia's more distinctive perspective, it is instructive to summarize what can be said at this point about some of the central questions posed in this chapter. What type of party system do Justices Brennan and Stevens prefer? Do they have a coherent theory of politics that is distinct from that of Justice Powell, on the one hand, and Justice Scalia, on the other? The answer is clearly "no." All of the justices favor a broad-based two-party system; their differences concern only its relationship to patronage. From the evidence of the patronage cases alone, the most one can say is that Justice Powell has an image of the American two-party system as more disciplined and accountable than it has ever been, whereas Brennan and Stevens are less wedded to a precise and unchanging image of the party system necessary to sustain American democracy. These justices are open instead to an image of a democratic society that is bound to our constitutional structures but perhaps not to a particular form of party or electoral system. Moreover, the justices voting with the majority in each case are much less fearful of third parties and interest groups than are the dissenters. Instead, the justices in the majority worry more about control of government by a single party or group.

Justice Scalia's theory of politics, insofar as it can be discerned from his dissents in the patronage cases, deserves separate consideration.

Rutan: Tinkering with Institutions That Have Worked?

Justice Scalia's theory of originalism, which limits interpretation of the Constitution to the rights clearly in it at the time of the Founders and leaves all other questions to the legislature, is a two-edged sword. If this theory consigns all matters beyond a very limited few to decision by the people's representatives rather than by the courts, it appears ultimately democratic. This interpretation sits uneasily, however, with Scalia's elaborate apologia for the institution of patronage in his dissenting opinions. This apologia rings instead with a Burkean tone, cautioning that institutions that have worked over generations should be preserved; their very longevity works in their favor (Burke 1955 (1790), 99).

Justice Scalia's argument from the age of the tradition of patronage may also be reframed in the less value-laden language of modern structural functionalist theory. In *Social Theory and Social Structure*, Robert Merton argued that any informal social structure that persists despite efforts at reform must fulfill important functions that are not being served by formal structures; in the case of political machines, he pointed to their "latent functions" of centralizing power (which I discussed above) and providing a route of upward mobility for the lower classes (Merton 1949, 72–73, 76–77). This formulation may provide some content to the "wisdom of the ages." On the other hand, what if the particular informal structure, institution, or tradition did not in fact operate as it is assumed to have operated? What if patronage never performed the functions claimed or, if it once did, had ceased to do so?

The assertion about the role of patronage in the social and economic advancement of the lower classes—originally made by Justice Powell and elaborated upon by Justice Scalia—is a good example. The argument is that the practice of patronage had the effect of bringing successive newcomer groups into the American political process, democratizing politics and giving those groups an avenue of upward mobility through government jobs. A constitutional prohibition on patronage now, Scalia argues, "prevents groups that have only recently obtained political power, especially blacks, from following this path to economic and social advancement" (*Rutan v. Republican Party of Illinois,* 497 U.S. at 108).

In fact, however, this long-assumed correlation between patronage and social mobility is an inaccurate description of the realities of patronage politics. African Americans, for example, were not allocated jobs in Chicago in any proportion to their numbers, and the jobs they did get were not the white-collar jobs that lead to the suburbs within a generation (Kleppner 1985, 64–90; Preston 1984, 92). Moreover, the policies and services that African Americans needed to change the quality of their lives as a group—for example, the allocation of public goods such as quality education and decent parks in the areas where they lived—were not forthcoming from the machine (Kemp and Lineberry 1982, 18–23). These outcomes were the direct result of patronage and its tendency to centralize power in one party. By contrast, in other parts of the country, where African American voters could provide the balance of power in closely contested elections between more equally balanced parties, minority groups had room to bargain to their advantage (Keiser 1989, 327–37; Key 1949, 298–314).

An even more basic challenge to the dissenters' assumptions about the function of patronage is presented by comparing the patterns of mobility of Irish Americans with those of other ethnic groups. One study concludes that the blue-collar patronage doled out by political machines *inhibited* the economic and social advance of Irish Americans by channeling them into relatively low-paid and low-status public jobs when other groups (Germans and Scandinavians, for example, despite language problems) were making substantial gains in the private sector (Erie 1988, 7–8, 89–90, 241–42). In short, the prohibition of patronage amounts to tinkering with an institution that worked only for some people—and may have been a mixed blessing for the in-groups as well.

At base, Justice Scalia's approach to deciding the patronage cases boils down to a very conservative position that favors preservation of the status quo, even if that status quo has operated systematically to exclude large minority groups. The constitutional jurisprudence of fundamental rights and strict scrutiny is aimed at precisely this type of situation—the protection of minorities against majority tyranny. In the patronage context, the connection between the First Amendment and the democratic functioning of a representative government is transparent: The suppression of First Amendment rights through patronage resulted in the exclusion of minority groups from the political process.

Finally, if the "wisdom of the ancients" is based on faulty assumptions, as it appears to be, what is the appropriate institution to evaluate and change a tradition that is not working? Justice Scalia would say that the legislature is. Unlike judges, however—who are selected by merit and freed by life tenure from a continuing concern with the political powers-that-be—members of the legislature often owe their professional lives to the very parties that desire the continuance of patronage. Voting to abolish patronage would be, for them, a vote directly against self-interest, which deprives them of the necessary perspective about the effect of patronage on the political system as a whole. Indeed, even observers who believe that decisions about patronage should be made on the basis of a cost-benefit calculation conclude that judges are in a better situation to make these calls than are legislators (Hasen 1993, 1330–32).

The Surprising New Majority in the Patronage Contracting Cases

The Supreme Court's decision in the *O'Hare Truck Service* case extends the First Amendment protection of the earlier patronage cases into the context of government contracts. What is the implication of this extension for the political process? The most obvious connection to examine is that between large campaign donations and the granting of public contracts. Even before *Elrod* was decided, commentators had begun to point out that today's elections require infusions of money to buy television ads and finance mass mailings, rather than city workers to go door to door (see e.g., Sorauf 1960, 31); contract patronage is the form of patronage best adapted to raising these funds. Contract patronage was the route taken when other forms of patronage were foreclosed by the Court; this trend was exacerbated by the decrease in government employment after 1980 and the privatization of many functions previously performed by government workers.

From 1982 to 1992, for example, the rate of increase in Illinois state employment declined, while spending on government contracts doubled (Gibson and Gratteau 1992). It seemed clear that the governor's office, after *Rutan*, was diverting patronage into other channels. The use of "pinstripe patronage"—rewarding political supporters with contracts, leases, and bond sales—was notorious (Gibson and Gratteau 1992; Freedman 1994, 125). For example, the state's landlords included major donors to gubernatorial campaigns, and the rents paid for state offices were often inflated as a result (Gibson and Gratteau 1992). In short, many observers believe that the primary dangers of inefficiency and corruption are now presented by patronage contracts (see, e.g., Hasen 1993, 1333). Even if television advertising has now become central to political campaigns, surely we do not want to solve the problems of campaign finance by covertly passing these costs through to taxpayers or to the beneficiaries of services for which the government contracts.

In contrast to the situation involving more traditional patronage jobs, no one argues that patronage contracting played a role in democratizing the political process or increasing participation in politics. Notably missing from Justice Scalia's dissent, as well, are the earlier arguments about the dangers presented by special interests. Indeed, who are these contributors in exchange for contracts except special interests? Instead, the defendants' arguments focused solely on the effect that prohibiting patronage would have on the administration's ability to ensure the efficient provision of services and thus to remain faithful to its electoral mandate. The local government defendants in the patronage contracting cases had argued that their ability to reward and punish by granting, withholding, or withdrawing contracts on political grounds was essential to their accountability in this sense. Contracting out government work involves assigning tasks to private bodies that are neither accountable to the public nor under the government's direct supervision. A garbage collector, for example, might no longer be a municipal employee; he or she may work for some private refuse firm instead. The defendants insisted that the partisan link was necessary to ensure the effective implementation of the administration's policy.

Where public tasks such as these are performed pursuant to a contract, however, the administration can ensure efficient and faithful implementation of policy simply by the power to terminate that contract for inadequate performance under its terms. Furthermore, the well- established exception for policymakers should apply to the awarding of contracts based on political affiliation, just as it does to governmental employees.[3] According to the *Elrod/Branti* Court, the top officials in the sanitation department, for example—that is, those who are in policymaking positions and for whom "party affiliation is an appropriate requirement for the effective performance of the public office involved" (*Branti v. Finkel*, 445 U.S. at 518)—may have to be Republican. If those who are in charge of designing and directing the implementation of the policies by which this crucial municipal service is performed are not clearly supportive of the administration's political program, they may indeed sabotage it. That description is not true, however, for a non-policymaking employee or a contractor who merely performs services under the terms of a contract that is itself designed by in-house policymakers to embody and implement the administration's policies and programs.

Suppose, for example, a mayor hires a public relations consultant on a contract basis and charges her with describing and publicizing the goals of the administration in relation to a project supported by their mutual party and opposed by another party or candidate. Surely that contractor could be categorized as a policymaker, just as she would be if the public relations function were being performed in-house. If she switches her allegiance to a candidate opposing the mayor, however, and no longer supports the project personally, the mayor should be able to fire her at will. If not, the administration can be saddled with a policymaker who does not share its goals. In short, if political affiliation is an appropriate qualification for the job, and if political affiliation is a factor in the firing decision, that connection should end the inquiry in a case involving an independent contractor as well as an employee.

THE SUPREME COURT'S PERFORMANCE
IN THE PATRONAGE CASES

How has the Court performed overall in these cases with respect to the questions about political parties, elections, and representation that are central to this chapter? In addressing these questions, it is important to remember that judges are neither social scientists nor legislators who take testimony about the impact of their decisions. The social science that appears in Supreme Court decisions is likely to be only as good as the briefs submitted in the case before it, and few litigants—perhaps especially local governments—have the money to pay for social science research on an hourly basis. Thus, although a good deal of excellent social science literature about the effects of patronage has appeared in recent years, very little of it is cited in the patronage cases. The opinions instead refer repeatedly to dated studies cited in previous opinions, only occasionally adding a few new ones. (One suspects that the educational background and reading habits of the justices and their current clerks play a role in the selection of studies cited.)

Despite these limitations, it is possible to discern in the patronage cases the lines of intellectual debate appropriate to evaluating the effect of the decisions on the American political system—namely, the justices' fundamental agreement about the value of a broadly based two-party system and the disagreements between the majorities and the dissenters about the threats posed to that system by the existence of patronage or its demise. The opinions in these cases discuss the effect of patronage on the freedom of debate necessary to representative government and patronage's relevance to local elections in the present day, its role in the integration of minorities into the political and socioeconomic system, and its relationship to the accountability of government to the electorate—giving the lie to the notion that current patronage law has been derived by abstract logic from prior First Amendment jurisprudence. Moreover, the conclusions reached by the majorities in the patronage cases are largely congruent with those that empirical social science research would suggest. In recent years, however, this debate has been constrained and forced into digressions by Justice Scalia's rigid ideological approach to questions of constitutional interpretation more generally, making empirical realities often appear largely irrelevant.

ENDNOTES

1. This control was possible even for positions that were nominally covered by civil service because civil service exams were held infrequently and the results posted long after most applicants had found other jobs (Allswang 1986, 118–19); when it was then not possible to fill a position from the civil service list, employees would be hired on a temporary basis and reappointed on that basis for as long as twenty years (Tolchin and Tolchin 1971, 40–41; Allswang 1986, 142–43; Knauss 1972, 101–3).

2. In *Branti*, the Court articulated the following test to distinguish between policymaking positions—which are available for patronage appointments—and nonpolicymaking positions, which are covered by *Elrod*'s prohibition: whether "party affiliation is an appropriate requirement for the effective performance of the public office involved" (*Branti v. Finkel*, 445 U.S. at 518). The lower courts have wrestled with the *Branti* definition of a policymaking employee since 1980, often with inconsistent results (Martin 1989).

3. Justice Kennedy creates some uncertainty on this point when he asserts that where both affiliation and speech are involved, the *Pickering* balancing test will automatically apply—raising the possibility that the government could be prevented from firing a high-level policymaker because a court saw an element of speech intermixed with what otherwise would be a "pure" affiliation case (*O'Hare Truck Service v. City of Northlake*, 719).

··· 8 ···

Entrenching the Two-Party System:
The Supreme Court's Fusion Decision

Douglas J. Amy

One of the most basic political issues facing every democracy is the question of what kind of party system is most desirable. In lieu of a positive assessment of the Supreme Court's patterns of decisions, Cynthia Grant Bowman attributed to the Court a broad agreement about the desirability of a stable two-party system.

Is the United States better off, however, with the two-party system that has been our tradition than with a multiparty system in which major and minor parties routinely elect members to office, as has been common in most other Western democracies? This question is important because the type of party system has significant effects on the basic processes of representation. Among other things, the form of the party system affects which candidates get elected, the extent of choices offered to voters, and the quality of representation in legislative bodies. Champions of our two-party system assert that it gives voters clear choices and produces a more accountable and stable government. Many citizens continue to identify with our major parties, and most politicians staunchly defend the traditional system. Proponents of multiparty systems claim that they encourage higher voter turnout, create more political competition, and produce more diverse and representative legislatures. Moreover, a growing number of Americans are frustrated with the Democrats and Republicans and want to see other parties challenge them at the polls. Who is right? Perhaps more important, how do we decide?

As with most political controversies, the Supreme Court has played an important and continuing role in shaping our party system—primarily through rulings concerning election procedures. The nature of party systems is determined in large part by the rules that govern elections. For example, rules determining ballot access have a direct effect on the number of viable political parties. If a state refuses to grant automatic ballot access to minor parties and requires them to collect large numbers of signatures on petitions, it discourages these parties and reinforces the two-party system. Not surprisingly, ballot access laws have often been challenged on constitutional grounds and have ended up in the Supreme Court. More recently, the Court looked at a similar election rule relating to the use of "fusion" ballots. The ruling tells us a great deal about the Court's current thinking about party systems, as well as the side with which it aligns itself in the debate between two-party and multiparty systems.

The authors of other chapters in this volume are relatively sympathetic to the Court's ad hoc, narrow, and fact-specific resolution of issues pertaining to parties. Yet some found reason to challenge or question the premise—the value of a strong and stable two-party system—that undergirds those decisions. This chapter, in contrast, is highly critical of the Court and its unfounded acceptance of a party duopoly. The Court's fusion decision reveals an impoverished understanding of how different party systems work, as well as their political consequences. The Court's weak grasp of the theory and practice of party systems casts serious doubt not only on this specific decision but also on the Court's general role in shaping the nature of the party system in the United States.

THE FUSION DECISION

On April 28, 1997, the Supreme Court decided by a 6–3 margin that states had the right to ban the use of fusion in elections (*Timmons v. Twin Cities Area New Party*, 520 U.S. 351 (1997)). Fusion is the practice of placing a candidate on the ballot as the nominee of several different parties. Typically, a minor party will nominate the same candidate as one of the major parties, allowing voters to cast their ballots for that candidate under the minor party's name. In this case, the New Party in Minnesota had chosen as its candidate for state representative in 1994 a person who was already the incumbent candidate for a major party, the Democratic-Farm-Labor party. The candidate accepted the New Party's nomination and signed an affidavit of candidacy for the New Party. State officials refused to accept the affidavit and the New Party's nominating petitions, however, relying on a state law banning the use of fusion. The New Party took Minnesota to federal court, asserting that the fusion ban violated its members' associational rights under the First and Fourteenth Amendments to the Constitution—in particular, their right to nominate the candidate of their choice. The district court ruling in favor of the state was reversed by the Eighth Circuit Court of Appeals. The Supreme Court overturned the appellate opinion, reinstating the ban.

The *Timmons* decision can be analyzed on several levels. On a constitutional level, the Court was balancing the associational rights of parties with the rights of states to regulate their elections. Legal scholars have thoroughly examined the constitutional issues (Kirschner 1995); those issues are not the main focus of this chapter. Instead, I consider the broader political implications of the fusion decision—how it sheds light on the Court's current thinking about two of our most basic representational institutions: our party system and our electoral system. For in this case, the Court weighed in with an unexpected and provocative defense of the two-party system and the electoral rules that support it. In particular, it concluded that states are justified in maintaining electoral laws—such as a ban on fusion—that favor the two major parties over minor parties. In support of this position, the Court invoked the specter of a chaotic multiparty political system. It suggested that a move from a two-party system to a multiparty system would increase political factionalism and seriously undermine political stability in the United States. In *Timmons*, the Court ventured boldly into the areas of political science and political theory, making a number of pronouncements about various electoral and party systems and their political effects.

The main purpose of this chapter is to investigate, and to assess the accuracy and validity of, the assertions about parties and elections that underpin the ruling in *Timmons*. Of particular interest are the Court's views about multiparty systems and the alleged threats they pose to stable and efficient government—views on which the entire decision hinged. An examination of the oral arguments and written opinions in this case indicates that the Court relied heavily on outmoded and inaccurate views of multiparty systems. These questionable views cast doubt on the rationale of the Court's decision and suggest that the Court would benefit by familiarizing itself with current scholarship in the area of parties and elections.

The Political Context

To appreciate the wider implications of the *Timmons* ruling, it is important to understand the political background of the case. Americans have

become increasingly alienated from the two major parties and more supportive of minor parties and independent candidates. Only about a quarter
of voters now strongly identify with the Republican and Democratic parties, and large numbers are dissatisfied with the choices offered by these
parties. Recent polls also show that up to two-thirds of the electorate
welcome the idea of new party challenges to the major parties. In addition,
a growing number of minor parties—including the Libertarian party, the
Reform party, the U.S. Green party, and the New Party—have offered
candidates for office in the 1980s and 1990s. Not since the 1920s have so
many Americans cast votes for candidates from third parties. This trend
has led one prominent political scientist to observe that

> one of the best-kept secrets in American politics is that the two-
> party system has long been brain dead—kept alive by support
> systems like state electoral laws that protect the established parties
> from rivals and by federal subsidies and so-called campaign reform.
> The two-party system would collapse in an instant if the tubes were
> pulled and the IV's were cut. (Lowi 1992, 28)

One of the electoral arrangements that sustains the two-party system
is our single-member-district, winner-take-all voting system. As political
scientists have long noted, this system creates a hostile environment for
minor parties (Duverger 1954; Downs 1957; Lijphart 1984). Minor party
candidates find it almost impossible to amass the majority or plurality of
the vote necessary to win in this system. Minor party supporters who vote
for their party's candidate typically waste their votes and may inadvertently contribute to the election of the major party candidate they least
like. This "wasted vote" problem makes it difficult for minor parties to
attract supporters and thrive. As a rule, minor parties have flourished only
in multimember-district electoral systems, such as the proportional representation (PR) systems common in Europe. These systems allow parties
to elect candidates who receive as little as 5–10 percent of the vote.

Like proportional representation, fusion is a way around the wasted
vote problem. It allows a minor party to nominate a candidate who is in a
position to win. More important, votes cast for a major party candidate on
a minor party ballot line enable the minor party to exert some leverage
on the candidate by arguing that a portion of his or her support comes
from the minor party members. The New Party, for example, hoped to
move Democratic candidates farther to the political left. Fusion was an

important political strategy in the New Party's efforts to become more politically viable.

This case is not the first time fusion has been used to bolster the political fortunes of minor parties. Fusion was a common feature in many midwestern and western states during the late eighteenth century—the golden age of minor parties in the United States. It allowed supporters of minor parties such as the Progressives, Grangers, and Populists to participate effectively in elections and to make their concerns heard by candidates elected to office. As one historian has concluded,

> [fusion] helped maintain a significant third party tradition by guaranteeing that dissenters' votes could be more than symbolic protest, that their leaders could gain office and their demands might be heard. Most of the election victories normally attributed to the Grangers, Independents, or Greenbackers in the 1870s and 1880s were a result of fusion between those third party groups and Democrats. (Argersinger 1980, 288–89)

The Republican Party, fearful of the advantage that fusion gave to the Democrats, led an effort to abolish this electoral tactic, and thirteen states passed bans on fusion between 1897 and 1907. Eventually, fusion was banned in forty-one states, contributing to the demise of the Populists and other minor parties (Argersinger 1980, 304). New York is one of the few states that still uses fusion—and the Liberal and Conservative parties there attribute much of their longevity to its availability.

Thus, the *Timmons* case is another skirmish in an ongoing battle between minor and major parties. State legislatures dominated by the two major parties have long used electoral rules—particularly ballot access rules—to discourage competition from minor parties. Fusion was yet another attempt to open the door to the political system and allow smaller parties a fairer chance to elect their candidates. As the New Party's executive director, Dan Cantor, explained, "It is no exaggeration to state that fusion voting is the key to a durable multiparty system in a country (like ours) that does not have proportional representation" (Cantor 1996).

The Court's Approach

In reaching its decision in *Timmons*, the Supreme Court employed the same approach it has used in cases involving ballot access laws. The issues implicated by ballot access and fusion are similar; both situations involve state ballot regulations that can significantly affect minor parties. Typically, states have limited the ballot access of minor parties by setting early filing dates and onerous petition requirements. These efforts have led to a series of constitutional challenges (Issacharoff, Karlan, and Pildes 1998, 245–54).

In evaluating the constitutionality of these ballot access laws, the Supreme Court has developed a balancing test, best articulated in *Anderson v. Celebrezze*, 460 U.S. 780 (1983). The Court has tried to weigh the burden that the law imposes on the associational rights of parties against the interests of states in regulating elections. Specifically, the Court has first evaluated the character and magnitude of the injury to the rights of parties, then measured it against the precise interests advanced by the state as justification for the injury. In *Munro v. Socialist Workers Party*, 479 U.S. 189 (1986), the Court upheld the constitutionality of a Washington state requirement that candidates could qualify for the general election ballot only if they received at least 1 percent of the vote in the primary. It concluded that the state had a strong interest in preventing ballot overcrowding and frivolous candidates, as well as in reserving the general election ballot for "major struggles." It also found that the 1 percent threshold did not unreasonably burden the minor parties' constitutional rights. On balance, the Court found that Washington state's ballot restriction was constitutionally acceptable.

The Supreme Court utilized this same kind of balancing test in *Timmons*. The Court first examined the New Party's claim that the fusion ban widely encumbered its associational rights under the First and Fourteenth Amendments. The New Party argued that the ban severely interfered with its right to select the candidate who best represented its views and to engage in electoral activity to attract the support of the broadest possible base of voters. The six-member majority of the Court (Chief Justice Rehnquist, along with Justices O'Connor, Scalia, Kennedy, Thomas, and Breyer) rejected these arguments and determined that the fusion ban placed little real burden on the constitutional rights of the party. The majority found that although the party's preferred candidate would not appear on the ballot under the party label, this circumstance did not interfere with the ability of the party or its members to endorse, support, and vote for that candidate. Nor did it interfere with the party's ability to nominate and vote for its own separate candidate. In examining the state's interest in the fusion ban, the Court determined that it had a legitimate right to use election regulations to prevent voter confusion and political instability. It concluded that these interests were sufficient to justify such a ban.

Of most interest for this chapter's purposes is the second aspect of the Court's decision: its evaluation of the state's interests in banning fusion. It is there that the Court's assumptions about party systems are most evident—and most open to question. It is there that the Court made its most important and controversial political claims. It is useful to begin the analysis with the arguments offered by the state of Minnesota, for the Court's treatment of those arguments provides an initial indication of the unfortunate caliber of political science used in this decision.

Voter Confusion and Overcrowded Ballots

Minnesota argued that the main justification for banning fusion lay in the state's interest in preventing voter confusion, overcrowded ballots, and ballot manipulation. Writing for the majority, Chief Justice Rehnquist agreed with these claims. Even a cursory examination of Minnesota's arguments reveals, however, that they are weak and have little empirical support. Consider the alleged problem of voter confusion. Minnesota argued, for example, that voters confronted with a fusion ballot might become bewildered and believe that they had to fill in every line where a candidate's name appeared for their vote to count. Such a problem could easily be prevented, however, by the use of clear instructions on the ballot—as one Justice pointed out during oral arguments. More important, the history of fusion in the United States indicates that voter confusion has not been a problem. In an *amicus* brief submitted in the case, twelve university professors concluded, "There is no evidence, in either the historical experience of nineteenth-century fusion or the contemporary experience of fusion in states like New York, that the practice confuses voters." The majority ignored these arguments.

Another variation of the confusion argument posits that if a single candidate appears on the ballot representing several parties, voters would have trouble distinguishing where that candidate stands. In fact, however, it is more likely that fusion would actually give voters more useful information about the candidates and their positions. Voters would be better informed about a candidate who is nominated by the Democratic and the Liberal parties than one simply running as a Democrat. In this sense, fusion would contribute to more knowledgeable voters, not confused ones.

Minnesota also contended that fusion would lead to ballots over-crowded with a great number of minor parties, many of them frivolous. The state hypothesized that fusion would allow members of the major parties to create dozens of "bogus" minor parties with issue-oriented names (such as the No New Taxes party, or the Conserve the Environment party) to "send a message" to the voters. This hypothesis is mere speculation, however. There is no evidence that such efforts have occurred when fusion has been used in the past. Moreover, if the state is concerned about the possibility of frivolous parties on the ballot, it has the traditional option of using ballot access regulations to ensure that parties demonstrate a reasonable level of public support before being put on the ballot.

The fact that Minnesota's justifications for the fusion ban were almost entirely based on hypothetical scenarios lacking empirical foundation was not lost on some members of the Court. In response to Minnesota's contention during oral arguments that fusion would create voter confusion, Justice Stevens remarked, "You have to be pretty dense to be confused on this one" (Greenhouse 1996). In his dissenting opinion, Stevens characterized the state's concerns about voter confusion and ballot manipulation as "farfetched" and concluded that "the parade of horribles that the majority appears to believe might visit Minnesota should fusion candidacies be allowed is fantastical, given the evidence from New York's experience with fusion" (*Timmons v. Twin Cities Area New Party*, 520 U.S. at 609).

The Real Issue: Preserving the Two-Party System

Chief Justice Rehnquist, writing for the majority, did not base his support of the fusion ban solely on Minnesota's relatively flimsy arguments about ballot integrity and voter confusion, however. Instead, he offered a new and stronger political rationale:

> States also have a strong interest in the stability of their political system. This interest does not permit a state to completely insulate the two-party system from minor parties' or independent candidates' competition and influence. . . . That said, the States' interest permits them to enact reasonable election regulations that may, in practice, favor the traditional two-party system and that temper the destabilizing effects of party splintering and excessive factionalism. The Constitution permits the Minnesota Legislature to decide that political stability is best served through a healthy two-party system. (*Timmons v. Twin Cities Area New Party*, 520 U.S. at 603)

Rehnquist's position was remarkable in several ways. First, the need to preserve the two-party system was not even argued in Minnesota's brief. No evidence on this issue was presented in the lower courts, nor did the District Court decision upholding the ban mention it. Second, the argument was extraneous. Because the Court had already decided that the fusion ban did not substantially violate the New Party's constitutional rights, it could have simply relied on Minnesota's claims of voter confusion and ballot integrity to uphold the ban. Rehnquist was clearly going out of his way to make this argument.

Most remarkably, the Supreme Court had never gone this far in arguing that states had a legitimate interest in using biased electoral rules to maintain a two-party system. *Timmons* is not the first case in which the Court has approved of electoral rules that hurt minor parties; it has routinely upheld burdensome ballot access laws. *Timmons,* however, "goes decidedly beyond earlier cases in [the Court's] endorsement of the two-party system" (Issacharoff, Karlan, and Pildes 1998, 261). In essence, the holding in *Timmons* suggests that if states do not actually ban minor parties, it is constitutionally acceptable for them to adopt electoral rules that discriminate against these parties—all in the name of preserving a two-party system.

This argument is clearly the most provocative—and most political—aspect of the decision. Traditionally, the legitimacy of elections as a democratic institution has rested on the ideal that they are free and fair contests between candidates and parties. In blessing state attempts to use electoral rules to stack the deck in favor of particular parties, the Court violates this crucial principle of fair competition.

To many observers, the Court's defense of the two-party system seemed curiously out of step with a great deal of public opinion about our party system. At a time when more and more Americans are abandoning the major parties and questioning the worth of the two-party system, the Court chose to endorse electoral rules that serve to protect the privileged position of these parties.

Threats to the Two-Party System

Why, then, did the Supreme Court deem this defense of the two-party system necessary? Many of the justices appeared concerned about the waning health of our two-party system and were cognizant of the potential threats to its vitality. For example, Justice Souter cited studies of declining party loyalty as evidence that "it may not be unreasonable to infer that the two-party system is in some jeopardy" (*Timmons Twin Cities Area New Party*, 520 U.S. at 614). Souter concluded that if the disappearance of the two-party system would demonstrably undermine political stability, a ban on fusion might indeed be permissible.

Several justices also worried about other, more serious, threats to the two-party system. For them, overthrowing the ban on fusion represented a slippery slope; if the Court upheld a constitutional challenge to this particular election rule, it could lend support to attacks on other rules that favor the two-party system. In oral arguments, for example, Justice Breyer noted that single-member electoral districts were the biggest burden on minor parties. If the Court overturned a lesser burden such as the ban on fusion, Breyer queried, would it not then be compelled to strike down single-member-district arrangements (Lowi 1996)? Chief Justice Rehnquist raised a similar point in the majority opinion: "Many features of our political system—e.g., single-member districts, 'first past the post' elections . . . —make it difficult for third parties to succeed in American politics. But the Constitution does not require states to permit fusion any more than it requires them to move to proportional representation elections" (*Timmons v. Twin Cities Area New Party*, 520 U.S. at 600).

Chief Justice Rehnquist and Justice Breyer were correct in identifying single-member districts as the most important electoral feature supporting our current two-party system. Most political scientists agree that this arrangement is the primary reason that minor parties have had little sustained electoral success in the United States. The adoption of multi-member-district, proportional representation elections would be a much more serious threat to the two-party monopoly than fusion.

In fact, a major point of Justice Stevens' dissenting opinion was that fusion does not actually present much of a threat to the two-party system. Fusion only encourages minor parties to form coalitions with major parties to support the latter's candidates; it does not result in the election of minor party officials to legislatures. In contrast, the adoption of proportional representation would pave the way for the routine election of minor party candidates. It would also almost certainly result in the splintering of the major parties and the creation of the multiparty legislatures that the justices fear.

The justices were undoubtedly aware of the movement afoot calling for the adoption of a PR system in the United States. A bill has been introduced in Congress to institute PR elections for members of the

House of Representatives. This option has been raised explicitly in several federal cases on voting rights as well. In *Holder v. Hall*, 512 U.S. 874 (1994 at 913), for instance, Justice Thomas observed in a concurring opinion that some voting rights advocates are now criticizing the current strategy of creating majority-minority districts and instead are urging the adoption of proportional representation elections. Thus, the Court's unexpected defense of the two-party system really may have been a preemptive strike aimed at other threats to our traditional party system that are looming on the political horizon.

THE SPECTER OF MULTIPARTY SYSTEMS

Regardless of the Supreme Court's motives or focus, we are left with the central political question: Should electoral arrangements that favor the two-party system be granted constitutional protection? The Court's affirmative answer to this question rested directly on a series of claims about the political effects of particular party systems—claims that have more to do with political science and political theory than with constitutional law. In particular, the Court found that a move toward a multiparty system would undermine an orderly and efficient political system. In the Court's view, multiparty systems foster political instability by encouraging "party splintering" and "excessive factionalism." In addition, multiparty governments are likely to be weak and inefficient. The specter of a chaotic multiparty democracy played a major role in the *Timmons* decision. The Court viewed the fusion ban as helping to preserve our two-party system and avoid the serious political problems associated with multiparty systems.

Do multiparty systems have the political dangers attributed to them? The Supreme Court offered surprisingly little justification for its conclusions. The ill effects of multiparty systems were simply asserted, with no effort to buttress them with evidence or argument. Similarly, there was no attempt to substantiate or validate the alleged political advantages of the traditional two-party system; these benefits were merely taken as fact. Referring cursorily to several other Supreme Court decisions, Chief Justice Rehnquist observed that "The stabilizing effects of such a [two-party] system are obvious" (*Rutan v. Republican Party of Illinois*, 497 U.S. 62 (1990)); he asserted perfunctorily that "there can be little doubt that the emergence of a strong and stable two-party system in this country has contributed enormously to sound and effective government" (*Davis v. Bandemer*, 478 U.S. 109 (1986)).

The political inferiority of multiparty systems is not nearly as "obvious" to many political scientists as it is to the Court. A large volume of work has been generated in the realm of party and electoral systems—which the Court in *Timmons* largely ignored. Scholars have scrutinized the political effects of multiparty systems and the proportional representation elections usually associated with them. Their findings cast serious doubt on the Court's assertions that these systems are politically dangerous.

In the remainder of this chapter, I examine the Court's key claims about these alternative electoral and party systems in light of this scholarly work. I focus particularly on the three specific political problems that fall under the Court's general fear of "instability": party splintering, weak coalition governments, and excessive factionalism.

Party Splintering

Most electoral scholars concur that a move away from our traditional single-member-district, winner-take-all elections would encourage some splintering of the two major parties. This evolution would certainly be true if we were to adopt proportional representation elections. A Christian Coalition party might well break off from the far right of the Republican Party; a leftist party might split off from the Democrats. Why, however, is this kind of splintering a major political problem? Chief Justice Rehnquist never explained.

Critics of multiparty systems have pointed to the overproliferation of parties in countries such as Israel and The Netherlands; at times these countries have had more than a dozen parties in their parliaments, and long, arduous negotiations have been required just to form a government. Such situations are not common in multiparty systems, however, and they can be controlled easily by the careful design of the electoral system. All proportional representation systems have thresholds—a minimum percentage of the vote that a party must get to elect anyone to office—and the setting of these thresholds allows for the regulation of the effective number of political parties (Taagepera and Shugart 1989, 126–41). In Germany, for instance, the threshold is 5 percent; this threshold acts to keep the number of the parties in the Bundestag to a reasonable number—usually about three to five. In contrast to this system of "moderate proportional representation," the electoral systems in Israel and the Netherlands have involved extreme forms of PR with very low thresholds (under 1 percent). These unusual *forms* of proportional representation—not PR per se—encouraged the creation of so many small parties. Proposals for PR in the United States have involved the moderate form, with very high thresholds—often between 10 percent and 25 percent—that would prevent excessive party splintering. The most likely result is that the Democrats and the Republicans would remain the two largest parties, with one, two, or three other parties joining them in the legislature. Hence, the Court's fear of rampantly proliferating political parties would seem to have little foundation.

Weak Coalition Governments

Another charge against multiparty systems is that, regardless of the number of parties, they are plagued by the problem of weak coalition governments. In two-party systems, one party usually controls the legislature with a clear majority of the seats, seemingly making it easy to pass legislation and govern effectively. In multiparty systems, typically, no single party holds the majority of seats in the legislature, so a ruling coalition of parties must be formed. The conventional wisdom is that these coalitions are weak and unstable, leading to government breakdown or gridlock. As Justice Stevens put it, "Systems of proportional representation may tend toward . . . fragile coalitions that diminish legislative effectiveness" (*Timmons v. Twin Cities Area New Party*, 520 U.S. at 380).

Once again, little systematic evidence supports this common allegation. Invariably, Italy is raised as an example of this problem. For several decades, Italy was plagued by unstable legislative coalitions that frequently broke apart over policy disagreements. If this kind of instability were the inevitable result of multiparty systems, however, one would expect to see it not just in Italy but in most European democracies that use PR. Instead, virtually all other PR countries—including Norway, Germany, Austria, Iceland, Ireland, Luxembourg, the Netherlands, Belgium, Denmark, and Finland—have enjoyed stable governments. Experience indicates that there is nothing inherent in proportional representation elections or multiparty governments that causes debilitating political instability.

It is true that many countries with single-member-district elections and single-party majorities do rank high on measures of government durability. For example, one study found that the United Kingdom had only nineteen governments between 1945 and 1992, compared to fifty-one for Italy. That same study, however, also found that the U.K. was only the sixth most stable country during that period—and that the five most stable countries (including Austria, Ireland, and The Netherlands) all used proportional representation (Issacharoff, Karlan, and Pildes 1998, 774). In a study of twenty-two Western democracies, Lijphart (1984, 157) found that "in our set of countries with long records of reasonably stable democracy, the majority have multiparty systems." Such findings severely undermine the assumption that multiparty democracies are constantly flirting with political disorder.

There also is little evidence that multiparty PR systems chronically suffer from legislative gridlock. In fact, gridlock is a problem more commonly attributed to the U.S. Congress than to European multiparty democracies. Despite being controlled by single-party majorities, our Congress has often found itself unable to act decisively on divisive political issues. It has taken decades, for instance, for Congress to pass effective legislation to ensure civil rights, combat acid rain, and balance the budget. Coalition governments have also been hobbled at times by differences between coalition partners; as a rule, however, European multiparty parliaments have been known for the rapidity and efficiency of their legislative processes. As Vernon Bogdanor of Oxford University has observed, "The truth is that the effectiveness of a government is not fundamentally dependent on either the existence or the absence of coalitions. The same range of policy outcomes is possible under coalitions as under single-party governments" (Bogdanor 1984, 139).

In general, then, the experiences of multiparty democracies indicate that the Supreme Court's concerns about weak coalitions and lack of governability are greatly exaggerated. Even if there is—in Justice Souter's words—"a state interest in preserving a political system capable of governing effectively," the record clearly demonstrates that multiparty systems can fit the bill.

Factionalism

The Supreme Court's third concern about multiparty systems is the encouragement of excessive "factionalism." Factionalism has many meanings, one of which is the splintering of parties discussed above. Perhaps of greater concern, however, is the general tendency to exacerbate group conflict in society. Critics of multiparty systems fear that they will further "balkanize" the American electorate, allowing political groups to frequent their own small and isolated political parties. The two major parties, these commentators argue, "serve as vital, umbrella-like, consensus-forming institutions that help counteract the powerful centrifugal forces in a country teeming with hundreds of racial, economic, social, religious, and political groups" (Sabato 1988, 5). In contrast, a multiparty system would allow political groups to go their own way into their own political parties (an African American party, a Green party, a Christian party, etc.), intensifying rather than moderating the conflicts between them.

An examination of multiparty systems in practice, however, reveals that they too encourage negotiation and compromise between political groups—but at a different point in the election process. In a two-party system, these negotiations usually take place *before* the election. During conventions and primaries, the groups in our large umbrella parties try to settle their differences and build an effective electoral coalition. In contrast, in a multiparty PR system, the political bargaining takes place in the legislature *after* the election. After the various groups elect their representatives, they then engage in negotiation and coalition building.

Some scholars have even argued that making multiparty legislatures the locus of political negotiation may be the most effective way to deal with factional conflict (Lijphart 1991, 81). Two-party systems usually produce legislatures with less diversity than in the larger society, hampering their ability to manage political conflict. Only majorities are represented; minority political groups are left out or underrepresented. In a multiparty legislature, however, all political factions are at the table; this diversity allows serious negotiations and dialogue to take place, increasing the possibility that an effective compromise can be worked out. As Lijphart has argued, proportional representation and multiparty systems are much better suited to societies with deep political divisions because they allow "the greatest possible inclusion of representatives of (different) groups in the decision-making process" (Lijphart 1991, 81).

Ironically, whereas our Supreme Court worries that a multiparty system will worsen political conflict, such a system is widely regarded abroad as the best way to mitigate extreme political factionalism and bolster political stability. When South Africa—a country torn apart by violent political and racial conflicts—emerged from apartheid and adopted a democratic form of government, all sides agreed that proportional representation elections and a multiparty system would be the best political arrangement for its diverse society. The recently completed agreement for a new political system for Northern Ireland—another area suffering from violent political conflict—includes a provision for proportional representation and a multiparty system. The hope is that this approach will finally allow for fair representation of Protestants and Catholics, thereby undermining the political frustrations that prompted some of them to take up arms.

ARE MULTIPARTY SYSTEMS IN THE STATE'S INTEREST?

In *Timmons*, the Supreme Court not only overstated the negative political effects of multiparty systems, it also ignored their political benefits. One searches the majority decision in vain for any inkling that a multiparty system might have any positive political effects. Justice Stevens did observe in his dissent that minor parties might encourage greater competition in ideas and governmental policies. This benefit, however, may be only the tip of the iceberg. Some scholars have maintained that multiparty PR systems have a host of important political advantages over single-member-district, two-party systems—advantages that can be plausibly described as being in the state's interest.

One well-documented benefit of proportional representation elections and multiparty systems is increased voter participation. High levels of participation increase the democratic legitimacy of the elected government. European democracies have long had much higher rates of voter turnout than the United States—often averaging 80 percent to 90 percent, as opposed to 50 percent here. Blaise and Carty (1990) have demonstrated that a significant portion of that difference is attributable to the presence of PR and multiparty systems. They estimate that if we were to have these systems in the United States, turnout would increase by 10–15 percent—resulting in millions of additional voters going to the polls. A wider menu of parties encourages higher turnout because it is much easier for voters to find a candidate or party that actually reflects their particular political views and, consequently, about whom they can get excited. Voters also can be reasonably assured that their votes will count in proportional representation elections, instead of being wasted as they often are in single-member-district systems.

Multiparty systems may also actually contribute to political stability in important ways. For example, a two-party system can produce wild swings in policies even when public opinion shifts only slightly. This dynamic was evident after the 1994 Congressional elections, when the

Republicans took over the U.S. House of Representatives with only 51.3 percent of the vote and promptly began to promote their "revolutionary" policy agenda. In multiparty PR systems, small changes in voter preferences tend to produce correspondingly small seat changes and policy changes. Elections in such systems usually do not result in a complete turnover of the parties in power; they produce a reshuffling of parties, with some of the new majority coalition participants having served in the previous coalition. The consequence is greater stability and continuity in policy, with incremental changes rather than abrupt shifts (Seidle 1994, 291). This stability explains why, in Great Britain in the 1970s, members of the business community supported a change to proportional representation and multiparty coalition governments. They were frustrated with trying to do business in a policy environment that was constantly shifting between the free market approach of the Conservatives and the socialist policies of the Labour party.

There is also a great deal of evidence that PR and multiparty systems produce legislatures that are much more representative of the public. Electoral scholars have demonstrated repeatedly that single-member-district election systems inevitably underrepresent smaller parties and overrepresent larger parties (Lijphart 1984, 163–68). For example, in the 1994 U.S. House elections in Iowa, the Republicans won 58 percent of votes and the Democrats 42 percent—but the Republicans were allocated all five of the seats in the state. In Great Britain, the Conservative party enjoyed almost two decades of parliamentary majorities without ever receiving more than 44 percent of the vote. In other words, the country was ruled by a party that most people voted against—a violation of many people's basic conception of how democracies should work. In multiparty PR systems, major and minor parties receive seats in numbers that correspond more accurately to the strength of their support among the voters. The legislatures therefore better reflect the prevalence and the variety of political views among the electorate.

Multiparty systems also provide greater protection for minority rights—one of the hallmarks of our democratic system. Political minorities—ideological, racial, religious, or otherwise—typically have a difficult time realizing representation in our winner-take-all election system. A multiparty PR system clearly makes it easier for such groups to elect some representatives to office. The elected representatives are then in a much better position to voice minority interests and concerns than if they were relegated to positions outside the government.

In addition, multiparty systems arguably beat two-party systems at their own game with regard to providing majority rule. The majority coalitions in these systems usually represent a much larger proportion of the voters and a much broader cross-section of public opinion. Thus, "multiparty systems are better able to bring [a] national majority into the governing process . . . a governing majority that is far more representative of the majority view of the public than would result from the mere giving over of governance to the victorious party in a two-party system" (Lawson 1997, 62–63).

Lawson (1997) also notes that, given the low turnout in our two-party system, the party that wins the majority of seats rarely represents the majority of eligible voters. In the 1994 election in which the Republicans took over Congress, less than 15 percent of the eligible voters actually voted for the Republican candidates who constituted the new majority in the House. (Voter turnout for House elections in 1994 was 39 percent. Only 23 percent of the eligible electorate cast votes for the candidates who won, and only a little more than 50 percent of those voted for Republican winners.) It is difficult to construe such results as "majority rule"—and they cast serious doubt on the legitimacy of these elected bodies. In multiparty PR systems, higher turnout rates and higher levels of effective votes are much more likely to ensure that the legislative majority actually represents a majority of the electorate.

This brief survey of some of the putative advantages of a multiparty PR system is not meant to prove its superiority over the present two-party system. It does demonstrate, however, that the Supreme Court's view of the relative merits of these competing party systems is distorted and one-sided. It also demonstrates that the Court's view of what constitutes the state's interests in partisan and electoral systems is overly narrow. Although states obviously have a clear interest in promoting ballot integrity and political stability, it is equally obvious that they have a strong interest in promoting political competition, encouraging political participation, strengthening majority rule, protecting minority rights, and increasing government legitimacy—all of which may be encouraged more by a multiparty system than by a two-party system.

CONCLUSIONS AND RECOMMENDATIONS

One observer of the oral arguments in *Timmons* remarked, "It seemed that all the justices were remembering their political science classes from

30–50 years ago, and having a good old time asking questions" (Cantor 1996). Unfortunately, this description is an all-too-accurate characterization of the quality of political science used by the Court in this case. Many of the justices' assumptions about the effects of various party systems and electoral systems were outdated, misleading, and often simply mistaken. The Court ignored the large body of scholarly work in this area that suggests that single-member districts and two-party systems are not requirements for a healthy and stable democracy. What is most disturbing about the Court's decision in this case is not that it is wrong but that it is so simplistic and ill informed. The Court arbitrarily adopted a position in favor of the two-party system without much explanation and without seriously grappling with the complex theoretical and empirical issues involved.

Interestingly, at one point in his majority opinion, Chief Justice Rehnquist attempted to exonerate the Court from any responsibility to base its decision on firmer intellectual ground. He argued that because the Court first decided that the fusion ban did not impose any severe burdens on the New Party's associational rights, Minnesota was therefore under no obligation to prove that there were "compelling" state interests to justify the ban. In other words, because the New Party had not suffered any substantial harm, the Court would not require any strong justification for the ban—nor would it "require elaborate, empirical verification of the weightiness of the State's asserted justification" (*Timmons v. Twin Cities Area New Party*, 520 U.S. at 601). Apparently, the state needed only to *speculate* about the possible harms of fusion or a multiparty system to make a persuasive case.

Although this excuse may make some sense in the context of constitutional law, it makes little sense from any other perspective. In this case, the Court moved in dramatic fashion to wrap the two-party system in the shroud of constitutional legitimacy and to justify election rules that are biased in favor of that system. Undoubtedly, the *Timmons* decision will be taken into account when the Court reviews other challenges to electoral rules discriminating against minor parties. For this reason, the most lasting legal significance of the decision may not be its effect on the viability of fusion practices but the effect of the Court's hostility toward minor parties and multiparty systems on future cases involving election regulations. Law professor Richard Hasen concluded that the *Timmons* decision will make it

> much more likely that courts will uphold ballot access laws imposing onerous requirements on third parties . . . [and] . . . will make

it easier for states to entrench the two-party duopoly through campaign finance laws, policies regulating access to public television,
patronage practices, partisan gerrymandering, and potentially a
wide variety of other measures. (Hasen 1998, 341)

As a portent of things to come, Hasen noted that the Supreme Court
declined to review a case in which the Florida Supreme Court upheld a
state law that subsidized the filing fees of major party candidates only. The
Florida court argued that the law "is reasonably related to the state's
important interest in strengthening and encouraging major parties, and
thereby discouraging minor parties, as a means of preventing factionalism
and the multiplicity of splinter groups" (*Libertarian Party of Florida v.
Smith*, 118 S. Ct. 57 (1997). Clearly, the *Timmons* decision will only
encourage this kind of blatant judicial hostility toward minor parties.

Given the important legal and political implications of *Timmons*, it
is unfortunate that the Supreme Court did not make more of an effort
to construct a sounder theoretical and empirical foundation for its decision. In particular, the Court need not have relied on speculation about
the effects of multiparty systems. Other Western democracies have long
experiences with multiparty systems, so plenty of information about the
political results of these systems is available. In future decisions concerning election rules and minor parties, the Court would do well to consult
this record of multiparty democracy. Furthermore, when the Court looks
abroad, it need not rely on isolated examples of nontypical countries such
as Italy and Israel; instead, it should tap the more comprehensive and
systematic analysis of multiparty systems in the political science literature.

The Supreme Court should reconsider the political role it plays in
decisions affecting party and electoral systems. It is now all too willing to
confer on legislatures broad discretion in determining what constitutes
fair election laws. Indeed, the Court has bent over backward to assign to
state legislatures only the best intentions and the public interest. There
can be a vast difference, however, between what legislators believe is in
the state's interest and what the public believes is in its own interest. The
majority of American voters desire more parties and more choices at the
polls, in stark contrast to legislative attempts to discourage viable minor
parties. Instead of regarding the public's waning support for the major
parties as an indication that we need to open the party system to more
competition, the Court took it as evidence that the two-party system is in
need of protection from competition.

The Court should adopt a much more skeptical eye when it considers how legislators define state interests in election system cases. It would do well to heed Justice Thurgood Marshall's approach in an earlier ballot access case, when he argued for a stricter form of judicial scrutiny in cases in which legislatures dominated by the major parties are making electoral laws: "The necessity for [a higher standard of review] becomes evident when we consider that major parties, which by definition are ordinarily in control of legislative institutions, may seek to perpetuate themselves at the expense of developing minor parties" (*Munro v. Socialist Workers Party*, 479 U.S. 189, at 201 (1986)). State legislatures clearly have an inherent conflict of interest concerning electoral laws. Because these legislatures are composed almost entirely of partisans of the two major parties, it is in their self-interest to create regulations that discourage minor parties. History confirms that these institutions have been all too willing to use electoral laws to stifle competition and place obstacles in the way of minor parties. For this reason, the Court should take an especially hard look at any assertions of "state interests" concerning elections. These claims may serve to protect not the legitimate interests of the public but only the interests of the two major parties seeking rationalizations for their efforts to stack the electoral deck against minor parties.

A good example of how state interest arguments require heightened scrutiny can be found in the dissents in *Timmons*. Justices Stevens, Ginsburg, and Souter all took an appropriately skeptical approach to the arguments put forth by the state of Minnesota. They rightly discerned that the state's arguments about voter confusion and ballot overcrowding were self-serving and had little empirical justification. Justice Souter regarded the state as primarily interested in preserving the advantages of the two major parties, not in safeguarding representative government. In oral arguments he noted that, in the eighteenth century, the ban on fusion was adopted as part of a "very widespread effort simply to maintain the hegemony of the two parties. They weren't worried about voter confusion. They didn't want new parties." In light of this history, he found the state's justifications for the fusion ban unpersuasive (Greenhouse 1996).

Unfortunately, no justice applied this same critical approach to the crucial arguments about the need to preserve the two-party system. Even the dissenting justices accepted unquestioningly Chief Justice Rehnquist's assertions about the political perils resulting from alternative electoral and party systems. Justice Stevens, for example, all too readily agreed that "systems of proportional representation may tend toward factionalism and fragile coalitions that diminish legislative effectiveness" (*Timmons v. Twin Cities Area New Party*, 520 U.S. at 611). In the future, all state claims about the political effects of various electoral and party systems should be greeted with a critical eye; the state should be forced to provide persuasive arguments and solid evidence to support them.

Ultimately, the Supreme Court must better appreciate its special role in cases involving electoral systems and party systems. It cannot afford to accept at face value the arguments put forth by state legislatures, whose inherent conflicts of interest render them incapable of objectively evaluating what is in the public interest. In areas such as fusion, campaign finance, ballot access, and term limits, legislatures simply cannot be trusted as guardians of the democratic process. The temptation for legislators to place their own interests ahead of the public interest can be overwhelming. The courts typically are the only institutions that can serve as a check on the major parties' efforts to pass self-serving legislation that undermines the workings of a representative democracy. The Supreme Court must take a more careful and informed look at these cases to ensure that crucial decisions involving our most basic representation institutions are based on political reality, not political myth.

··· III ···

The Court and Political Reform: Friend or Foe?

"We are now forming a republican government. Real liberty is neither found in despotism or the extremes of democracy, but in moderate governments."
—Alexander Hamilton, *Debates of the Federal Convention* (1787)

"The more I see of the representatives of the people, the more I admire my dogs."
　　　　—Alphonse de Lamartine, *Letter to John Forster* (1850)

The analysis in Part II of this volume reveals the Supreme Court's inability to conform the gaggle of party cases to an organized, doctrinally consistent pattern. It certainly bares a lack of consensus over parties and their role in our democracy—a lack of consensus shared by the larger culture. It also reveals a deeper rift in our understanding of the political system generally. In short, with respect to parties and politics, we are torn between a politics that is hierarchical, elitist, and controlled and one that is progressive, participatory, democratic, and open.

This debate entails a conflict over the first principles of representation. It takes us back to the clash of the "delegate" and "trustee" models of representation. Is one better represented by a system that is highly sensitized or attuned to identifying the precise wishes of the citizen and reflecting those wishes as closely as possible? Or is one better represented by a system that, though arguably less directly responsive, may be better constituted to make rational determinations about the best interests of the citizenry as a whole?

The framers opted for a less inclusive, more hierarchical system of elections and politics. That view has yielded to the inexorable expansion of the progressive model; the latter would strip away intermediary party organizations or other obstacles to direct popular sovereignty and widespread participation. The progressive model, with its plebiscitary view of elections and its stress on individual political rights over those of collectives, holds increasing sway. The preferred values are democratized parties, an open political system, direct involvement, and expanded voter choices and candidate alternatives. In short, we have witnessed the withering of republican principles of government—priorities that were at the heart of the framers' vision.

This trend has placed the Supreme Court squarely in the middle as it contemplates the constitutional permissibility of various reforms. All roads to reform lead to and through the Supreme Court. As the public's increasing dissatisfaction with parties and politics has led to progressive reforms in a variety of shapes, the Court frequently finds itself reviewing questions of reform and popular participation.

In the Court's resolution of these conflicts, it too is speared on this dual tradition. Its guide to the ruling constitutional values alternates between the progressive and pluralist understandings of government. The chapters in Part II reinforce the Court's responsibility for delineating the appropriate constitutional balance between the competing values of open, democratic participation and the state's interest in stability. In *Morse v. Virginia Republican Party*, the Court had to balance the right of parties to control nomination processes with the right of individuals to participate in them. In the patronage cases, the Court was the agent of reform—stripping away the long-standing practice of party patronage, which it perceived as hindering individual rights of expression and association. In both of these instances, the progressive gains of individuals came at the expense of partisan organizations. In the *Timmons* decision, by contrast, the Court was a tool of retrenchment, stifling a relatively minor reform of the two-party system.

Part III (chapters 9–11) explores these issues in greater detail. Any analysis of political reform must begin with the role of money in elections. Nothing has shaped public perceptions or generated more public skepticism toward politics than the ways in which we fund our elections. Those practices raise questions about the fundamental fairness and effectiveness of the entire electoral process. The current quagmire owes much of its existence to the formative role played by the Court and its interpretation of the First Amendment. Likewise, any solutions are sure to require judicial endorsement.

Chapter 9 explores the constitutional issues surrounding this debate. It begins with *Buckley v. Valeo* (1976) and the Supreme Court's treatment of money as the functional and constitutional equivalent of political speech. The Court eventually moved toward a novel constitutional theory of political representation aimed at leveling the group playing field; it sought to equalize group influence on campaigns by making spending rights contingent on the representative characteristics of types of groups. Though well intentioned, this group-equalizing strategy was quickly rendered futile by the development of new fundraising and spending practices. More recently, the *Colorado Republican Committee* decision (1996) reveals that the Court continues to search for a coherent doctrinal approach that will reflect the pragmatic realities of modern campaign spending. David Ryden raises a series of theoretical questions that the Court must address as it considers various reform proposals. Running counter to the current of conventional sentiment, Ryden concludes that the remedy may lie with a party-conscious constitutional approach to campaign financing that elevates the associational and speech rights of political parties in hopes of mediating other influences in funding campaigns.

Chapter 10 examines the Supreme Court's attitudes toward the initiative and referendum process, as well as their significance for political participation and representative democracy. Ballot initiatives are an increasingly popular democratic check on the legislative process. They also leave minorities with less protection against the raw power of potentially hostile majorities than the legislative process provides. Recent high-profile plebiscites have focused widespread attention on the threats posed to minority rights, as initiatives have attempted to make English the official language in Arizona, repeal affirmative action in California and Texas, deprive illegal immigrants in California of government benefits, and repeal gay rights legislation in Colorado. In analyzing the constitutionality of plebiscites, Brad Smith uses the absence of meaningful empirical evidence to debunk arguments that plebiscites systematically harm minority groups. Smith contends that initiatives are no more likely than legislative enactments to harm minorities. In his view, the failure of legislatures to acknowledge constitutional constraints on their authority is a greater threat to minority rights than the relatively small number of voter initiatives passed each year. Plebiscites are a means of reining in legislatures and judges that go beyond these constitutional bounds. The political philosophy underlying *Romer v. Evans* (1996) ultimately fosters disrespect for rights in general—and in the process undermines the representative process.

Chapter 11 confronts themes similar to those of chapter 10. Just as initiatives are designed to give citizens more direct input into and control over policymaking, so too are term limits meant to limit the power and tenure of entrenched legislators. Like initiatives, term limits reflect suspicion of representative governance, which relies on the judgment, wisdom, and independence of elected officials. Jeff Polet draws on *U.S. Term Limits v. Thornton* (1995), the Supreme Court decision striking down Arkansas's term limits statute, as the basis for his critique of the Court's representation jurisprudence. Polet focuses on two noteworthy aspects of the case. One is the Court's paternalistic view of representation, as it extinguished one of the most widely embraced grassroots reforms in decades. Even more significant was the impoverished view of federalism underpinning the decision. Implicit in the Court's rejection of congressional term limits was an understanding of the democratic experiment as a simple relation between the federal government and the undifferentiated whole of the American people. Unfortunately, this one-dimensional view of representation leaves little room for attention to critically important linkages in the forms of mediating institutions—state and local governments, political parties, groups, and the like. A more balanced and functionally derived federalism would make greater allowance for the recognition of all of these entities, thereby generating a more representative political process.

The tension between hierarchical and progressive models of democracy is present in each of these chapters. At the same time, the essays in this section confront the most basic questions regarding our political structure. Can we have a system of representation in which political resources are so disparate as to raise doubts about whether some voices are heard (and therefore represented) at all? What kind of democracy is most advantageous, and how "representative" should it be? The pervasive use of the initiative process takes the debate of direct versus representative democracy out of the textbook and into the realm of practical application. And what role does federalism play? Are we represented only as individuals or as an undifferentiated whole? Do states, communities within those states, and smaller groups within those communities warrant recognition? If so, to what extent? The Court's decisions in these cases do not always explicitly broach these topics. The ways in which the conflicts are resolved, however, have concrete and far-reaching ramifications for the representativeness of the system.

··· 9 ···

To Curb Parties or to Court Them?
Seeking a Constitutional Framework
for Campaign Finance Reform

DAVID K. RYDEN

Item: The 1996 presidential campaigns easily set record highs for the solicitation and spending of so-called "soft money"—the unregulated contributions given by wealthy individuals, business, labor, and other collective interests to the political parties. As the 2000 presidential race continues, so does the surge in soft money, with candidates raising funds at an unprecedented clip.

Item: The 1997–98 off-year congressional election cycle likewise established new fundraising and expenditure records for a midterm election, mostly as a result of the expanded participation of parties. The two national committees spent a total of $193 million, and overall party spending in 1998 was more than double party expenditures in the previous off-year elections of 1994.

Item: As this book goes to press, pressure is building in both houses of Congress for a major reform of the campaign finance system. The key components of the two most popular measures (the McCain-Feingold bill in the Senate and the Shays-Meehan version in the House) focus on "issue advocacy" and soft money; in other words, the reform efforts are intended to limit the input and influence of groups and political parties.

Item: Meanwhile, a recent federal district court opinion in Colorado cast aside all federal limits on political parties' spending on their congressional and presidential candidates (*FEC v. Colorado Republican Party*, Civ. No. 89n1159). The court found such limits to be an unconstitutional impingement on party speech rights. The effect of the decision, if it were to survive on appeal, would be to effectively remove all campaign spending constraints on the political parties. Many anticipate that this case may well find its way to the U.S. Supreme Court for review.

Item: Elsewhere, the Republican National Committee and the Ohio Democratic Party have joined together in a lawsuit in federal court to challenge the laws that regulate political party spending of soft money. They contend that they have the right to raise unlimited amounts of money from any source and to spend it as they see fit (even in coordination with a candidate), provided they do not expressly advocate voting for or against a particular candidate (Rosenkranz 1999).

Item: On January 24, 2000, the Supreme Court issued an opinion that reaffirmed the much-maligned *Buckley* campaign finance framework (*Nixon v. Shrink Missouri Government PAC*, No. 98–963). By a 6–3 margin, the Court upheld the constitutionality of contribution limits as a tool for remedying real or perceived corruption of the political process. In *Nixon*, the Court rejected the notion that any and all limits on contributions violate the First Amendment, in the process removing a major obstacle to future legislative reforms.

What is to be made of this flurry of developments on the campaign finance front? First, they point to a remarkable shift that has occurred in the past few years in the relative influence of various actors in the funding of campaigns. In short, there has been a significant movement from candidate-centered elections toward a party-centered and interest group-centered system of funding elections (Magleby and Holt 1999). Second, this movement is regarded with dire concern by most observers, who interpret it as further evidence that campaigns and elections are dominated by narrow special interests to the exclusion of the people. Consequently, as the momentum builds to reform campaign spending, most of the attention is aimed at the strategies employed by—and which empower—political parties and interest groups. Finally, at the center of the reform landscape stands the judiciary, in particular the Supreme Court. All roads to reform lead to, and through, the courts. Given the focus of those reforms on political parties and groups, it is virtually certain that the Court will be forced, sooner or later, to decide the constitutional parameters bounding the role and influence of political parties and groups in financing political campaigns and elections.

These observations frame our exploration of the constitutional questions surrounding campaign finance reform. The swirl of revelations regarding fundraising practices in the 1996 campaigns, combined with unabated spending in the most recent election cycle, have intensified efforts to overhaul the campaign financing system. Genuine reform faces formidable obstacles—including bona fide differences over the means and ends of such reform, as well as the habitual aversion of legislators to seriously alter a system that serves them well. No less an obstacle is the Supreme Court; its seminal decision in *Buckley v. Valeo*, 424 U.S. 1 (1976) still serves as the basic constitutional framework for campaign finance regulations. Any reform will ultimately occur only within the context of what the Court will allow under the First Amendment.

The campaign finance jurisprudence illustrates in striking fashion the Supreme Court's role in shaping the functional operation of our political system. Few observers harbor illusions that the Court is some pristine institution safely insulated from politics. Rarely, however, do we fully appreciate its formative impact on politics at a practical level. With regard to voting rights, district line drawing, funding of campaigns, ballot access, patronage, and other aspects of representation, the Court wields the ultimate check. Its decisions bear directly on how well the system—and the government it produces—rises to the challenge of representing the panoply of voices and interests that constitute our society. The Court's powerful determinative influence on the nitty-gritty of real-world politics compels, therefore, that it be grounded in sound principles of representative government. It is fair to ask, then, whether the Court has exhibited the requisite appreciation for the complexities of political representation? Simply put, are its decisions constructed on a firm theoretical foundation?

Felix Frankfurter, vigorously dissenting from the Court's decision to enter the reapportionment fray in *Baker v. Carr*, 369 U.S. 186 (1962), rued that it required the Court ultimately to choose "among competing theories of political philosophy" (*Baker v. Carr*, 369 U.S. at 300). Without revisiting the wisdom of the plunge into redistricting, Frankfurter's comment proved prescient. The Court is ill-equipped to decide controversies related to campaigns and elections unless it does what Frankfurter foresaw as a requirement: adopt some working theoretical assumptions regarding politics and representation. Constitutional questions pertaining to the electoral process require that the Court act to some extent as political scientist and settle on some basic foundational building blocks derived from democratic theory.

This chapter assesses whether the constitutional principles elucidated by the Supreme Court in the sphere of campaign financing adequately reflect the demands of representation. A textual analysis of opinions from

Buckley v. Valeo to *Colorado Republican Federal Campaign Committee v. FEC*, 518 U.S. 604 (1996), reveals a theoretically impoverished judicial understanding of representation.[1] A constitutional reconceptualization of representation is needed, one more reflective of its complexities.

My assessment hinges on four observations. First, the Court has been cramped by its free speech approach to campaign financing restrictions, to the neglect of the ancillary right of association. *Buckley*'s focus on individual speech rights slighted the importance of collective association and action in achieving meaningful political participation. Second, the Court's occasional acknowledgment of group activity focused exclusively on collective speech rights, without reference to broader associational rights as a path to effective representation. It sought to equalize group speech, evaluating campaign spending regulations by how well they achieved parity in the volume of group voices in the political debate. The inequities in group spending evident in today's campaigns indicate the futility of this approach. Third, the Court has decided these cases virtually without reference to the goal of effective political representation, although the nature and quality of representation are directly implicated by the rules of campaign finance. A more coherent constitutional framework would balance the doctrinal focus on speech with a heightened recognition of the rights of association not simply as a corollary of speech but as an essential means of pursuing broader aims of meaningful political representation. Finally, not all political association is equal in achieving representation—and neither should be the right of association designed to further that end.

I conclude by suggesting that political parties—contrary to dominant public perceptions—are functionally superior to other group actors as systematic channels of representation. This conclusion may compel a party-conscious approach to campaign finance jurisprudence.

THEORIES OF REPRESENTATION IN CAMPAIGN FINANCE JURISPRUDENCE

The Supreme Court over the past two decades has relied on three alternative understandings of representation in weighing the constitutional propriety of legislative efforts to regulate money. The first approach, exemplified by the ruling in *Buckley v. Valeo*, was primarily individualistic in its thrust. The regulations imposed by Congress redressed inequalities in individual political access—a goal with which *Buckley* was largely consistent (Gottlieb 1982, 205, 208). The Court explicitly repudiated legal attempts to equalize group voices in the political process.

In the 1980s, the one-dimensional, individualistic assumptions of *Buckley* were supplemented by group-centered efforts to level the campaign playing field. The judicial gloss applied to Congress's regulatory scheme sought parity of group speech; the means to that end was legal categorization of groups and equalization of the resources they could expend. A rational group-based system of representation has proven an empirical impossibility, however—as evidenced by the failure to effectively handicap or control group influence in recent elections.

The third alternative—broached but not embraced in *Colorado Republican Federal Campaign Committee v. FEC*—is based on a "responsible party" model of politics; it would unfetter political parties from campaign restrictions in hopes of elevating their place in the financing scheme. This approach is premised on the importance of political association, especially party activity, in effectuating representation. Party structures are regarded as the best means of simultaneously serving the political interests of individuals and collectives; hence, they provide an institutional response to the multidimensional demands of representation. This alternative is implicated by the current context, and the Court will almost surely be asked to revisit it soon.

BUCKLEY AND THE INDIVIDUALISTIC SPEECH ORIGINS OF CAMPAIGN FINANCE REGULATION

The Federal Election Campaign Act (FECA) of 1971 ushered in the era of modern campaign finance regulation. Modified in 1974 by a series of post-Watergate amendments, FECA placed strict limits on what individuals and groups could give to—and spend independently on behalf of—candidates, parties, and political action committees (PACs). FECA imposed ceilings on total campaign spending and on how much of their own money candidates could spend. The regulations were challenged as impermissible burdens on First Amendment rights of political expression and association. By the time the Supreme Court had rendered its constitutional judgment on FECA, the restrictions had a much different look.

The *per curiam* opinion in *Buckley* dissected and reconstructed FECA, striking key provisions but not the entire statute. Although limits on what individuals and PACs could contribute were constitutional, limits on expenditures made independently on behalf of a candidate were not.

Disclosure requirements and overall contribution caps for individual donors passed muster; the ceilings on total campaign spending and the
candidate's expenditure of his or her own funds did not.

The *Buckley* decision was couched almost exclusively in terms of free
speech. Treating money as the practical equivalent of speech in the
political arena, the Supreme Court reasoned that expenditures were a
purer, more direct form of speech than campaign contributions—and
therefore were entitled to greater First Amendment protection. Limits
on independent expenditures, overall spending, and candidate expenditures amounted to substantial, direct restrictions on the right to political
expression, and were impermissible (*Buckley v. Valeo,* 424 U.S. at 58–59).
Furthermore, independent expenditures that were not coordinated with
the candidate had less potential to corrupt the beneficiary than contributions and were therefore less open to regulation.

At the core of the Court's decision in *Buckley* was an individualistic
perception of politics, a perception that was dismissive of group activity.
Determined to protect free speech in the form of campaign spending, the
Court concerned itself with the speech of individuals. The preferential
treatment accorded independent expenditures over campaign contributions reflected an implicit bias favoring individual over associational activity.[2] By elevating expenditures above contributions, the Court discounted
the possibility that one's money might be used more efficiently by an
organization or party.[3] Although the Court paid lip service to the right of
association, it saw association merely as ancillary to political speech (*Buckley v. Valeo,* 424 U.S. at 25). Associational rights were cast in individualistic
terms, their aim to "amplify the voice of [the association's] adherents"
(*Buckley v. Valeo,* 424 U.S. at 22). Indeed, to the Court, political association was a negative where "the actuality and potentiality of corruption have
been identified," and must be limited (*Buckley v. Valeo,* 424 U.S. at 28).

The individualistic thrust of *Buckley* was more readily apparent in
the Court's explicit rejection of group-conscious regulatory measures. The
Court renounced the goal of equalizing groups' ability to wield political
influence:

> It is argued, however, that the ancillary governmental interest in
> equalizing the relative ability of individuals and groups to influence
> the outcome of elections serves to justify the limitation(s). . . . *But
> the concept that government may restrict the speech of some ele-
> ments of our society in order to enhance the relative voice of others*

is wholly foreign to the First Amendment. (*Buckley v. Valeo,* 424
U.S. at 48–49; emphasis added)

The Supreme Court thus repudiated the idea that the political playing field could be leveled by handicapping group expenditures. If the
individual freedom to speak is roughly equal, group voices cannot be
guaranteed an identical chance to be heard through political spending. As
one commentator stated, "The Court was prepared to take a substantial
risk of collective inequality to satisfy a desire for individual fairness"
(Gottlieb 1982, 204).

Subsequent cases cemented the Supreme Court's preoccupation with
individual speech rights.[4] In *California Medical Association v. FEC,* 453
U.S. 182 (1981), the Court upheld FECA limits on contributions to multicandidate committees. The Court's skepticism toward associational activity was evident in its characterization of donations to associations as
"speech by proxy" that was less protected under the First Amendment
than direct expenditures. The right of political association was defined
solely by its service to the speech rights of the contributing individual,
without regard for the recipient association (*California Medical Association v. FEC,* 453 U.S. at 196). This narrow, "one-dimensional, sum-of-its-
parts view of political association" ignored the unique functions and rights
of the association, as well as the heightened political effectiveness that
individuals gained through them (Gottlieb 1982, 207).

THE DEMANDS OF REPRESENTATION:
A THEORETICAL FRAMEWORK

One cannot evaluate the Supreme Court's representation jurisprudence
without some theoretical framework or set of assumptions to serve as a
qualitative guide. The most striking characteristic of political representation is its sheer complexity. Representation cannot be distilled down to a
single definition or set of ideas. It incorporates a host of concepts and
interpretations—each with some measure of validity, depending on the
given context (Pitkin 1967; Birch 1971; de Grazia 1951).

For example, representation springs from a variety of sources. *Formal* representation is grounded in the practices and processes of the
electoral system. This form of representation occurs when voters formally
authorize representatives to act on their behalf by voting them into office—or hold them accountable by voting them out. The Supreme Court's

early focus on individual voting rights and "one-person, one-vote" jurisprudence emphasized formalistic representation. Representation also has
a *substantive* dimension: namely, legislative activity and outcomes. This
form of representation entails representatives, individually and collectively, pursuing policies desired by the represented (Ryden 1996, 14–19).
Although formal representation encompasses electoral arrangements
through which representatives are selected every second, fourth, or sixth
year, substantive representation occurs through the various channels by
which people petition their representatives between elections, to move
them to act on their behalf. *Descriptive* representation is achieved when
the representative mirrors or embodies the salient characteristics of those
she or he represents. This sharing of relevant traits is assumed to be
accompanied by corresponding attitudes, interests, and policy positions,
which can then be advanced in a deliberative representative body. Race-
conscious redistricting practices are the most striking example of descriptive representation. Finally, representation is *relational*; it exists in the
personal relationship between legislator and constituent and is cultivated
through visits to the district, constituency service, and pork-barrel politics.

Overlaid on these types of representation is the array of political
actors through whom representation is sought and realized. These actors
include individual citizens and voters, as well as parties, interest groups,
and other collectivities with political interests and agendas. There is also
representation of the "people" or the "public"—that ambiguous whole
that encompasses the national interest or common good. Individual and
collective dimensions also exist on the other side of the equation—in who
is doing the representing. Congress comprises 535 independent offices,
each engaged in its own set of representative activities. Those individual
legislators coalesce into parties, which operate within government to push
policies representative of party voters, activists, and organizations. Interest groups represent the interests of individuals or associations of which
they are composed. The picture is complicated further by blocs of voters,
interest groups, and caucuses within parties. Finally, representation as an
activity occurs collectively when the entire legislative body passes legislation or takes other action.

In short, political representation is complex and multifaceted—"a
labyrinth of concepts and forms that synthesize an array of activities and
participants through institutional and structural means" (Ryden 1996, 5).
It is a myriad of activities, behaviors, and perceptions that link the governors and the governed (Eulau and Prewitt 1973, 443). It involves:

many people and groups . . . operating in the complex ways of large-scale social arrangements. What makes it representation is not any single action by any one participant, but the overall structure and functioning of the system, the patterns emerging from the multiple activities of many people. (Pitkin 1967, 221–22)

Even this cursory delineation makes clear the limits of what we can reasonably expect from the Supreme Court. The Court is unlikely to adopt a single theory of representation—nor would we want it to, in light of these intricacies. "The most that we can hope to do . . . is to be clear on what view of representation a particular writer is using, and whether that view, its assumptions and implications, really fit the case to which he is trying to apply them" (Pitkin 1967, 227–28).

The Supreme Court is capable of identifying the dimensions of representation theory that best fit a given problem or situation, provided it is cognizant of the host of representational concepts and forms. Any conceptual framework for analyzing constitutional questions must acknowledge the richness, complexity, and variety of the faces, forms, and manifestations of political representation. We should expect the Court to choose the doctrinal path that best comports with the complex reality of political representation and opens the channels of representation so that the multiplicity of modes and actors that compose the labyrinth of representation are free to operate.

The Theoretical Limitations of *Buckley*

The individualistic free speech approach of *Buckley* captured little of this complexity. Group theories emphasize associational affiliations as principal determinants of one's political interests, motivations, and effectiveness. Individual activity in a large-scale democracy gains significance when individuals merge with others of like mind. Meaningful individual participation hinges on the influence of the collectivities to which one belongs and the groups that *represent* one's interests.

The descriptive pluralist model of government ties sound policymaking to the widespread participation of, and competition between, organized collective interests. The greater the number of group interests with access to policymakers, the healthier and more representative the policy outcomes. Consequently, the electoral process should be cognizant of and accommodating to the host of *group* interests in politics.[5] Given the assorted interests in our society, the Supreme Court's individualistic approach in *Buckley* was superficial. Its focus on speech alone oversimplified the numerous ways in which political representation is advanced and the multiple entities through whom it is accomplished. It minimized the representative benefits of organized, institutionalized political behavior.

Group theory and pluralism require more than simple constitutional acknowledgment of group activity, however. Although pluralist critiques have recognized the essential importance of group activity, they have also identified threats to representation from marked group inequality. The pluralist ideal entails full and free group competition that produces optimal public policy; the reality is one of inequality and disequilibrium. Disparities in political resources skew the system heavily toward well-endowed groups, to the detriment or outright exclusion of others—hence the gulf between pluralism in theory and pluralism in practice. Although formal recognition of group activity is necessary to assure individual efficacy, inequities between groups in a pluralist democracy undermine the underlying objective of individual equality.[6]

In jurisprudential terms, the question is how to approach representation questions doctrinally to accommodate the array of group interests in society while promoting individual equality. What institutional arrangements would empower the individual in politics *and* address the shortcomings of pluralist representative structures? What structures might enhance the representative potential of groups without sacrificing basic standards of individual equality?

BUCKLEY RECAST: JUDICIAL LEVELING OF THE GROUP PLAYING FIELD

Dramatic changes in campaign funding forced the Supreme Court to confront directly the propriety of group involvement in elections. The *Buckley*-bifurcated FECA rules did little to stem the escalating prominence of money in campaigns, and unease over the influence of money prompted further regulatory efforts. The rapid proliferation of political action committees, especially in the realm of business and industry, suggested that those with too much influence were gaining even more. The dominant perception was of campaign finance rules that aided rather than restrained wealthy groups' capacity to dominate debate in the policymaking arena (Epstein 1980; Wertheimer 1980).

The judicial response to this perceived crisis was a startling embrace of a neopluralist, group-based constitutional analysis, as the Supreme Court departed from its earlier denunciation of attempts to balance group voices.[7] Congress paved the way by requiring corporations to fund political activities through separate, segregated funds with money solicited only from employees and members. The law inferred that a corporation's right to speech (by spending) should bear some relation to the popularity of the ideas it expressed. As these regulations invited fresh constitutional challenges, the Court was drawn into a perilous course that involved gauging the rights of groups to participate financially in campaigns on the basis of their associational character.

In subsequent cases, a judicial strategy took shape that sought to equalize group influence by monitoring and calibrating the expenditure of group resources. The Supreme Court demarcated varying speech rights for different types of associations based on their representative capabilities; it differentiated between groups in their right to collect and spend money for political purposes on the basis of their representative character. Yet the meting out of group speech rights was propelled less by a clear understanding of group theory than by a sense that the funding of campaigns had gone badly awry. The Court found itself reacting to a perceived political crisis with no overarching theory of representation to guide it.

The first hints of a departure from *Buckley* came in *First National Bank of Boston v. Bellotti*, 435 U.S. 765 (1978). In dicta, the Supreme Court speculated that the regulation of corporate spending might be justified if "corporate advocacy threatened imminently to undermine democratic processes, thereby denigrating rather than serving First Amendment interests." The potential for "the relative voice of corporations" to overwhelm other voices might warrant limiting their voice (*First National Bank of Boston v. Bellotti*, 435 U.S. at 789).

That possibility hardened into reality in *FEC v. National Right to Work Committee*, 459 U.S. 197 (1982). The National Right to Work Committee (NRWC) had admittedly ignored the FECA requirement to segregate funds for corporate political activities, accepting contributions from nonqualifying donors. In ruling against NRWC, the Court cited the interest in avoiding corruption of the political process. It added, however, a justification directly counter to *Buckley*'s disavowal of group equalization efforts. For the first time, the Court examined the nature of the political association as a legal measure for gauging group influence through spending.

The Court held that different organizational structures and purposes required "different forms of regulation in order to protect the integrity of the electoral process" (*FEC v. National Right to Work Committee*, 459 U.S. at 210). The Court sanctioned Congress's judgment that "the special characteristics of the corporate structure require particularly careful regulation" (*FEC v. National Right to Work Committee*, 459 U.S. at 210) because corporate wealth might otherwise dominate political debate. The prohibition against the use of general corporate treasury funds for campaign activities was a legitimate prophylactic measure to "ensure that substantial aggregations of wealth amassed by the special advantages which go with the corporate form of organization should not be converted into political 'war chests'" (*FEC v. National Right to Work*, 459 U.S. at 207). This ruling signified a marked shift from the focus on individual equality toward endorsement of legislative manipulation of group input to level the political playing field.[8]

In *FEC v. National Conservative Political Action Committee*, 470 U.S. 480 (1985), the Supreme Court went further. The National Conservative Political Action Committee (NCPAC) was a nonprofit corporation that spent heavily in support of President Reagan's 1984 reelection bid; in the process, it exceeded FECA caps on spending by independent committees. The Court struck down the limitations as applied to NCPAC, showing a newfound appreciation for the political benefits of group involvement. That appreciation was narrowly confined, however, to association as a means of speech. Association was simply a way for individuals to pool their resources to enhance the volume of their speech in the political marketplace. Although "freedom of association [was] clearly implicated" by the regulations, organizational rights existed only to "[amplify] the voice of their adherents" (*FEC v. National Conservative Political Action Committee*, 1985, 494).

In its NCPAC ruling, the Supreme Court warmed to the task of group classification for purposes of governing campaign finance. It railed against the indiscriminate lumping of poorer, smaller associations with larger, for-profit corporations. The spending limits were overbroad, applying "equally to an informal neighborhood group that . . . spends money on a presidential election as to the wealthy and professionally managed PACs involved in these cases" (*FEC v. National Conservative Political Action Committee*, 496). Wealthy PACs warranted more stringent treatment than "informal discussion groups that solicit neighborhood contributions to publicize their views" (*FEC v. National Conservative Political*

Action Committee, 498). In the Court's view, campaign finance rules should address the disparate abilities of various group voices to make themselves heard. NCPAC was created expressly for participation in political activities and lacked the evil of "traditional economically organized corporations" (*FEC v. National Conservative Political Action Committee,* 500). Therefore, NCPAC could not exert undue corporate influence that warranted restraining its political voice.

The group distinctions grew increasingly subtle in *FEC v. Massachusetts Citizens for Life,* 478 U.S. 238 (1986). Massachusetts Citizens for Life (MCFL) was prosecuted by the Federal Election Commission (FEC) for publishing and disseminating a preelection newsletter without first establishing a separate, segregated fund. The Supreme Court found the restrictions unconstitutional, reasoning that MCFL posed no threat of unfair deployment of corporate wealth to advance political causes (*FEC v. Massachusetts Citizens for Life,* 478 U.S. at 259). Because MCFL was created solely for political purposes, it could not wield the "corrosive influence of concentrated corporate wealth" (*FEC v. Massachusetts Citizens for Life,* 478 U.S. at 257). Because MCFL did not threaten "the integrity of the marketplace of political ideas" (*FEC v. Massachusetts Citizens for Life,* 478 U.S. at 257), its political speech could not be constitutionally restrained.

The Supreme Court's opinion in *FEC v. Massachusetts Citizens for Life* reflected a wholesale abandonment of *Buckley's* aversion to aiding some group voices by muting others. The Court's rationale was increasingly sophisticated, however. It was guided by the notion that expenditures of group resources should correspond to the level of support underlying the ideas being expressed. Organizational wealth by itself did not compel regulation because the "[r]elative availability of funds is . . . a rough barometer of public support" (*FEC v. Massachusetts Citizens for Life,* 478 U.S. at 258). Hence, "all who participate in the political marketplace [need not] do so with exactly equal resources" (*FEC v. Massachusetts Citizens for Life,* 478 U.S. at 257). The key inquiry was whether the group spending was indicative of the intensity and strength of support for the underlying ideas. Was the volume of an association's speech a valid benchmark of the popularity of the ideas advanced? Or did it reflect wealth amassed in the economic marketplace without a nexus to the group's political ideas? MCFL's resources were "not a function of its success in the economic marketplace, but [of] its popularity in the political marketplace (*FEC v. Massachusetts Citizens for Life,* 478 U.S. at

259). The money collected and spent presumably was an accurate measure of the strength of pro-life opinions among MCFL members. As such, it was "representative" in character—and legal regulation of it was less justified.

THE ILLUSORY GOAL OF GROUP PARITY
IN POLITICAL CAMPAIGNS

The Supreme Court's ruling in *FEC v. Massachusetts Citizens for Life* featured a full philosophical embrace of group-centered representation. It revealed a group-differentiating constitutional jurisprudence that was based on how accurately group expression represented members' political preferences. It also marked the high-water mark of a bold legal experiment in ameliorating political inequality. Congress and the Court in tandem created tiered group rights in the financing of elections. FECA, with its judicial gloss, pursued parity of group influence by gauging and controlling the volume of group voices in the public forum. Given the prominence of money as the animating force of contemporary campaigns, Congress's and the Court's efforts to "level the playing field" were understandable, even laudable. The thirst for money in costly modern-day campaigns provides an unparalleled opportunity for a political presence (Jackson 1988; Alexander 1992; Malbin 1980). Campaign spending allows individuals, groups, and political parties to seek and gain access to power. It also distorts the representativeness of political actors and institutions. A wealthy individual can wield as much clout as a large group of people of modest means. In short, those with more money enjoy inordinate political influence.

Does the neopluralist drive to legally compartmentalize groups stand up, however, to the theoretical framework presented above? Is it an adequate response to the theoretical and practical challenges of representation? *Austin v. Michigan Chamber of Commerce*, 494 U.S. 652 (1990) exposed a deep philosophical divide on the Supreme Court. Ignoring a state law that required a segregated fund for corporate political activities, the Michigan Chamber of Commerce ran an advertisement for a candidate in a special election for the Michigan House of Representatives. Relying on *FEC v. Massachusetts Citizens for Life*, the Court characterized the Chamber as a business association rather than a political advocacy group—and as such, properly subject to the regulatory measure (*Austin v. Michigan Chamber of Commerce*, 494 U.S. at 662).

The majority opinion elicited skepticism from Justices Kennedy and Scalia, both of whom questioned the Court's ability to make sophisticated distinctions that would actually advance the elusive goal of political equality. Justice Kennedy derided the statute as "value-laden, content-based speech suppression that permitted some nonprofit groups, but not others, to engage in political speech" (*Austin v. Michigan Chamber of Commerce*, 494 U.S. at 695). The First Amendment barred government from "shap[ing] the political debate by insulating the electorate from too much exposure to certain views" (*Austin v. Michigan Chamber of Commerce*, 494 U.S. at 706). Justice Scalia rejected the notion "that too much speech is an evil that the democratic majority can proscribe" (*Austin v. Michigan Chamber of Commerce*, 494 U.S. at 680). Scalia facetiously proclaimed that: "To assure the fairness of elections by preventing disproportionate expression of the views of any single powerful group, your Government has decided that the following associations of persons shall be prohibited from speaking or writing in support of any candidate: _____" (*Austin v. Michigan Chamber of Commerce*, 494 U.S. at 680). Scalia scornfully described as "illiberal" the premise that expenditures must reflect actual support for the political ideas espoused, calling it a "one man–one minute" proposal (*Austin v. Michigan Chamber of Commerce*, 494 U.S. at 685). The objective of equalizing the political debate, though noble, was something government "cannot be trusted to do" (*Austin v. Michigan Chamber of Commerce*, 494 U.S. at 692).

The Supreme Court took an extended hiatus from campaign financing after *Austin*. Justices Kennedy and Scalia's objections hinted, however, at the theoretical, empirical, and practical questions plaguing group representation theories. Empirically, the Court's step onto the slippery slope of group categorization, carried to its logical conclusion, suggested a descent into a quagmire. The empirical reality is that only individuals furnish distinct, definable, functional units by which to gauge political activity. Groups exist in countless associational forms and varieties. Calibrating the volume of a group's political voice to reflect the depth and breadth of its members' preferences creates formidable challenges in identifying, typing, ranking, and weighting these collectivities.

First, which groups are entitled to greater representation? Only those having suffered past exclusion? If so, what kinds and levels of disadvantage are deserving of legal remedy? Groups can be distinguished by structure or organization, political resources, internal procedures, or the goals underlying their formation. They can be differentiated by their functions and activities, their degree of permanency, or their political agenda. Relevant distinctions exist between partisan organizations and interest groups, for-profit and nonprofit corporations, public interest and business organizations, and organizations formed around an economic interest and groups of sociologically designated people. Can a nonarbitrary scheme of group-based representation account for these distinctions? Ordering and handicapping of groups appears to present insuperable difficulties.

Second, if the ultimate goal is parity of group influence, what about equalization of other political resources (May 1987)? Other possible benchmarks of a group's representative character include organization and leadership, substantive interests, scope of agenda, decision-making procedures, member roles, and the like. Should we also neutralize groups with advantages not necessarily traceable to money but to organization, political expertise, access to the media, or prestige? These problematic questions raise doubts about whether implementation of a fair system could ever be possible (Ryden 1996, 76–82).

Given these and other objections, it is not surprising that the Supreme Court's group speech equalization efforts have suffered from a notable lack of measurable success. The dramatic growth in PAC spending—culminating in the "soft money" orgy of recent elections—should have shattered any illusion that parity of group speech can be achieved through existing campaign financing regulations. Current fundraising practices have nullified legal efforts to handicap the influence of groups. Exponential increases in independent spending and in soft money funneled through partisan organizations for "party building" activities have badly outstripped the Court's neopluralist efforts. Indeed, the widening disparities in group voices leave the Court's efforts looking quaintly well-intended but hopelessly naive.

THE LIFE OF THE PARTY: THE COURT, POLITICAL PARTIES, AND CAMPAIGN FINANCE REGULATION

One moral that could be drawn from the Supreme Court's struggles is that it ought to avoid the temptation to engage in political theorizing. The naysayers would argue that constitutional doctrine and political theory are an ill-formed fit; the political realities are too complex to be easily translated by the Court into effective legal principle. An alternative conclusion is that the Court simply needs to engage in better theorizing. Recent developments have raised a third potential theoretical basis for campaign finance regulation, built around a party government model of politics. Proponents of a party-conscious regulatory regime argue that political parties have been absent from the Court's analysis of free speech and associational rights. The Court has been hampered by a crabbed understanding of the right of association, defining it solely as a means of "amplifying the voices" of the members of the association and ignoring what it means with regard to gaining *representation*.

Political association is more than simply amplified individual speech. Rather, it is a means of pursuing political representation. Association is aimed at putting into office a candidate who will *represent* a group's members. Although contributions pay for speech (in the form of political advertisements), they also fund a host of associational activities—voter registration drives, "get out the vote" efforts, voter guides, candidate recruitment, rallies and campaign events—aimed at electing the person who will best *represent* individuals belonging to that party or group. Financial support also is used to gain access to candidates and policymakers, so that an organization's lobbyist might better persuade that person to *represent* the interests of its members. The right of association, then, is a crucial path to achieving effective political representation, and this right should be at the center of the Supreme Court's doctrinal approach to campaign financing.

How might this expansive view of associational rights affect the Court's jurisprudence? First, it would provide a useful common analytical framework or basis for discussion. Second, it might help correct common perceptions of PACs as bordering on criminal and group involvement in politics as inherently evil. Third, elevating the right of association as a tool of representation would better equip the Court to draw meaningful constitutional distinctions between types of associational activity. Freedom from restrictions in the electoral/campaign financing realm should correspond to the extent to which the association serves the ends of representation. Finally—and most significant for the purposes of this discussion—it would lead to constitutional recognition of partisan organizations as unique channels of representation; constitutional emphasis on associational rights and benefits would highlight political parties as institutional means of integrating individual and group voices and facilitating their access to the public square, thereby maximizing effective participation for all.

Party advocates rue what they consider the failure of the Supreme Court to acknowledge constitutionally the functional benefits of party systems.[9] Until recently, political parties had been largely absent from campaign financing cases. The fault was not necessarily entirely the Court's; it is naturally limited to the cases it hears, and those cases tended not to directly involve political parties. Yet the indirect impact of the Court's decisions worked to the parties' detriment. From *Buckley* to *Austin*, the Court significantly altered the ground rules of campaign financing with virtually no consideration of political parties. Its focus on groups as conduits for individual speech rendered parties indistinguishable from—even subordinate to—other associations and groups (Ryden 1996, 2). Throughout, the Court tended to equate the electoral role of PACs with that of political parties, reinforcing the message that "parties were no more important to electoral representation than other political groups" (Maveety 1991, 174–75).

Although the cases before the Supreme Court rarely implicated political parties directly, the respective interests of parties and groups were clearly in tension, if not in competition. The expansion of the speech rights of PACs came at the expense of political parties, as group constitutional rights were extended to areas of electioneering traditionally considered the exclusive realm of the party organizations. The broadening of group access helped to undermine the parties' unrivaled dominance of elections. In this sense, then, the PAC decisions were "antiparty" (Maveety 1991, 168).

Colorado Republican Campaign Committee v. FEC

The Supreme Court was forced to confront the legal status of political parties, however, in *Colorado Republican Federal Campaign Committee v. FEC*, 518 U.S. 604 (1996).[10] The case grew out of a 1986 U.S. Senate race in Colorado. The state Republican Party ran radio ads against Democratic Congressman Tim Wirth, a declared candidate for the seat. When Democrats complained that the cost of the ads exceeded FECA limits on party spending, the FEC sued. In addition to raising technical statutory defenses, the Republican Party asserted that campaign spending limits *as applied to political parties* were unconstitutional in their entirety. This frontal challenge to restrictions on parties presented the Court with a natural vehicle for considering party structures as a third constitutional path to fair, effective representation.

The decision was a mixed blessing for political parties. The result was a boon to the parties, but it was rendered with little acknowledgment of their functional benefits. The Court neither closed the door on, nor availed itself of, a partisan-centered constitutional doctrine. Although the Court decided by a 7–2 vote in favor of the Colorado Republican Party, a plurality of justices did so on narrowly circumscribed grounds. Confining their decision to the specific facts of the case, these justices declined to reach the larger issue of whether parties could constitutionally be subject to spending restriction. The plurality of justices (Breyer, O'Connor, and Souter) concluded that the spending by the Colorado Republican Party in this setting was "independent" of any specific candidate because the party had not yet nominated one. Because the spending did not constitute a "coordinated" expenditure made in consultation with a candidate, it was not subject to the statutory limits.

Justices Kennedy, Rehnquist, Scalia, and Thomas were inclined to go much further, however, and would have found all campaign spending constraints on political parties unconstitutional. Justices Kennedy and Thomas in particular anticipated a party-centered constitutional theory of representation. Observing that "political parties have a unique role" in advancing "their members' shared political beliefs," Kennedy continued:

> A political party has its own traditions and principles that transcend the interests of individual candidates and campaigns; but . . . candidates are necessary to make the party's message known and effective. . . . It makes no sense, therefore, to ask, as FECA does, whether a party's spending is made "in cooperation, consultation, or concert with" its candidate. The answer in most cases will be yes, but that provides more, not less, justification for holding unconstitutional the statute's attempt to control this type of party spending. . . . Party spending "in cooperation, consultation, or concert with" its candidates of necessity "communicate[s] the underlying basis for the support," . . . the hope that he or she will be elected and will work to further the party's political agenda. . . . The party's speech, legitimate on its own behalf, cannot be separated from speech on the candidate's behalf without constraining the party in advocating its most essential positions and pursuing its most basic goals. (*Colorado Republican Federal Campaign Committee v. FEC*, 629–30)

Likewise, Justice Thomas found the anticorruption justification nonsensical in the party context because "the very aim of a political party is to influence its candidate's stance on issues and, if the candidate takes office or is reelected, his votes." When political parties achieve that aim, it is hardly "a subversion of the political process' (*Colorado Republican Federal Campaign Committee v. FEC*, 646).

Implicit in the positions of Justices Kennedy and Thomas was a constitutional approach to campaign finance rooted in the model of responsible party governance. That model is premised on vigorous party structures as a comprehensive response to the myriad of representational demands. It sees political parties as functionally superior to other group players in performing representative democratic tasks. Political parties are uniquely constituted to represent individuals and collectives. Through their management of campaigns and elections, political parties aggregate, shape, and channel individual participation; they also serve as vehicles of collective influence by giving groups a forum in which to air concerns. Unlike other groups, political parties mediate and reconcile a host of interests. Whereas other groups polarize or compartmentalize the polity, political parties meld different voices and interests into a reasonably coherent platform. By recruiting and supporting candidates to couple with that platform, political parties serve as representational linkages between individuals, groups, and office holders. Between elections, political parties serve as integrative institutions within government, bringing a modicum of direction and cohesiveness to the administration of power. Majority and minority parties set agendas, define issues and alternatives, and manage the conflict that is at the heart of politics. Without political parties to organize and run the government, the government would be far less connected with, and responsive to, the represented.

The difficulty with the "responsible party" model, of course, is that real political parties do not fit the model. The parties do the tasks described above imperfectly—and some of them rather poorly. Nevertheless, even flawed, imperfect parties differ significantly in nature and character from other collective interests. The issue is whether political parties' organizational and functional attributes serve the multiple demands of representation enough to compel a party-informed constitutional jurisprudence. At the very least, the Supreme Court is dangerously indifferent toward the institutional safeguards of representative democracy that political parties provide. A better sense of the structural component of party subsystems would inform the Court's representation jurisprudence.

This oversight is magnified by the "campaign money equals speech" framework. It obscures parties' unique representative capabilities and renders them indistinguishable from other political groups. It reveals "an almost studied ignorance of the interdependence of the organizational, electoral, and governmental functions" of partisan organizations (Maveety 1991, 183). A constitutional alternative to the lukewarm attitude toward parties expressed in *Colorado Republican Federal Campaign Committee v. FEC* would be a serious endorsement of associational rights for parties in the context of campaign financing. Political parties have been found in other contexts to be a "politically salient, cohesive class" entitled to constitutional protection (*Karcher v. Daggett*, 462 U.S. 725, 749 (1983); *Davis v. Bandemer*, 478 U.S. 109 (1986))—including the First Amendment right of association (*Tashjian v. Republican Party of Connecticut*, 479 U.S. 208 (1986); *Eu v. San Francisco County Democratic Committee*, 489 U.S. 214 (1989)). However, for that right "to be a doctrinal tool that furthers responsible party government, it must be applied with a goal in mind" (Maveety 1991, 184). The Supreme Court must seek to further effective representation through party activities in the sphere of campaigns and elections.

Although explicit assignment of associational rights to political parties would not necessarily remove all congressionally imposed FECA constraints,[11] it could preserve a necessary counterweight to the rampant influence of PACs. Enhancing the prominence of political parties would not banish groups from the arena, but it would keep them operating within the constraining framework of the party structures. In short, it would bring us full circle to the group/pluralist theory of Bentley, Truman, Dahl, and Key that welcomed spirited group activity but always placed it squarely within the context of a strong two-party system (Schattschneider 1960).

ISSUES AND OBJECTIONS: ANSWERING THE SKEPTICS

The constitutional treatment of political parties in funding campaigns is hardly an abstract theoretical discussion. Indeed, political parties appear to be the point at which the latest developments in campaign spending, reform efforts, and constitutional disputes will intersect. Largely as a result of the decision in *Colorado Republican Federal Campaign Committee v. FEC*, political parties have moved to the center of the financing system. Soft money has taken on greater strategic importance as party spending has increased exponentially in the past two election cycles

(Magleby and Holt 1999). Party fundraising and spending are almost sure to rise in the absence of additional statutory or constitutional shackling.

Current congressional activity—and the public opinion it reflects—is pulling in the opposite direction. At this writing, the reform with the greatest weight of support is the proposed ban on soft-money contributions to the parties. Were such a ban to pass, the courts would certainly be called on to reconcile it with political parties' constitutional rights. Already, a lower court ruling in Colorado has recently thrown out all federal limits on political parties' spending on their congressional and presidential candidates, finding these limits an unconstitutional impingement on party speech rights (*FEC v. Colorado Republican Party*, Civ. No. 89n1159). If this ruling were to survive an appeal, the result would be akin to the removal of all party spending limits. A similar challenge to constraints on party spending is being raised in federal court in Ohio.[12]

The relationships among the Supreme Court, the Constitution, and political parties are especially timely in light of these developments. These developments also raise a host of practical questions pertaining to political reform and the Court as agent of, or obstacle to, reform.

First, does not special constitutional treatment for political parties artificially do for parties what they seem unable to do for themselves, which is to maintain a position of primary influence in and control of elections? Favorable legal/constitutional treatment should not relieve the parties themselves of the responsibility for fulfilling their representative tasks. The onus remains on political parties to achieve intellectual coherence, definition, and organizational cohesion/integration to make their relevance to the system manifest. The dissipation of the party link to voters reinforces the need for internal reform and improvement. This development, however, does not extenuate the need for a friendlier legal/constitutional environment within which political parties can operate.

Second, does not the party-based prescription fly in the face of our constitutional approach to parties? Why should there be special constitutional protection for entities not mentioned in the Constitution and, indeed, to which some framers were even hostile? The Constitution itself is not hostile to political parties—only silent on them. The framers were expert at planting certain values in the Constitution but leaving open how those values would be cultivated. A pro-party doctrine views political parties as critical to the accomplishment of important constitutional values—namely, authority, accountability, responsiveness, and representative democracy.

Third, is it the proper purview of the Supreme Court to decide that a party-centered system is somehow more desirable than candidate-centered elections (Briffault 1996)? Or are issues implicating party responsibility better left to the judgment of the legislative branch? The Court's struggles in this realm suggest caution in advocating a more activist Court confronting multifarious and confounding issues such as these. Such activism may be necessary, however, only because the legislative branch's self-interest in perpetuation of power renders it manifestly incapable of fairly or evenhandedly entertaining these questions.

Fourth, is an explicit constitutional recognition of collective First Amendment rights—in this case with respect to political parties—likely in light of the Supreme Court's less hospitable attitudes toward group rights generally (as evidenced by recent Fourteenth Amendment decisions in race-conscious redistricting and affirmative action)? Party proponents would argue that the very opposite is true: A party-grounded jurisprudence is consistent with the Court's growing concern with the polarizing, fragmenting tendencies of group rights. Political parties facilitate group activity while reconciling and mediating multiple group interests. Political parties, and parties alone, are able to mitigate this tension.

Fifth, does not the unprecedented role of political parties in the 1996 and 1998 campaigns and their stunning success in raising and spending soft money indicate that they do not need special constitutional status? In fact, the current climate may compel greater legal protection of political parties, not less. Political parties are the likeliest targets for incumbent officeholders searching for superficial reforms to appease the public. Office holders untethered from political parties stand ready to eliminate the soft money provision that is central to party influence. This development would lead to campaigns even more centered on the candidates themselves, making representative governance even more elusive and illusory.

Sixth, what are the implications for minor parties, which already face a legal regime that is stacked against them? Does the interest in a stable, two-party system justify tiered associational rights? Or does fairness compel equal treatment? Minor parties perform many of the same representative functions as do the major parties. Yet legal obstacles in campaign financing, ballot access, fusion, and other areas distort elections and muffle the degree to which minor parties represent public attitudes and positions. Consistent adherence to party rights would begin to rectify the oppressive legal treatment of minor and third parties.

Finally, how can this legal approach be reconciled with dominant public perceptions that parties (as well as interest groups and PACs, for that matter) are the scourge of politics and not a boon—and that their relative role should be diminished rather than enhanced? The effort to rebuild public trust and confidence in political parties and politics must occur on several levels; it should include more sophisticated and even-handed media coverage, internal party reform, a better-informed public, and politicians muting their own disparagement of the house in which they reside. A legal regime that leaves room for party rejuvenation rather than stifling it is one more piece of the puzzle.

These questions legitimately deserve more attention than can be devoted here. Political parties in our democracy are constrained by con-stitutional indifference, a historic tradition of weak parties, and wide-spread public hostility. The objections lose much of their force, however, if one is mindful of the distinct functional attributes that political parties bring to representative government. If we are unable to recognize the value of political parties, we may continue to stumble toward more well-intended, but myopic, reforms that only hasten the erosion of our repre-sentative institutions and structures.

ENDNOTES

1. There is inherent ambiguity in attributing to "the Court" any single doctrinal or theoretical approach. Space constraints limit the extent to which this chapter can address important empirical distinctions within the Supreme Court in its campaign finance jurisprudence. The reader should be mindful of those distinc-tions, however, especially in light of personnel changes on the Court since *Buckley* and in view of the splintered nature of its pronouncement in *Colorado Republican Federal Campaign Committee v. FEC.*

2. This focus on individualism paralleled the Supreme Court's early voting rights cases. For an extensive discussion of the Court's heavily individualistic approach to questions of representation and voting rights during the Warren years, see Maveety (1991).

3. Campaign organizations are run by media professionals, consultants, pollsters, strategists, and others who strive to maximize the impact of contributors' finan-cial resources. Independent expenditures are often less effective in transmitting the desired message and may even counter the strategy of the campaign itself. Nevertheless, the Supreme Court was willing to limit the associational use of money but not independent individual efforts. Congress, unfortunately, re-sponded to *Buckley* by taking the Court's lead and further dampening the role of political parties and associations in campaign financing. *Buckley* resulted in a

set of 1976 amendments to FECA that further limited what individuals and PACs could contribute to political parties and other political committees.

4. The individualistic approach to associational rights was echoed in *Citizens Against Rent Control v. City of Berkeley*, 454 U.S. 290 (1981). A Berkeley city ordinance that limited contributions relating to ballot measures was invoked against an unincorporated association that opposed a ballot initiative to impose rent controls. Although the Supreme Court struck down the provision, the associational rights at stake were those of *"individuals* to support concerted action by a committee advocating a position on a ballot measure" (at 298, emphasis added). *Citizens Against Rent Control v. City of Berkeley* shielded the exercise of associational activities but signaled no "change in the Court's failure to appreciate the ways in which an association functions as anything more than the sum of its members' efforts" (Gottlieb 1982, 206).

5. For a thorough exposition of group theories in American politics, from Bentley to Truman to pluralist theorists such as Robert Dahl and V. O. Key, see generally Ryden (1996, 67–76).

6. A string of classic works exposed the flaws in the pluralist vision from a variety of perspectives (see Schattschneider 1960; Olson 1965; McConnell 1966; Lowi 1979). Even enthusiasts of pluralism such as Robert Dahl openly confronted its practical weaknesses (Dahl 1982).

7. *Neopluralism* in this context is the creation of a group-based set of representation rights. It entails the conferral of various degrees of formal representative status on particular identifiable groups in an effort to redress inequities in the pluralist system. A statement of the theoretical basis for group representation can be found in Young (1990). Lani Guinier is illustrative of the neopluralist desire to modify the electoral system to ensure formal representation for a variety of groups or interests (see generally Guinier 1994). The goal of Young and Guinier is to give disadvantaged groups a voice in the political debate through formal legal mechanisms that would equalize group influence. See also Grady (1993).

8. This shift to group-conscious remedies paralleled the Supreme Court's inclusion of group factors in other areas of representation rights and issues (Maveety 1991, 19–38). For an analysis of the similarities between the neopluralist campaign financing decisions and the establishment of a "group right to representation" in the voting rights/redistricting cases, see Ryden (1996, chapter 3).

9. The Supreme Court's neglect of political parties is not limited to campaign finance. In a wide range of cases—involving issues from patronage and ballot access disputes to party primaries and partisan gerrymandering—the Court has repeatedly displayed a disturbing lack of appreciation for the value of party subsystems as means of representation. At times, political parties are treated on a par with or subordinate to other political groups; at other times, they are excluded from consideration altogether (Ryden 1996).

10. The appellate opinion in this case illustrates the sheer lack of understanding that courts have demonstrated regarding party functions. The 10th Circuit upheld an FEC finding that the Republican Party had exceeded FECA limits on coordinated expenditures by parties (*FEC v. Colorado Republican Federal*

Campaign Committee, 59 F. 3d 1015 (10th Cir. 1995). The appellate panel treated political parties as no different (and arguably worse) than other group participants in process. Party limits were necessitated by the need for "the prevention of corruption and the appearance of corruption spawned by real or imagined coercive influence" on the process. Citing the "opportunity for abuse" when contributions "derive from sources inherently aligned with the candidate," the opinion noted "the dangers of domination that underlay the Supreme Court's acceptance of the constitutionality of contribution limits . . . in political party expenditures" and the "risk of actual corruption or appearance of corruption from large coordinated expenditures by political parties."

11. Raising the level of scrutiny for restrictions on political parties would not necessarily exempt them from campaign regulations or reform efforts. For example, "responsible party" proponents view soft money as a legitimate form of party building that reinforces political parties' capacity to function as representative entities. When the line between "party building" and express advocacy of a particular candidate becomes as blurred as it did in 1996 and 1998, however, the increased potential for narrow interests to "corrupt" candidates by funneling huge sums through political parties may warrant regulation or reform. My prescription would include, among other measures, a strict redefinition of party building, an FEC that has the power to enforce the existing rules, and instantaneous and complete disclosure.

12. In its most recent decision, the Supreme Court surprised some by reaffirming the basic framework of *Buckley* (*Nixon v. Shrink Missouri Government PAC*, No. 98–963, decided January 24, 2000). In *Nixon*, the Court by a 6–3 vote upheld states' authority to attack the threat of corruption by limiting campaign contributions. The Court rejected the argument that *all* restrictions on contributions violate the First Amendment. The reach of the decision is open to varying interpretations. It also does not impact directly the constitutionality of constraints on political party spending. But it demonstrates that the Court is not prepared to jettison the framework established in *Buckley*.

··· 10 ···

Plebiscites and Minority Rights:
A Contrarian View

Bradley A. Smith

One vexing aspect of democracy is the tension between majority rule and respect for the rights of minorities. Americans have attempted to resolve this tension by creating a variety of checks on unbridled majority power. These checks include a federal system of government with independent executive, legislative, and judicial branches; limits on government functions to certain enumerated powers; and bills of individual rights, backed by judicial review. In addition, all fifty states and the federal government provide for government by elected representatives, rather than direct citizen voting on lawmaking.

Twenty-six states, however, also provide for some type of statewide direct democracy—plebiscites by which voters can directly enact or repeal laws and state constitutional amendments.[1] Plebiscites can serve as an effective means for the citizenry to reestablish its power over a legislature that may be unduly beholden to a small, well-organized minority. Plebiscites also operate outside the checks and balances that normally apply to lawmaking, however. Laws passed by plebiscites do not require the approval of two legislative chambers and an executive. Plebiscites generally are not limited to any particular enumerated powers, and voters can insulate their decisions from judicial review under state constitutions by fashioning the bill as a state constitutional amendment. Because of this apparent lack of constraints, some observers fear that direct democracy allows—and even encourages—the majority to trample the rights of individuals, especially those in disfavored, identifiable (in Supreme Court parlance, "insular") minority groups (Burke 1993; Gunn 1981; Bell 1978).

Until recently, direct democracy had received scant attention from scholars. Three political trends have created renewed interest in the subject, however. The first trend is the growing use of direct democracy.

Whereas only 302 measures appeared on state ballots during the 1950s and 1960s (Persily 1997), 230 statewide measures appeared on state ballots in the election of 1988 alone (Eule 1990, 1517). Moreover, there is substantial public support for broadening the initiative process, including the implementation of plebiscites at the national level (Eule 1990, 1507).

The second trend is the use of direct democracy to decide social issues. Early in the twentieth century, plebiscites were used primarily to decide economic policies. In recent years, however, ballot initiatives have been placed before voters to limit affirmative action, make English a state's official language, and repeal legislation prohibiting private discrimination against homosexuals, among other things (Persily 1997).

Finally, there has been a ratcheting up of the level of direct citizen lawmaking. Initiatives are being used not merely to pass laws but to place policy choices beyond simple legislative review by writing policy preferences into state constitutions. This development has raised the stakes in ballot campaigns by allowing temporal majorities to insulate policy preferences from future legislative majorities and from judicial review under state constitutional standards (Garrett 1997).

When laws passed by plebiscite are alleged to violate the U.S. Constitution, courts must decide whether a law passed by popular vote should be entitled to the same level of deference as one passed by the legislature (Garrett 1997; Schacter 1995). If plebiscites are more likely than other legislation to violate minority rights, as some commentators argue, they ought to be put to a more stringent test when they are reviewed for constitutionality (Eule 1990; Gunn 1981; Bell 1978). Indeed, some commentators have even suggested that all plebiscites are unconstitutional under Article IV of the Constitution, which guarantees to each state a "republican" form of government (Hamilton 1997; Rogers and Faigman 1996).

For the most part, the Supreme Court has strained to avoid deciding these issues. For example, it refused to hear an appeal of California's Proposition 209, approved by voters in 1996, which abolished that state's affirmative action programs (*Coalition for Economic Equity v. Wilson*, 521 U.S. 1141 (1997)). In another case, the Court held that a lower court's decision to strike down a voter-initiated amendment to the Arizona Constitution that proclaimed English to be the state's official language should be vacated on grounds of mootness, thus avoiding a decision on the merits (*Arizonans for Official English v. Arizona*, 119 S. Ct. 850 (1999)).

In 1996, however, the Court decided *Romer v. Evans*, 517 U.S. 620 (1996), a high-profile case arising from a 1992 voter-approved initiative amending the Colorado state constitution. Amendment 2, as the initiative was called, prohibited all branches and departments of the Colorado state government, including political subdivisions such as municipalities and school districts, from enacting or enforcing any law or regulation entitling any person to "quota preferences, protected status, or claim of discrimination" on the basis of "homosexual, lesbian, or bisexual orientation, conduct, practices, or relationships."

Amendment 2 had its genesis in a series of events during the 1980s. In that decade, several states and local governments enacted ordinances or adopted policies prohibiting discrimination on the basis of sexual orientation. Colorado was in the vanguard of this movement. The cities of Aspen, Boulder, and Denver adopted ordinances prohibiting discrimination against gays and bisexuals in housing, jobs, and public accommodations. In 1990, the governor of Colorado, by executive order, prohibited job discrimination in state hiring based on sexual orientation and implemented sensitivity training on homosexuality for state employees. In 1991, the Colorado Civil Rights Commission urged the legislature to extend state civil rights law to ban private discrimination based on sexual orientation (Tymkovich, Dailey, and Farley 1997).

In 1992, citizens upset by these developments placed Amendment 2 on the ballot as a proposed amendment to the Colorado Constitution. Amendment 2 aimed to repeal gay-protective legislation implemented by the governor and municipalities and to prevent any further adoption of such policies by the state or local governments. In November 1992, Colorado voters approved the measure by a 54–46 margin.

In many respects, Amendment 2 illustrated all that is allegedly wrong in plebiscitary voting. The amendment targeted legislation passed to protect a single minority group—the often-reviled homosexual community. Because the measure was framed as a constitutional amendment, opponents were unable to raise state constitutional objections to it. There is evidence that voters were confused into thinking that the amendment targeted affirmative action rather than basic antidiscrimination laws. There were also indications of appeals made to homophobic sentiments in parts of the public (Schacter 1997).

After Amendment 2 was approved by Colorado voters, it was challenged in court under the equal protection clause of the Fourteenth Amendment to the U.S. Constitution. After a lengthy journey through

Colorado state courts, the case reached the U.S. Supreme Court, which held in May 1996 that Amendment 2 violated the equal protection clause.

In its immediate impact, *Romer v. Evans* was a major victory for the gay and lesbian minority—and arguably for all Americans concerned about privacy and freedom. The Supreme Court's opinion may be unsatisfying, however, to observers concerned about the broader ramifications for direct democracy, for at no point does the opinion address any larger concerns about the use of plebiscites and their possible effect on minority groups. Thus, people who see plebiscites as a political threat to minorities may continue to do so. If this view is correct, *Romer* does not do nearly enough to protect minorities, and the Supreme Court should take a firmer stand to abolish or limit the use of plebiscites.

Opponents of *Romer* argue, however, that the Supreme Court showed too little deference to the will of the people of Colorado. They view the decision as a raw exercise in judicial power. This belief is fostered by *Romer*'s equal protection analysis. In particular, the Court's treatment of the voters' intent and the legitimate state interests behind the law ranges from careless to insulting. The decision also assumes that the effort to embed policy choices in the state constitution is illegitimate and a sign of the voters' irrational animus towards homosexuals—whereas such efforts, in fact, are part and parcel of politics. Amendment 2 supporters see *Romer* as precisely the type of special interest usurpation of power that plebiscites are designed to circumvent.

In this chapter, I examine the arguments made by observers who see plebiscites as a unique threat to minorities; I conclude that the decision in *Romer*, if not clearly wrong, is at least not very convincing. Although the Supreme Court was correct in not placing plebiscites under added constitutional scrutiny, I further conclude that the Court's reasons for striking down Amendment 2 are unconvincing and reveal a palpable lack of understanding of the political process.

This conclusion does not imply that I do not share the concerns of Amendment 2 opponents. I believe that the modern political and constitutional paradigms, which—properly applied—would have supported the constitutional validity of Amendment 2, are seriously flawed. Yet these paradigms are paradigms that the Supreme Court and many Amendment 2 opponents have helped to create. *Romer* stands as an arbitrary attempt by the Court to avoid some of the nastier consequences that flow, in part, from its own decisions about the constitutional constraints on the exercise of political power. Because it is arbitrary, it is and will be viewed by proponents of the measure as illegitimate.

In summary, I conclude that there is a serious threat to individual liberties posed by issues such as Amendment 2. By failing to recognize the extent of that threat and their own role in creating it, however, opponents of the amendment have erred in concluding that plebiscites per se are the problem. Their arguments at once go too far and not nearly far enough. The true, long-term threat to rights comes less from the increased use of direct democracy than from the broader erosions of the traditional checks of federalism and limits on government power. On these fronts, *Romer* is not only not helpful but is counterproductive.

DOES DIRECT DEMOCRACY UNIQUELY THREATEN MINORITIES?

The Problem of Faction

A primary concern for the drafters of the U.S. Constitution was to control the effects of "faction." James Madison defined a faction as a group "united and actuated by some common impulse of passion, or of interest, adverse to the rights of other citizens, or to the permanent and aggregate interests of the community" (Hamilton et al. [1788] 1961, 78). The problem for the drafters of the Constitution was to prevent factions from using government power to obstruct the common good and the rights of other citizens.

There is a tendency today to think of factions in terms of modern interest groups and to view factions only as a minority of the people exerting pressure at key points in the legislative process to frustrate the will of the majority. Madison, however, defined a faction as a group, "whether amounting to a majority or a minority of the whole . . ." (Hamilton et al., 78). Moreover, for Madison, minority factions were less to be feared than a faction consisting of a majority of the people. A minority faction, Madison argued in *Federalist 10*, can be defeated at the polls by a regular vote. A majority faction, on the other hand, might "sacrifice to its ruling passion or interest both the public good and the rights of other citizens" (Hamilton et al., 80–81). To people concerned about minority groups, it is the majority faction, not the minority "special interest," which is to be feared. Moreover, observers alarmed by the growing use of plebiscites argue that majority factions are most dangerous in a direct democracy because of the absence of many of the safeguards of indirect, representative democracy (Eule 1990; Bell 1978).

Madison shared this fear of direct democracy. In his view, a "pure democracy" was much more prone to the evils of majority faction than a representative democracy. He argued that a direct democracy "can admit of no cure for the mischief of faction." He favored representative government because it allowed views to be "refine[d] and enlarge[d]" by passing them through a chosen body of citizens. Under such a system, laws might well be "more consonant to the public good than if pronounced by the people themselves" (Hamilton et al., 82).

This view does not automatically imply, however, that legislative lawmaking is always preferable to direct democracy. Madison equally recognized that a legislature could come under the control of what he termed "men of factious tempers, of local prejudices, or of sinister designs," who would "betray the interests of the people" (Hamilton et al., 82). Madison's response was that this result would be less likely in a large republic than in a small one.

Suppose, however, that a minority faction, after gaining control of the legislature, were to maintain its position against the wishes of the majority through manipulation of the perks and powers of office (Felton 1993). In this scenario (perhaps unforeseen by Madison), a limited dose of pure democracy—as exists in many of the states today—may serve as a more direct cure to such a "betrayal of the interests of the people." Indeed, this result is precisely what was intended when direct democracy was introduced during the "Progressive" era (Persily 1997; Magleby 1984). It may not be un-Madisonian at all to view limited direct democracy as a partial cure to the problem of control by a minority faction.

The question, then, is whether plebiscitary democracy, as a limited adjunct to the legislative process, is supportive of or harmful to minority rights or to the constitutional guarantee of republican government.[2] Modern opponents of direct democracy argue that it does away with checks on majority rule that normally protect minorities. Some critics contend that plebiscites should be considered per se violations of the republican government clause (Hamilton 1997; Rogers and Faigman 1996). Others assert that, at minimum, actions taken by plebiscite should be subject to a higher level of judicial scrutiny than actions taken by state and local legislatures (Leong 1997; Eule 1990; Gunn 1981; Bell 1978).

It is not enough, however, merely to show that the legislature generally turns out laws superior to those enacted by plebiscite or that some plebiscite measures damage certain minority groups. The claim is that plebiscites uniquely threaten the rights of identifiable minority groups in a manner that calls for their abolition or restriction through judicial action. This argument requires showing that plebiscites systematically discriminate against identifiable minority groups in a manner that legislative enactments do not.

The Case Against, and For, Direct Democracy

Critics of plebiscites argue that where minority rights are concerned, legislative lawmaking is superior to direct democracy in two ways. First, the legislative process makes it more difficult for majorities to enact antiminority legislation. Second, legislative lawmaking creates an environment in which majorities are less likely to seek to do so.

The first argument is a simple claim that goes to the basic structure of American government. With the exception of Nebraska, every state in this country has a bicameral legislature. Because each chamber of the legislature reflects different constituencies, it is especially difficult for any particular faction to elect a majority in both houses. Moreover, the minority group often need not control an entire house of the legislature to defeat a majority faction on particular legislation; it will be enough merely to control one or two key committees. In addition, state governors have the power to veto laws, which can normally be overridden only by a supermajority of the legislature. Arguably, these checks enable a minority group to stop harmful legislation before it becomes law (Bell 1978; Eule 1990).

In practice, however, it is doubtful that this governmental structure provides substantial benefits to identifiable minority groups. It is at least theoretically possible for a minority of just more than 25 percent to gain control of at least one legislative chamber, thereby enabling that minority to block legislation.[3] Of course, even in this most favorable case, any minority of less than 25 percent will gain little from the legislative process as opposed to plebiscites. In fact, because most members of the legislature will have been elected by more than 51 percent of the voters, and because many members of the minority group will vote for losing candidates, a minority group normally must be considerably greater than 25 percent of voters to gain control of a legislative chamber (Baker 1991).[4] As the percentage of minority voters needed to control the legislature approaches 50 percent, the difference between legislative and plebiscitary outcomes fades.

Similarly, the gubernatorial veto is relatively insignificant as a means for minority groups to block legislation. As a general rule, governors use the veto power sparingly. Furthermore, a governor will normally have been elected by more than 50 percent of voters from the same statewide constituency that votes on a plebiscite. Thus, although it is true that a veto offers one final chance for a group to block legislation, it is doubtful that many measures that would gain a majority in a plebiscite would be vetoed if passed instead by the legislature (Baker 1991, 717–19).[5]

More important, the ability to check legislation may not always favor minority group interests. Minority groups seek not only to defeat but to pass and repeal legislation. In doing so, they face the same legislative hurdles described above. For example, for many years the civil rights movement in this country was substantially hampered by the possibility of a Southern filibuster in the U.S. Senate. If a passionate, conservative Christian minority steadfastly opposed to homosexual rights exists in the legislature, gay rights activists may find it easier to pass protective legislation through a plebiscite. Just as a bicameral legislature and governor make it easier to block legislation harmful to any particular minority, they may make it easier to block legislation beneficial to that minority group. Ultimately, then, it is hardly clear that minorities uniformly, or even usually, benefit from bicameralism and the separation of powers.

The legislative process may also protect minorities indirectly, however, by creating a climate in which legislation targeting the rights of minorities is less likely to pass. The legislative process creates this climate by providing a measure of the intensity of opposition that is absent from plebiscites and by providing for reasoned debate, compromise, and accountability.

Plebiscites provide voters with a stark choice—yes or no—and then aggregate vote totals. No distinction is made between the mild supporter and the passionate opponent; there is no measure of intensity. If 51 percent have a mild preference for legislation that is strongly opposed by the remaining 49 percent, the legislation will pass in a plebiscite. Although this aspect of plebiscites is not necessarily bad, most Americans believe—on utilitarian or other grounds—that intensity of opposition ought to be considered at some point in the process.[6] Representative government seems to provide reasonable accounting for intensity. Voters who rarely agree with any candidate on all policies or priorities must weigh the various positions of candidates, and the importance of particular issues, in deciding how to vote. The issues on which a voter has the strongest feelings will play a dominant role in determining how the vote is cast. Thus, where the majority has a very mild preference on an issue, a candidate is unlikely to gain many votes by trumpeting the majority position; few voters in the majority will feel strongly enough to make the issue a decisive, or even primary, factor in selecting a candidate. Taking a strong position in favor of the legislation, however, is likely to cost the candidate votes among passionate opponents of the legislation. In this way, minority groups, through their intensity of opposition, can head off harmful legislation or least force the majority to compromise on points of particular importance to the minority.

This intensity may also be felt directly in the legislature. Representatives who feel strongly about an issue, or who know that their constituents do, may be especially dogged in opposition on the floor. Here, the ability of minority group representatives to head off harmful legislation is assisted by the other great features of representative democracy: deliberation, compromise, and accountability.

Representative democracy includes, as an instrumental part of the process, formal deliberation and debate. Madison favored such debate for its ability to "refine and enlarge" opinion (Hamilton et al., 82). Hamilton felt that the legislative process allowed for "more cool and sedate reflection" (Hamilton et al., 432). Deliberation assures that different views are heard and that measures are well conceived to address the alleged problem. Even when debate does not prevent the legislative passage of a bill, the minority may be able to persuade the majority to rewrite its most objectionable parts or to soften its impact.

A natural outgrowth of this deliberation and cooling of passions is compromise. Majority legislators, informed by their minority colleagues about potential problems or effects of legislation in ways that voters are not, are then able to craft and amend legislation to deflate opposition or to enlarge majorities. Legislators are more likely than most voters to understand that complete victory is rarely attainable and to recognize that they will have ongoing dealings with the vanquished on other issues upon which they may need support and compromise. Legislators may also recognize the possibility of finding themselves in the minority on a future issue.

Finally, legislators are publicly accountable for their votes. Some observers argue that this accountability protects minorities (Hamilton 1997; Eule 1990). This theory is based on the premise that it is unfashionable to state one's racism or antiminority views publicly, whereas such votes may be cast without cost in the privacy of the voting booth (Bell 1978). Thus, the legislative process prevents antiminority sentiments that might otherwise be voted into effect through the anonymity of the plebiscite.

All of these arguments echo those of Madison, Hamilton, and other framers of the U.S. Constitution; they may provide compelling support for the wisdom and efficacy of legislation over direct democracy. It is far less clear, however, that they make the case that plebiscites, especially as a limited adjunct to representative government, systematically disadvantage identifiable minority groups. Indeed, in making these arguments, opponents of plebiscites adopt an idealistic vision of the legislature and a pessimistic vision of plebiscites.

For example, although plebiscites do not allow voters to register the intensity of their opinions at the ballot box (just as legislative intensity does not show up in the roll call vote), it is incorrect to assume that voter intensity plays no role in a plebiscite. One side's relative intensity may lead its partisans to vote in greater numbers or to work harder on the campaign. If both sides are free to raise contributions and spend money in unlimited sums, the intense minority may raise as much or more campaign money as sponsors of an initiative. (For example, in Colorado's Amendment 2 campaign, anti-Amendment 2 forces substantially outspent proponents of the measure.) This money can then be used to attempt to persuade the voters who do not begin with particularly strong preferences and are open to persuasion. Similarly, it is a mistake to assume that voters with a mild preference will vote without considering the passionate opposition of other voters. If voters do not take the strongly held and expressed views of others into consideration, the implication is that those voters do feel strongly about the issue—suggesting that even in the legislative process, the intensity of support might not have made a difference in the outcome.

Plebiscites do not provide for legislative debate, but they do allow for deliberation by the people. Large sums of money are often spent to influence the public on the merits of ballot proposals, and high-profile efforts such as Amendment 2 draw substantial media coverage. Indeed, the types of issues believed to threaten minority rights usually result in the most public discussion. Even outside Colorado, Amendment 2, like California's Proposition 209 a few years later, prompted far-ranging debate on radio programs, in letters to the editor, and in everyday conversation.

Critics of direct democracy note that this debate takes place largely after the measure is approved for the ballot, so that compromise or consideration of other options is impossible. These critics deride the quality of public deliberation of ballot measures, arguing that voters know little more than bumper sticker slogans (Rogers and Faigman 1996). Many proposals run dozens of pages and involve complicated issues from offshore drilling rights to insurance regulation, requiring reading and comprehension skills far beyond those of the typical voter (Eule 1990; Lowenstein 1982). Simplification of these issues in media reports and advertising may not make them more comprehensible.

This type of public debate may not be the "cool and sedate reflection" that the founders had in mind. Sadly, however, such "cool and sedate" debate is no longer an important component of modern legislatures, either. Representatives often vote with little or no understanding of the issues; they also vote on so many issues that, even with staff support, they know relatively little about many of them. The typical legislator spends less time studying issues than in pursuing reelection through constituent work. Most legislators leave issues to be debated in committees and then vote on the recommendation of committee members or along the party line (Baker 1991, 748–49). In this case, modern legislators may not be much different from common voters, who tend to rely on the opinions of informed friends and colleagues (Tymkovich, Dailey, and Farley 1997, 316). Moreover, far more information is available to local opinion leaders—in books and newspapers, over the Internet, and through radio and television—than was likely available 200 years ago to the most dedicated legislator.

Other critics argue that public debate is easy to manipulate (Riker 1991), and evidence confirms efforts to mislead and confuse voters on ballot issues as much as to educate them (Lowenstein 1982). Schacter (1997) argues that Amendment 2 was passed largely because voters were confused between affirmative action for gays, which they opposed, and laws protecting gays from discrimination, which they supported.

Yet this confusion is not a one-way street that systematically disadvantages minorities. For example, in November 1997, citizens placed an initiative on the ballot to amend the Houston city charter to provide that "the city . . . not discriminate against or grant preferences to any individual or group on account of race, sex, color, ethnicity or national origin. . . ." City officials changed the language so that the question actually presented to voters was, "Shall the city . . . end the use of affirmative action for women and minorities. . . ." The measure was defeated, 55 percent to 45 percent. Polls showed, however, that voters would have favored the measure had the original language been used (Robinson 1997). Within days of the vote, a federal judge struck down one of the county's major affirmative action plans because it provided for quota preferences, not merely affirmative action to find and promote qualified minorities (*Houston Contractors Association v. Metropolitan Transit Authority*, 984 F. Supp. 1027 (1997). The judge further indicated that the city's programs were similarly flawed (Tedford 1997). The change in the initiative language seems clearly to have been intended to hide the quota nature of the city's programs from the electorate. In short, both sides can play the disinformation game. Although this example may suggest a weakness in plebiscites as a method for making laws in general, it does not mean they are systematically bad for minorities.

If the purpose of deliberation is to effect compromise, however, this debate may come too late. Voters in a plebiscite have no opportunity to select a middle ground or to approve parts of a measure while rejecting its more extreme provisions (Gillette 1988). Nevertheless, it is not true that plebiscites leave no room for compromise. When a group puts a measure before the electorate in the form of a plebiscite, it will normally see broadened public support by moderating its proposal to assure a statewide majority (Tymkovich, Dailey, and Farley 1997, 317).

Moreover, legislative compromise is not a one-way ratchet protecting minority groups; it can be used to harm a minority group as well. Suppose, for example, that a legislature is considering two items. Legislator A strongly favors the first and mildly opposes the second. Legislator B mildly opposes the first but strongly favors the second. Legislator C, representing a minority group, strongly opposes both. If each legislator accurately reflects public opinion in his or her district, both measures would be defeated in plebiscites. In the legislature, however, A and B could trade votes, with A voting for issue two in exchange for B's vote in favor of issue one. In this scenario, each issue passes, and the process of legislative compromise harms, rather than benefits, the minority group (Baker 1991).

Moreover, a legislator may easily escape accountability for antiminority votes simply by invoking the greater good of a broader legislative agenda. Accountability might also work against minorities in the legislative process. Although the initiative process may remove the disincentive for a racist voter to act on his or her opinions, the legislative process may give the nonracist representative an incentive to support legislation disadvantaging minorities, if that will gain votes among racist members of a constituency. This scenario is particularly likely if the legislation is phrased in neutral language. Additionally, voters in a plebiscite must actually cast the vote to disadvantage a minority. This fact may have the effect of forcing voters to more fully confront the motivations for their intended votes. In a society that publicly condemns racism and hostile attitudes toward minorities, this internal check on voter conduct should not be dismissed. Such voters may feel less concerned, however, about voting for a candidate who supports such legislation—someone who will do the "dirty work" for them. The voter may be able to justify such a vote emotionally on the basis of other policies supported by the candidate (Baker 1991, 735–36).

Thus, even if plebiscites make it harder for a minority to block legislation, it is not clear that this fact works to the systematic detriment of minority groups. Legislative issues and alliances change. Although plebiscites sometimes make it harder for a minority to block legislation, they may sometimes make it easier for a minority group to pass legislation (Baker 1991). For example, women's suffrage was brought about largely through initiatives (Baker 1991, 708). Conversely, homosexual activity was criminalized in virtually every state by acts of the legislature. Plebiscites did not create Jim Crow laws, segregate schools, intern Japanese Americans during World War II, ban interracial marriage, or limit the right to vote. Virtually all of the truly antiminority legislation in this country has been passed by legislatures, not plebiscites (Briffault 1985).

There is little empirical evidence that plebiscites have been used more than the legislative process to harm minorities (Charlow 1994; Baker 1991). Arguments to that effect rely on a handful of high-profile cases, such as Amendment 2 or Proposition 209. Such anecdotal evidence is not terribly convincing, given the large number of local and state initiatives. Many more initiatives never garnered enough signatures to make it to the ballot.

Ultimately, whether plebiscites are better or worse than the legislative process may depend on the nature of the proposed law (Garrett 1997). Plebiscites are probably inferior for determining complicated schemes of insurance regulation or campaign finance, but they may be preferable for relatively straightforward issues such as stadium subsidies. Even assuming that representative government is generally preferable to direct democracy, the case for direct democracy as systematically disadvantageous to minority groups is weak.

ARE PLEBISCITES UNCONSTITUTIONAL?

The courts must decide on the constitutionality of plebiscites against this background. Plebiscites, of course, are not provided for in the constitutional operation of the federal government. The founders eschewed direct democracy for the federal government because they saw it as an inferior lawmaking device compared to representative government. Instead, they guaranteed to each state a republican form of government (U.S. Constitution, art. 4, sec. 4). Even critics of direct democracy concede, however, that a state meets the requirements of the republican government clause as long as it is generally "representative" (Eule 1990).

Thousands of laws are passed each year by legislatures, compared to a relative handful by plebiscite. The initiative process is a minor adjunct to the basic task of lawmaking by state legislatures. These limited plebiscites are a legitimate structural impediment to factional control of the legislature. Indeed, they may actually increase some republican virtues in the citizenry by involving more citizens in the governing process or stimulating interest in public affairs by addressing issues otherwise neglected by the legislature (Baker 1991; Cronin 1989; Gillette 1988). Issues such as Proposition 209 and Amendment 2 seem to have had that effect.

Should Plebiscites be Reviewed under a Higher Standard of Judicial Scrutiny?

If plebiscites are not per se unconstitutional, scholars such as Eule (1991), Gunn (1981), and Bell (1978) argue that they should be reviewed by courts with less deference than usual, on the theory that they are constitutionally "suspect" (Leong 1997).

In traditional equal protection jurisprudence, the Supreme Court will require only that there be some rational basis behind a law for it to pass constitutional scrutiny. When the Court engages in this "rational basis" review, the law is almost always upheld (Lively et al. 1996). The Court will apply a heightened standard of review known as "strict scrutiny," however, if the allegedly infringed right is a "fundamental" right—such as the right to travel or vote—or the group complaining of unequal treatment is a "suspect class." Suspect classes are groups against whom any legal discrimination should be regarded as a probable violation of the equal protection clause of the Fourteenth Amendment because of historic animosity and discrimination. As a practical matter, suspect classes have been groups defined by race, ethnicity, and alienage (*Graham v. Richardson*, 403 U.S. 365 (1971)). Whereas "rational basis" review has usually meant that a regulation will be upheld, so few laws have survived "strict scrutiny" that the Court itself has questioned whether the standard is not "strict in theory, fatal in fact" (*Bernal v. Fainter*, 467 U. S. 216 (1984)). In recent years, the Court has applied a level of "intermediate" scrutiny to government laws that classify citizens based on sex (*Mississippi University for Women v. Hogan*, 458 U. S. 718 (1982)).

Neither strict nor intermediate scrutiny has been routinely applied to plebiscites (e.g., *Citizens Against Rent Control v. City of Berkeley*, 455 U.S. 290 (1981))—nor should it be. If plebiscites are not per se unconstitutional, the only serious argument for subjecting laws passed via ballot initiative to stricter scrutiny than those enacted by the legislature is that the former are systematically more likely to be unconstitutional. No serious empirical evidence supports such an assertion, however. Nor is there evidence to suggest that existing standards of judicial review are less likely to spot and strike down unconstitutional laws passed through plebiscites than unconstitutional laws passed by legislatures—although Bell (1978, 23) makes this argument, without factual support.

Separate standards of review for legislative and plebiscitary enactments could result in the anomalous situation in which a law passed in one state by the legislature is deemed constitutional, whereas the same law passed in another state by plebiscite is struck down. Although this method of constitutional interpretation is not impossible—consider, for example, that the Supreme Court determines the constitutionality of laws regulating pornography based on "community standards"—it probably is not a result with which most observers would be comfortable.

Most of the high-profile plebiscites that have been cited as examples of antiminority legislation, in fact, have been struck down under current standards of judicial review (e.g., *Romer v. Evans*; *Hunter v. Erickson*, 393 U. S. 385 (1969); *Washington v. Seattle School District No. 1*, 458 U.S. 457 (1982); *Reitman v. Mulkey*, 387 U. S. 369 (1967)).[7] California's Proposition 209 is the notable exception. *Romer* does nothing to suggest that present standards of review are insufficient; the opinion is one of the bluntest the Supreme Court has issued in striking down a law on equal protection grounds.

The contention that plebiscites are particularly threatening to minority rights is an overreaction to a handful of high-profile cases. In almost all of these instances, the affected minority group has found redress in the courts. Although democratic theory suggests that laws made through the representative process may be generally *better* than those enacted through plebiscites, there is little to suggest that representatives are regularly more considerate of minority interests. To the extent that laws passed by plebiscite may sometimes run roughshod over minority or individual rights, current standards of judicial review seem adequate to police them.

RIGHTS, ROMER, AND REFERENDA: WHERE IS THE REAL THREAT TO LIBERTY?

To this point, I have taken at face value the proposition that plebiscites may pose a unique threat to minority rights, and I have suggested that the evidence in support of this position is weak. This assessment does not imply that minorities cannot be threatened by particular plebiscites. There is little reason to think that minorities are systematically threatened by plebiscites as opposed to legislative enactments, however. Using *Romer* as a springboard, I suggest that the true threat to minority rights comes rather from broader political and judicial philosophies that have eroded other republican institutions and created an environment in which rights, and checks on legislative power, have generally lost their importance.

Romer Revisited

Having rightly refused to invoke a heightened standard of review for plebiscites per se, the Supreme Court in *Romer* faced the question of whether Amendment 2 involved a "suspect class" or a "fundamental right." Otherwise, the rational basis standard would be applied. The Court could have held that homosexuals should be viewed as a suspect class, based on a well-documented history of animosity and discrimination. This approach would have brought the case squarely within the framework of *Hunter v. Erickson, Washington v. Seattle School District No. 1,* and *Reitman v. Mulkey.* It also would have required the Court to overrule its 1986 decision in *Bowers v. Hardwick,* 478 U. S. 186 (1986), which held that a state could constitutionally criminalize homosexual conduct. This the Court was unwilling to do.

Alternatively, the U.S. Supreme Court could have followed the Colorado Supreme Court's example. The latter found that Amendment 2 violated a fundamental right to "equal participation in the political process"—a vague phrase that could mean almost anything. The U.S. Supreme Court wisely refused to open this Pandora's box. With no "fundamental right" at stake and no "suspect class" involved, the Court was left to examine the law under the rational basis standard—usually an automatic victory for the constitutionality of the law.

In *Romer*, however, the Court held that no rational state interest was served by Amendment 2 and that the amendment "seems inexplicable by anything but animus toward the class that it affects" (*Romer v. Evans*, 517 U.S. at 632, 1996). The Court wasted little effort explaining either proposition. Colorado's proffered rationales for Amendment 2—respect for citizens' freedom of association and the state's interest in conserving state resources to fight discrimination against other groups—were dismissed in a single sentence: "The breadth of the Amendment is so far removed from these particular justifications that we find it impossible to credit them" (*Romer v. Evans*, at 635).

In fact, there is little evidence that most Amendment 2 voters were motivated by what the Court called "a bare . . . desire to harm a politically unpopular group. . . ." Surveys taken at the time of the vote found that 77 percent of Colorado respondents opposed criminalizing homosexual conduct, 71 percent felt that landlords should not discriminate on the basis of sexual orientation, and 70 percent felt that employers should not refuse to hire on that basis (Gerstmann 1999). Eighty-one percent agreed that "homosexuals are not really different from anyone else" (Dailey and Farley 1996). These data hardly suggest mass voter animus toward homosexuals.

The Amendment 2 campaign itself demonstrated a high level of tolerance for homosexuals in Colorado. Amendment 2 opponents included the League of Women Voters, hundreds of religious leaders, the American Civil Liberties Union, and most of the state's newspapers (Tymkovich, Dailey, and Farley 1997, 293–94). As early as 1971, Colorado had become one of the first states to decriminalize homosexual sex. Certainly some supporters of Amendment 2 did harbor strong animus toward homosexuals as a group, and some pro-Amendment 2 campaigning may have included extreme rhetoric on the alleged perversions of homosexuality. The overall picture, however, is hardly that of an electorate paralyzed by homophobia, fear, or hatred (Balkin 1997).

In fact, rational bases exist for states to limit the reach of antidiscrimination laws. First, in an era of high taxes and record government expenditures, concern over enforcement costs is real. The relatively low added cost of enforcing particular measures regarding homosexuals diminishes, but does not change, this fact.

More important, the state asserted a legitimate interest in personal privacy and freedom. At common law, individuals retain the right to discriminate in most of their private dealings. The United States operates on the general principle that individuals should retain personal autonomy and freedom to engage in consensual economic and social relationships. The right to private property—including the right to exclude others—has long been viewed as a mainstay of personal freedom, privacy, and tolerance in this country (Duncan and Young 1995).

Laws that prohibit private discrimination in housing and employment intrude on well-established rights to free association and use of property and are among the most invasive laws a community can pass. Such laws mandate social and economic relationships that individuals would not otherwise choose. Housing and employment are two of the most dominant social relationships in ordinary life. Many people spend more time interacting and conversing with people with whom they work than with family. Denying individuals the right to employ whom they choose, on whatever grounds, is a substantial infringement on personal autonomy. The regulation of housing rentals—particularly owner-occupied duplexes, small apartment buildings, sublets, or roommate arrangements—has the potential to be equally or even more intrusive.

This intrusiveness can be viewed in the local ordinances that Amendment 2 sought to repeal. For example, under Boulder's ordinance, a coffee shop owner's wife gave some religious literature on homosexuality to a gay employee who had apparently made various personal problems known at work. The Boulder Human Rights Commission ordered the owner—who had not even handed out the "offending" literature—to undergo and sponsor "sensitivity training" sessions. Boulder's ordinance also prohibited churches or other religious organizations from refusing to hire individuals because of sexual orientation, even if homosexual behavior was contrary to official church doctrine. Aspen's ordinance required churches to open their facilities to homosexual organizations if they allowed any community organization to use the facilities. Under similar local ordinances in Wisconsin, a woman was fined for refusing to share her house with either heterosexual men or lesbian women because of her concern about unwanted sexual attention (Tymkovich, Dailey, and Farley 1997, 301–3). More recently, a New Jersey court enforcing an antidiscrimination statute required the Boy Scouts—a private organization opposed to homosexuality—to allow gay men to serve as scoutmasters (*Dale v. Boy Scouts of America*, 308 N.J. Super. 516 (1998)).

These infringements on personal rights of privacy, religion, and property may be worth the benefits of tough antidiscrimination laws. Laws prohibiting discrimination on the basis of race, sex, religion, national origin, and, more recently, disability, are now prevalent across the country. There are strong arguments that such protection should be extended to homosexuals. It is specious for the Supreme Court to claim, however, that no political body could rationally conclude that the benefits of extending such protections to homosexuals are not worth the costs.

An electorate might well take different—and wholly rational—approaches to different classes of people, depending on the perceived harm caused by discrimination to the class at issue and the perceived cost of forcing individuals to accept such behavior in what were once private, consensual relationships. For example, although there is substantial evidence of the harm that discrimination does to gay men and women (Jackson 1997, 456–57), Justice Scalia argued in his *Romer* dissent that gays had high disposable income, more political power than their numbers would suggest, and constituted a "politically powerful" minority (*Romer v. Evans*, at 636). Whatever the factual merits of Justice Scalia's position, his argument went unanswered by the majority of the Court.

Following Scalia's lead, an unrebutted electorate might rationally conclude that protection for homosexuals is relatively unnecessary, and, so not worth the regulatory costs imposed on others. Alternatively, the electorate might view the costs of protective legislation based on sexual orientation as particularly high because such legislation infringes not merely on traditional liberties to use and enjoy property but also on the religious liberties of many citizens. This is rarely the case regarding, say, military status—which has also been prohibited, in some instances, from being used as a basis for discrimination. These judgments may be debatable, but they certainly are rational conclusions. Having reached such a conclusion, one could then ban legislation based on sexual preference but not, perhaps, other grounds.

Politics, Plebiscites, and Minority Rights

Given the rational basis—other than fear and animus—for the passage of Amendment 2, the legitimacy of the Supreme Court's decision to strike down Amendment 2 must hinge on some other factor. The Court's opinion reveals two factors that gave it cause for concern. The first was that only sexual orientation was singled out for repeal by Amendment 2. Colorado governments remained free to pass protective legislation based on any other characteristic. In fact, the municipalities that had included sexual orientation as a protected characteristic also prohibited private discrimination on the basis of age, military or marital status, pregnancy, parenthood, custody of a minor child, and political affiliation. The Court took this fact as proof of antihomosexual "animus." As a matter of politics, however, the singling-out strategy behind Amendment 2 makes perfect sense.

The Supreme Court recognized that the state interests put forth in *Romer* would be perfectly acceptable to justify repealing all antidiscrimination laws at the state level (Dailey and Farley 1996). The Court does not claim that such laws are constitutionally mandated. Therefore, the Court's insistence that citizens opposing such protection must seek repeal of all such laws simultaneously is bizarre.

The Court has not held, for example, that no characteristic may be protected under antidiscrimination laws unless all characteristics are protected under such laws. Yet in *Romer* the Court insists that the same cost-benefit analysis—applied in the other direction—is prohibited by the Equal Protection Clause. In essence, the Court has made it impossible to terminate antidiscrimination provisions one law at a time. Yet allowing individual classifications to be repealed when they are no longer deemed worth the cost is a rational way to approach the issue. The burden on gay rights supporters to organize a plebiscite to repeal Amendment 2 would have been no greater than the burden on Amendment 2's original sponsors to place Amendment 2 on the ballot. Supporters of Amendment 2 and similar proposals may be excused for not understanding why the normal rules of politics do not seem to apply to them.

The Supreme Court's second concern was that Amendment 2 prohibited *local* governments from passing laws prohibiting discrimination on the basis of sexual orientation. Thus, even where problems were local, and the costs of enforcement would not fall on taxpayers outside of the locality, such ordinances were banned at the state level. The Court also interpreted this aspect of the amendment as evidence of unreasonable animus—and it might well be. On the other hand, it may be less the result of "animus" than a natural political reaction to a philosophy of government fostered by the Court's own failure to limit government power in the past—in particular by its failure to restrict the federal government to its properly enumerated powers.

Representative government is not the only republican institution the framers established to protect the rights of the citizenry from the passions of democracy. Separation of powers, federalism, and the concept of enumerated powers were all viewed as key bulwarks in the defense of liberty (Hamilton et al. [1788] 1961, 102, 292–93, 321, 330). The U.S. Constitution provided the federal government with certain enumerated powers, beyond which it supposedly has no authority to act. The Bill of Rights was added as something of an exclamation point to these limits. Like the federal government, most states practice a type of federalism. Though they retain a plenary police power, most states delegate substantial authority to cities, counties, townships, and other lower levels of government. There has long been considerable overlap in the powers of differing levels of government—for example, cities, counties, states, and the federal government have simultaneously built roads, allowing citizens who desire roads to lobby for them at several levels of government. Nevertheless, Americans historically have recognized that local, state, and federal governments have different responsibilities.

Since the 1930s, however, previously enumerated powers of the federal government have been stretched beyond recognition. This expansion of the federal government's authority has been effected with the acquiescence of the Supreme Court. First-year law students learn that the power the Constitution grants to the federal government to "regulate Commerce with foreign Nations, and among the several States, and with the Indian Tribes" now extends, according to the Court, to limiting how much wheat a farmer may grow on his own land to feed his own family and livestock. Such activity, though not actually "commerce . . . among the States," might somehow *affect* such commerce (*Wickard v. Filburn*, 317 U.S. 111 (1942)).

A similar lack of legislative discipline has now surfaced in the states. Most legislators, at any level of government, are virtually unrestrained in the types of laws they pass. Disfavored activities are banned—as with a recent California initiative banning all smoking in bars, regardless of the consent of owners and patrons. Favored activities are subsidized or mandated. In short, we have all but eradicated the idea that there are any ethical, procedural, or constitutional restraints on any act of government at any level (Barnett 1995). It is natural, then, that political battles will migrate toward higher levels of government because local defeat can always be salvaged by victory at the next higher level of government.

Thus, when voters in Aspen, Boulder, and Denver passed ordinances that limited the rights of citizens to use their property, live their lives, and uphold their religious beliefs in certain ways that discriminated against individuals on the basis of sexual orientation, it was natural that affected citizens looked to a higher level of government—the state—to overturn these ordinances. That the actual leadership of the pro-Amendment 2 forces should come from Colorado Springs (a city that had not passed such an ordinance) matters little. These citizens, too, were merely acting to enforce a preference for laws, just as California citizens have limited discrimination in cities they never intend to visit.

The decision of antigay rights forces to enforce their political preferences at the state level is what any group now routinely does when it lacks a local majority but retains a majority of the electorate at a higher level of government. Voters who supported Amendment 2 might be forgiven for not understanding why—had they defeated the local ordinances in Aspen, Boulder, and Denver—supporters of gay rights could have passed laws, binding on Amendment 2 supporters, at the state level. Amendment 2 supporters, however, having lost locally, could not take *their* case to the state level.

To say that plebiscites are not particularly dangerous to identifiable minority groups is not to say that majorities cannot act in derogation of minority rights. The charge that plebiscites disadvantage minorities must mean more than that the losers lost, however, for that is the nature of all political decisions. Rather, the majority's action must illegitimately burden the minority.

Critics concerned about the alleged threat that plebiscites pose to minority rights cite as examples proposals such as Amendment 2, Proposition 187, Proposition 209, "official English" proposals, cutoffs of public funding for abortion (Eule 1990; Hamilton 1997), and even reductions in property taxes (Aoki 1997). That such issues should be invoked as examples of the threat posed by plebiscites to minority "rights" demonstrates a general confusion about the very concept of limited government. There is no constitutional *right* to benefit from affirmative action or even to be protected by anti-discrimination laws. Indeed, those "rights," though enacted by statute to achieve valid and admirable ends, contravene centuries-old common law rights retained by people. There is no *right* to publicly funded abortions, and using compulsory tax payments to force people to fund a procedure that many regard as vile, or even as murder, may seem to the impartial observer to be a greater infringement of *rights* than does the refusal to provide funding. There is no *right* to high taxes and more government spending. Governments should not, in my view, discriminate in the provision of benefits on the basis of alien status. An effort to cut such benefits, however—as in Proposition 187—can certainly be interpreted as an attempt to reduce tax burdens as much as an effort to violate *rights*. The discrimination inherent in such a law may have far less to do with animosity or prejudice toward any particular racial or ethnic group than with a legitimate debate over the concept of citizenship and what it means to be part of the American body politic. Americans who support "English only" rules generally do so because they do not believe that they should be required to pay, with tax dollars, for foreign language use or classroom instruction.

I do not necessarily approve of any of these policy decisions, but it is odd to describe any of them as jeopardizing *rights*—at least in the Lockean sense in which rights have been traditionally understood. The Supreme Court's ready willingness in *Romer* to attribute support for such measures to bigotry and ignorance—a readiness shared by many scholars—is disturbing. If this is the reaction of legal "elites" to the public's efforts to reduce the role of government in their lives and to limit government encroachments on their traditional rights, the public will likely grow more suspicious of courts, legal scholarship, and government generally.

Nor should one assume that these traditional rights do not benefit minorities. Gays, too, pay a price for including sexual orientation as a forbidden grounds of discrimination. If the Boy Scouts are a public accommodation that must include gay scoutmasters, can gay organizations any longer exclude heterosexuals? Can gay bars refuse to hire heterosexual servers? If employees or guests joke about the "breeders" hired, will the bar be subject to "hostile environment" charges?

Many homosexuals, of course, have no difficulty accepting the logical implications of these questions—just as the majority of heterosexuals rarely concern themselves with the sexual preferences of others. One size does not fit all, however. *Romer* is a long-term defeat for gays because it affirms that sexual orientation *is* the public's business; efforts such as Amendment 2 to make it a purely private affair between consenting adults—whether lovers, landlords and tenants, or employers and employees—now violate the Equal Protection Clause. Where such personal matters are the public's business, no minority group can rest easy. In short, *Romer* further erodes respect for the concepts of enumerated powers, individual rights, and federalism. As such, it promotes further incursions on minority rights.

CONCLUSION

Critics now voicing concern about plebiscites have expressed little concern over ballot proposals to regulate handguns, although the Second Amendment explicitly protects the right of the people to keep and bear arms. These critics applaud initiatives aimed at limiting political speech in the name of campaign finance reform, although the First Amendment explicitly protects the right of free speech. They show relatively little concern when plebiscites are used to artificially lower prices on insurance or other goods, depriving stockholders of much of the value of their property, although the Fifth Amendment explicitly states that private property shall not be taken without compensation. Such policies may be good. The Constitution may even allow them—although millions of Americans think, with some justification, that it does not. When certain rights with clear textual basis in the Constitution are ignored by courts and scholars, however, while proposals are made to ban plebiscites because of the perception that they somehow tread on "rights" that have no obvious textual basis in the Constitution, millions of people rightly conclude that the Constitution is being purposefully interpreted in a politically partisan manner (see Barnett 1995).

Madison thought that representative government was superior to direct democracy in part because the former might offer more security for minorities (Macey 1994; Eule 1991). Perhaps, however, a more important check on majorities was the concept of enumerated powers, which is now rarely respected by legislators and barely enforced by the Supreme Court. Another check was the Bill of Rights, yet the Court has refused to enforce these rights equally—providing little protection to gun and property owners while granting what often appears to be stronger protection to topless dancers and atheists. The Ninth and Tenth Amendments, which reserve all unenumerated rights to the people and the states, are virtually ignored. This judicial slackness, aided by the complicity of many legal scholars, has fed the enormous growth in government. This growth has raised taxation to record levels and has steadily infringed on traditional, common law liberties. Adding insult to injury, the theory of jurisprudence apparently adopted in *Romer* holds that even a modest effort to reassert limits on government power can only be the result of animus toward those who would use government to coerce others.

Enumerated powers and the Bill of Rights were intended to take certain issues out of the political arena and to protect minority rights by limiting the ability of majorities to invoke the coercive power of government. Those checks have largely broken down. Everyone who cares deeply about minority rights should beware. With the erosion of traditional checks on majority power, if the majority cannot remove issues from the political process—as Amendment 2 attempted to do—it will surely find a way to enact its preferences through the political process, whether by plebiscite or other means. Therein lies the true threat to minority rights.

ENDNOTES

1. Direct democracy takes two forms. A referendum originates within a state's legislative body. The legislature places the proposal on the ballot, or, in some states, the citizenry may by petition demand a vote to repeal legislation passed by the legislature. An initiative originates with the "people"; a percentage of the electorate (usually 5 to 10 percent of those voting in the previous election) may propose a law or constitutional amendment, which is placed on the ballot for an up or down vote. Twenty-six states provide for at least one of these procedures; twenty-two provide for referenda and initiatives.
2. For the most part, direct democracy is little more than an adjunct to the legislative process for passing laws. In most states that allow for plebiscites, the vast majority of laws are passed by the legislature.
3. A bare majority of legislators can defeat legislation. If each of these legislators is elected by a bare majority of voters, then a little more than 25 percent of voters will elect a majority of that house of the legislature. This is particularly true for minorities covered by the Voting Rights Act because the Act, as interpreted by the courts, requires some "packing" of these minority voters into "majority-minority" districts. A majority-minority district is one in which election of a member of the minority group is likely because the district includes a substantial majority of minority voters. Because minorities usually win these majority-minority seats by large margins, the minority group's total electoral support must substantially exceed 25 percent before it could elect a majority of the legislature (*Thornburg v. Gingles*, 478 U.S. 30 (1986)).
4. The question of the extent to which intensity of opposition ought to be considered is old—ranging from the unrestrained majoritarianism of Rousseau, on the one hand, to proposals that no legislation should be passed or tax collected, absent unanimous consent, on the other. For the purposes of this chapter, I ask the reader's indulgence that some consideration of intensity of feeling is probably desirable, leaving aside the vital question of how much such intensity should be indulged by the majority.
5. Hamilton ([1788] 1961, 443) argues that the veto power would normally be used when the legislature acted against the will of the people generally.
6. In *Hunter v. Erickson* the Supreme Court struck down an Akron city ordinance that required a popular vote before any legislation could be passed to remedy

discrimination on the basis of race, religion, or ancestry. In *Washington v. Seattle School District No. 1,* the Court struck down a Washington law prohibiting local school districts from making school assignments in certain manners calculated to remedy past discrimination. In *Reitman v. Mulkey* the Court struck down a California constitutional provision that affirmatively allowed private discrimination on the basis of race. In each case, the Court struck down the law involved because it singled out a suspect class for discriminatory treatment.

··· 11 ···

A Thornton *in the Side: Term Limits,* Representation, *and the* Problem *of* Federalism

Jeff Polet

In the movie *Monty Python and The Holy Grail*, King Arthur happens upon a few peasants slopping muck in a field. Identifying himself as their king, Arthur soon finds himself in the awkward position of explaining to members of an "anarchical commune" why they ought to obey him. He regales them with the familiar story of Excalibur being presented to him by the Lady of the Lake, only to be taunted with the rejoinder that "supreme executive power comes from a mandate from the masses, not some farcical aquatic ceremony."

The notion of popular sovereignty remains one of the foundational ideas of our system of government—one we embrace at the youngest of ages. Belief in popular sovereignty is so deeply ingrained that it remains largely unquestioned, or its complexities unreflected upon, until much later in life. Small wonder, really, that many of us become cynical when we discover the "real" story of our representative institutions, which drastically skew our earlier untroubled ideas. We like our soup thin; complexity creates confusion, confusion creates indifference, and indifference creates a public hardly able to stand up to the rigors of democratic governance. The founders of this country understood well that a public untutored in the exigencies of democratic governance, a public not in possession of the virtues necessary to its functioning, would be unable to sustain such an experiment. One of the great questions of our regime was how to educate the public into responsible citizenry; one of the answers to this question was that uniquely American political hybrid—federalism.

221

FEDERALISM AND REPRESENTATIVE DEMOCRACY

Few of us are taught to think about federalism anymore. The idea seems archaic—a remnant of a distant and often oppressive past. If anything, we are likely to think about it negatively. Didn't federalism lead to the Civil War? Didn't it produce Jim Crow laws and segregation? Isn't it awkward and inefficient? Isn't it out of step with an economy that demands greater centralization, or with a technological age whose tele-communications, transportation, and market capabilities render state borders obsolete? Does it fit a public that shifts constantly across borders? If we think about federalism, we see it as part of a world well lost, the stock-in-trade of reactionary politicians who use the rhetoric of federalism to divest the federal government of its power and return power to the often backward politics of the states and localities. Federalism is the last refuge of political scoundrels who are unwilling to keep in step with the times.

Still, evidence suggests federalism is not dead. Recently, the Republican Party has successfully trumpeted a new federalism as part of its electoral strategy. Today more than ever, bright and creative governors are producing fascinating and impressive results with bold and often narrow policies. Indeed, the best governing in this country today arguably occurs in state capitals, not in Washington; when potential presidential candidates are discussed, most pundits look to governors' mansions, not Congress. Cities also are asserting greater responsibility for governing themselves, with impressive results.[1]

Although federalism in practice still possesses vitality, the theory of federalism is less well off. Seldom discussed in textbooks and its principles rarely debated, federalism appears moribund. This circumstance reflects a larger problem in our government: an unwillingness to invoke constitutional justifications when discussing policy issues. It is as if King Arthur had told the peasants, "Who cares why I'm your king? Just obey." When policy separates from any constitutional justification, obedience to the policy becomes a simple matter of coercion—which in the long run is likely to prove very unstable indeed.

If we cannot count on our schools or our books to teach us about the rigors of constitutionalism and the problems of federalism, to whom can we turn? In the past, one might have hoped that the president would use his pulpit to school the public. Instead, our presidents now typically use the rhetorical power of their office to provide us with laundry lists of services they will try to deliver. Interestingly, it has fallen to the Supreme Court to be the "Republican schoolmaster" the public requires (Wilson and Masugi 1998, Part I). There are certain obvious benefits to this situation; given the complexities of constitutional democracy, sorting through conflicting claims and issues requires much deliberation and judgment—qualities more political branches exhibit in tainted form.

Then, too, there is the issue of the nature of representative democracy. In this century, the Supreme Court has operated with a more plebiscitary view of democracy that is not particularly hospitable to mediating institutions. In fact, issues of federalism and representation closely dovetail with one another and, in practice, create a polity that individuates thinly and collectivizes thickly. It is the thesis of this chapter that the Court's ruling on Congressional term limits badly misconstrued the meaning of federalism, as well as the nature and purpose of democratic governance. It operated with a poor theory of representative democracy that demonstrated "little appreciation for the variable of collectives in the electoral equation, either in giving significance to individual voting rights or in engendering meaningful representation through participation" (Ryden 1996, 33). The Court's decision was grounded in two ideas: It saw the Constitution as a coherent and simple doctrine about politics, and its notion of politics was dismissive of the inherent and insoluble problems of democratic governance. Although the justices do have a theory of politics, it is poorly attuned to the ironies, ambiguities, and troubling contradictions of a constitutional system that refuses to bend immediately to public will.

Americans are socialized from an early stage to think of the Constitution as a venerable document—a document so well constructed that it would become a model for all nations (Richards 1996). Likewise, the founders are regarded as once-in-a-millennium geniuses who created a document of unparalleled efficacy. We believe that the Constitution embodies a coherent theory of politics and that proper interpretation of the Constitution involves understanding its meaning in light of the intentions of those who drafted it. We like to think of the law—despite our misperceptions of the behavior of lawyers—as a clean and tidy mechanism for maintaining order, devoid of ambiguity. Likewise, the Constitution, if interpreted properly, is expected to provide clear, incontrovertible answers to the problems we face.

Experience, on the other hand, teaches us that the meaning of the Constitution is anything but clear; that interpretation is anything but straightforward; that federalism is an awkward and, in many ways, poorly constructed system; that the doctrine of original intent (that is, that meaning is derived from understanding the intentions of the author) is not unambiguous; and that American law rests on an interesting paradox: Although premising itself on the rejection of tradition and any binding authority it might have, it generates within itself a necessary respect for tradition and authority. When the framers of the Constitution created their "new order for the ages" (MacDonald 1985), they operated with the assumption that political order could best be created and maintained when it was based on the sentiments of "the small and arrogant oligarchy of those who merely happened to be walking about." MacDonald argues that the making of the Constitution was "simultaneously a conservative and a radical act" (MacDonald 1985, 261), with the introduction of federalism the most radical element. Likewise, Madison wrote:

> But why is the experiment of an extended republic to be rejected merely because it may comprise what is new? Is it not the glory of the people of America that, whilst they have paid a decent regard to the opinions of former times and other nations, they have not suffered a blind veneration for antiquity, for custom, or for names, to overrule the suggestions of their own good sense, the knowledge of their own situation, and the lessons of their own experience? (*Federalist 14*)

One recognizes in this perspective one of the essential aspects of American culture—namely, the dominating influence of Protestantism, which itself is perpetually troubled by a founding event that involves the rejection of the authority of tradition. Like Protestantism, American political thinking has sought to resolve this problem of the authority of tradition by locating authority solely within a sacred text, with the same resulting problem. Problems of order are poorly resolved because of the conflicting and arbitrary nature of interpretation. Although this interpretation is a bit one-sided, it demonstrates the paradoxical nature of constitutional law.

FEDERALISM (MIS)APPLIED:
U.S. TERM LIMITS, INC. V. THORNTON

These issues are neither dead nor dormant in American politics. The way the Supreme Court resolves them has an enormous effect on the actual shape of the polity. One often finds remarkable things in unexpected places—a surprising example being the Court's decision in *U.S. Term Limits Inc. v. Thornton,* 514 U.S. 779 (1995). In *Thornton,* the Court ruled on the constitutionality of a term limits amendment to the Arkansas constitution. The amendment prohibited candidate(s) who had already served three terms in the U.S. House of Representatives or two terms in the U.S. Senate from appearing on the ballot for another term in that body.

On the face of it, the *Thornton* case would seem to be an unusual time for the Court to exercise its role as "constitutional schoolmarm." The sharp disagreement between the majority and the dissent reveals a great deal, however, about the fundamental tension and incompleteness of American politics—a system whose most distinguishing characteristic is its peculiar ambivalence regarding the ends we seek to make it serve (McClay 1996). Less important is the issue of term limits than "the means the Court used to come to this conclusion" (Heintz 1997, 693). Not only is the particular policy at issue; so too are ideas about the nature of American constitutionalism. In this instance, members of the Court staked out extreme positions in an attempt to give particular shape to the American political landscape.

The well-established maxim of interpretation would have judges avoid pronouncing on issues not germane to the case; in other words, judges should not go to places where they need not go. The Supreme Court's ruling in *Thornton* violates this principle. Rather than deciding the issue on its simple merits—perhaps as a ballot access case—the Court instead turned the case into a referendum on the nature of federalism, the meaning of the Tenth Amendment, and the basic principles of democracy. The most interesting aspect of this sojourn into political theory, however, is that the Court (both the majority and the dissent) relies on the very nontheoretical assumption that political problems admit of some final and formulaic resolution. As one observer writes, "What is at stake in this debate is not a mere matter of politics; it is a search for the ambiguous dividing line between state and federal power in cases of implied preclusion—in a sense, a search for the missing piece in the federal framework—a piece that is wrongly presumed to exist" (Richards 1996, 569–70).

In other words, although the Supreme Court may be operating with a theory of politics, it is not particularly conversant in political theory. Typically that is not a problem unless the Court decides that it can safely venture into those waters. There is a difference between a Court that operates within the constitutional framework and one that decides that it has a privileged understanding of that framework, defining it from without. In the latter case, the picture of the Constitution becomes distorted; allowing the Court to exercise exclusive definition of the American political landscape is akin to giving Hollywood the sole voice in defining American culture.

This assessment of the Supreme Court's behavior departs from the facile juxtaposition of judicial activism and judicial restraint. Neither of those terms illuminates much with regard to judicial behavior. For example, as the Court was striking down the Arkansas term limits amendment, it also was striking down a law criminalizing the possession of handguns at schools (*United States v. Lopez*, 115 S. Ct. 1624 (1995)). Both cases dealt with the relationship between the federal government and the states. Whereas the *Thornton* dissenters could best be characterized as "restraintists," however, the dissenters in *Lopez* would have to be classified as activists (Wilson and Masugi 1998, 224; Schwartz 1996). Those terms typically merely cover the political preferences of the particular judge; they do not tell us what those political preferences might be.

The issue is further complicated if the Supreme Court decides to substitute theorizing for judgment, rather than seeing the close interplay between the two. The doctrinaire interpretation of the Constitution, manifest in the sibling doctrines of restraintism and activism, acts as a broadsword rather than a stiletto, ignoring the ambiguity and duplicity of the law. David Nichols writes:

> In interpreting the constitutional powers and limits of the national government, both conservatives and liberals too often retreat to standards that require no judgment. . . . They supply a rule which takes the place of judgment. But we can apply such rules only when we believe that there are no competing claims to be reconciled and only when we believe there is no ambiguity in the character of the law or in its application to particular circumstances. We turn to such rules only when we fail to recognize that the role of the judge is based not just on the principle of the rule of law but also on the recognition of the limits of the rule of law (Wilson and Masugi 1998, 215–16).

To the extent that the Supreme Court is judging, then, it does so backwards—moving from the conclusion to the premises. Judges often operate by feelings and hunches rather than judgment and rational thinking, drawing on the body of history and precedent to justify their decisions. With this background in mind, we can turn to the substance of the Court's ruling in *Thornton*.

The people of Arkansas passed, 60 percent to 40 percent, an amendment to their state constitution that would bar incumbents who had spent three terms in the U.S. House of Representatives or two terms in the U.S. Senate from appearing on the ballot for another term in the house in which they served. The trial court held that the amendment violated Article I of the U.S. Constitution, which sets out qualifications for U.S. Representatives and Senators.[2] The state Supreme Court held that length of service in Congress amounted to another qualification for not holding office (the clause in the Constitution is phrased in the negative—though neither the dissent nor the majority was inclined to make anything of that). It affirmed the lower court finding of unconstitutionality. Term limits proponents argued Amendment 73 was not a disqualification from office but a ballot-access measure because the candidate could still win office in a write-in campaign. The purpose of the amendment was to level the playing field between incumbents and challengers; therefore, proponents argued, it served a valid public interest.

THE COURT SPEAKS

The U.S. Supreme Court heard the case in November 1994 and ruled in May 1995. Justice Stevens delivered the opinion for the five-member majority, with a concurring opinion by Justice Kennedy. Justice Thomas dissented, delivering what may be his most impressive opinion to date—a long, sprawling overview of American constitutionalism, joined by Chief Justice Rehnquist and Justices O'Connor and Scalia. The majority opinion was predicated on the need for a uniform national legislature (Wellington 1996); the dividing issue between the majority and the dissent turned on the nature of the federal legislature and the question of whose legislature it is. Justice Stevens remarked that the framers envisioned "a uniform National Legislature representing the people of the United States" (*U.S. Term Limits, Inc., v. Thornton*, 514 U.S., at 822). Thomas rejoined that "the ultimate source of the Constitution's authority is the consent of the people of each individual State, not the consent of the undifferentiated people of the Nation as a whole." (*U.S. Term Limits, Inc., v. Thornton*, 514 U.S., at 846). This issue implicates the nature of the federal experiment—it is as old as the nation itself and apparently still has not been resolved, even by the Civil War. The case involved two foundational principles of constitutional democracy: the nature of representation and the Constitution as a creation of the states as opposed to American citizens.

Even more important than the idea of uniformity, according to Stevens, was "the fundamental principle of our representative democracy"—namely, that "the people should choose whom they please to govern them" (*U.S. Term Limits, Inc., v. Thornton*, 514 U.S., at 795). This principle comprised two parts, according to Stevens. One part was the egalitarian belief that elections should be open to all. The second part was the belief that the people who choose whomever they want to govern them are understood here as the undifferentiated group of Americans. To the majority, these two parts are the bedrock of American constitutionalism. Nowhere does the Supreme Court engage in a reflection about the nature of democracy as a representative system.

The Constitution, Justice Stevens argued, is an exclusive source of office qualifications, which cannot be added to or subtracted from. This exclusivity guarantees that the states could not undermine the national legislature by setting qualifications at a level at which no candidate could possibly be elected. Granting this power to the states would put the national government at the mercy of the states. "In our view," Stevens wrote, "it is inconceivable that the Framers would provide a specific Constitutional provision to ensure that federal elections would be held while at the same time allowing States to render those elections meaningless by simply answering that no candidate could be qualified for office." The Constitution, he continued, "nullifies sophisticated as well as simpleminded modes" of undermining its principles (*U.S. Term Limits, Inc., v. Thornton*, 514 U.S., at 811).

FEDERALISM: THE MAJORITY VIEW

In so arguing, however, Justice Stevens postulated a theory of federalism that can hardly be called federalism at all. It is more nationalist in scope than that envisioned by any of the Framers—Hamilton included. Stevens asserted that representatives in the national legislature owe allegiance not to the people of the state or to political parties but to "the people of the nation" (*U.S. Term Limits, Inc., v. Thornton*, 514 U.S., at 822). Members of Congress have a direct relationship with the nation as a whole. Whatever the merits of the historical argument Stevens makes—and it is quite detailed—this claim alone is surprising to anyone familiar with the arguments of the Constitutional Convention or the text of the Constitution itself.[3]

Certainly, the Constitution is more nationalist in scope than contemporary anti-federalists might concede. An interesting, though problematic, reflection on these issues appears in Brinkley, Polsby, and Sullivan (1997). The authors argue that the anti-federalists "lost the constitutional battle at the end of the eighteenth century. Nothing has changed in two centuries to make them right at this stage" (Brinkley, Polsby, and Sullivan 1997, 14). This claim begs analysis at two levels. First, it is not clear that the anti-federalists lost in the sense that their ideas were negated, either historically or Constitutionally; many concessions had to be made, after all. To argue that the anti-federalists lost would be to deny the tension still present in American politics. Moreover, much has happened in the past two centuries that validates the anti-federalist views. Term limits were discussed at the Constitutional Convention—the Articles of Confederation, after all, did contain a term limit provision—but they were ultimately left out because incumbency was thought to be more advantageous to the government and the states. The new government needed stability more than anything. Two centuries later, stability is not the problem; entrenchment is. In this situation, term limits make more sense (Klarman 1997).

Furthermore, the Supreme Court has long had a legitimate role to play in protecting minority rights. In *Thornton*, however, the Court missed an opportunity to protect majority rights without significantly infringing on minority rights. One commentator, reflecting on the democratizing tendencies of term limits, was prompted to declare the Court's ruling an "outrage" (Klarman 1997, 513).

Indeed, the majority almost seems to treat incumbents as a suspect classification entitled to equal protection under the Fourteenth Amendment (Zywicki 1994, 138). Even in that case, however, term limits probably would have been overturned because laws rarely pass the strict scrutiny test[4] employed under the Fourteenth Amendment.

In fact, if the debate is over the nature of democratic principles, as Justice Stevens suggests, then one could plausibly postulate that term limits are as democratic as the current system, if not more so. Elhauge, Lott, and Manning (1997) argue that term limits would lower entry barriers and relieve the pressure to keep the incumbent. Moreover, it is ironic to overturn an amendment supported by 60 percent of the people, and overwhelmingly favored in opinion polls, in the name of the principle that people should be free to choose. The Supreme Court seemed to be saying that people may not put constraints on themselves. In the process, it created confusion about what counts as a democratic principle or what popular sovereignty is (Heintz 1997, 693).

The Supreme Court in *Thornton* made an ends of what is only a means, revealing the formal way in which it construes democracy. In short, the emphasis on egalitarianism and public choice are in fact foreign ideas grafted onto the Constitution, not ideas fundamental to its construction. One need only consider the peculiarity of elections to the House as compared with all the other branches of government to see the point. Even election to the House was not fully majoritarian or egalitarian.

Furthermore, nowhere in either the majority or the dissenting opinions is there any reflection on the nature of representation or the role of mediating groups in the process. The dissent, perhaps, comes a little closer by stressing the role of the states within the federal system, but even there no attention is given to the role of parties or other groups in shaping a theory of representation (Ryden 1996, chapter 1). The oversight is not just the Court's, however; commentators also miss this aspect of the Court's decision.[5] This omission is particularly notable because the potential effect of term limits on associational rights (one assumes this means the parties) was raised during oral arguments.

THE DISSENT: BRING BACK THE STATES

Whereas the majority in *Thornton* leans too heavily toward nationalism and individualism, the dissent errs in the other direction. In Justice Thomas's view, the union is purely an abstraction—a relationship of convenience between the states. "The notion of popular sovereignty," Thomas wrote, "that undergirds the Constitution does not erase state boundaries, but rather tracks them" (*U.S. Term Limits*, 514 U.S., at 849). The electoral college, the elections of Senators by state legislatures, and Article VII's requirement of state ratification all indicate that the Constitution was created by the states, not the people of the United States. Indeed, Madison argued in *Federalist 39*:

> That it will be a federal and not a national act, as these terms are understood by the objectioners—the act of the people, as forming

so many independent States, not as forming one aggregate nation—is obvious from this single consideration: that it is to result neither from the decision of a *majority* of the people of the Union, nor from a *majority* of the States. It must result from the *unanimous* assent of the several States that are parties to it, differing no otherwise from their ordinary assent than in its being expressed, not by the legislative authority, but by the people themselves. Were the people regarded in this transaction as forming one nation, the will of the majority of the whole people of the United States would bind the minority. . . . Each State, in ratifying the Constitution, is considered as a sovereign body independent of all others, and only to be bound by its own voluntary act.

Justice Thomas insisted that congressional override could only be applied when the states could not be trusted to support the federal government. In this instance, however, the states were merely trying to narrow the field of candidates to make the electoral process manageable (*Storer v. Brown*, 415 U.S. 724 (1974)), not to undermine the federal government. Indeed, Thomas argued, there is a world of difference between a self-imposed restraint and one that comes from above. Although the states do not possess "unbridled power" with regard to the authority given them in Article I, section 4, to regulate elections, they do have significant leeway in seeking to make elections fair. It is not clear then, that any right is violated by the term limits amendment, nor that the power of the federal government is threatened.[6] Only abstract principles of governance are brought into question. Again, this assessment is not really judgment but pontification.

CLASHING VIEWS OF THE TENTH AMENDMENT

Although notions of federalism and popular sovereignty drove the decision in *Thornton*, the key to the debate is the nature of the Tenth Amendment reservations of powers to the states. Justices Stevens and Thomas develop hard-line interpretations of the Tenth Amendment—neither of which does particular justice to its complexity. For Stevens, the Tenth Amendment only referred to powers enjoyed by the states prior to ratification of the Constitution. The states gained no new powers after ratification, nor were all previous powers assumed to survive. This analysis, as one commentator noted, is an entirely new Tenth Amendment rule (Schwartz

1996, 522). Among other things, it ignores the fact that many of the states did impose additional qualifications after ratification.

Justice Thomas, on the other hand, takes an equally radical approach to the Tenth Amendment. If a power is neither specifically given to the federal government nor specifically denied the states by the text of the Constitution, then the states enjoy that power. "The Federal government and the States," Thomas writes, "thus face different default rules: Where the Constitution is silent about the exercise of a particular power—that is, where the Constitution does not speak either expressly or by necessary implication—the Federal government lacks the power and the States enjoy it." Thomas overstates his case, however; in his view, the states could constantly tinker with the national government so long as such tinkering is not explicitly forbidden by the Constitution.

The balance was most notably addressed by the Court in the seminal case *McCulloch v. Maryland*, 17 U.S. 316 (1819), where Justice Marshall granted a broad sweep of power to the federal government via the "necessary and proper" clause of Article I, section 8. Justice Stevens's opinion in *Thornton* drew on Marshall's ruling, as well as the commentaries of Justice Joseph Story, whose *Commentaries on the Constitution* were a comprehensive attempt to create a national legal culture. In using Marshall and Story, however, Stevens drew upon the two men who were probably the most nationalist in orientation of anyone from early American history. This approach gives the majority's decision a decidedly nationalist, but not necessarily balanced, flavor.

The Federalist Papers are inconclusive on this issue. Madison and Hamilton were careful enough thinkers to realize that the problem admits of no easy solution. Candidate qualifications were a contentious issue at the Constitutional Convention (Farrand 1966, Vol. I, 217); the issue was not definitively settled even on completion of the text. Hamilton noted in *Federalist 59* that "if the state legislatures were to be invested with an exclusive power of regulating these elections, every period of making them would be a delicate crisis in the national situation." At the same time, he realized in *Federalist 60* that the interest of the states would be such that they would not want to undermine the federal electoral process and that giving too much power in this regard to the federal government would benefit certain sectors of society—notably, the wealthy, landed classes. The nationalist Hamilton believed that the federal government should not be given too much authority in regulating elections, because it would negatively affect local governance. Hamilton notes that the qualifications of the representatives to be chosen "are fixed in the Constitution, and are unalterable by the legislature."

Note once again the absence of a fixed point of historical reference on this issue; the writers of *The Federalist Papers* and the participants at the Constitutional Convention realized that federalism was an unfinished project that did not admit of formulaic resolution. Clearly, however, their idea of the importance of the states superseded our own. Thus, Justice Thomas probably gets the better of the historical argument, though it cannot be called an outright victory (Schwartz 1996, 524).

The debate in *Thornton* further turned on whether term limits are considered a qualifications issue or a ballot access measure. Justice Thomas refused to acknowledge that term limits constitute a further qualification. Even if they were, Thomas argued that the qualifications clause of the First Amendment was a floor, not a ceiling. The constitutional language was not meant to be exclusive; otherwise, Article VI would not have needed to stipulate that a religious test could not be used as a qualification. Moreover, many states added further qualifications after ratification—most notably, property qualifications. Any decision that regulates in any manner state restrictions on candidates would then become eligible for review. By focusing on the qualifications clause, the Supreme Court opened another realm of potential jurisprudence, including revisiting the much litigated redistricting cases. Such an analysis would also mean that states could not insist that candidates be mentally fit for office or have no criminal record.

To the majority, the measure appeared to be a ballot access restriction. To Stevens, the issue had more to do with "fundamental principles of democracy" than additional qualifications or the power of the states (*U.S Term Limits*, at 819). The issue was who may and who may not be included on the ballot. The Supreme Court had already ruled that the states do have a legitimate interest in regulating the ballot and narrowing the field of candidates. Allowing restriction of incumbents, however, would be the first step toward subverting the federal government altogether. Justice Stevens found it "inconceivable" that the framers would have insisted elections be held but allow states enough regulatory power "to render those elections meaningless by simply ensuring that no candidate could be qualified for office" (*U.S Term Limits*, at 811). Of course, that analysis pushes the logic of the Arkansas amendment much further than necessary. The majority appeared only interested in "whether state-imposed term limits are in a continuum with Armageddon (here, state refusal to hold federal elections at all), and not whether Armageddon was near at hand" (Sullivan 1995, 98).

Representation, and the right to control representation, Justice Stevens argued, belongs solely in the hands of the people of the United States. His analysis leaves no room for state limitations or other mediating agencies, such as political parties. *Thornton* is a strange decision in comparison to other ballot access cases. Typically, these cases involve candidates with little name recognition and shallow support. They deal with restrictions that confuse or attenuate meaningful choices for the populace. Incumbents, however, tend to have high name recognition and broad support, and no court has yet recognized them as a suspect class worthy of Fourteenth Amendment protection. Yet the majority in *Thornton* implies that incumbents may well be a protected class by insisting that it is as wrong to deny rights indirectly (here, the right to run for office) as it is to deny rights directly. Term limits proponents assert that those rights were not denied because the incumbent could still launch a write-in campaign. As Thomas demonstrates, moreover, incumbents who engage in write-in campaigns or are well funded tend to have a fairly high success rate.

The point behind term limits restrictions, though, is the belief is that the advantages of incumbency are so pronounced that challengers have little chance of winning the election. The purpose of Amendment 73, according to Justice Thomas, was to level the playing field and thus make the electoral process freer and more equitable (one of the fundamental principles espoused by Justice Stevens). Thomas writes:

> [N]o one knows exactly how large of an electoral benefit comes with having been a long-term Member of Congress, and no one knows exactly how large an electoral disadvantage comes from forcing a well-funded candidate with high name recognition to run a write-in campaign. But the majority does not base its holding on the premise that Arkansas has struck the wrong balance. Instead, the majority holds that the Qualifications Clauses preclude Arkansas from trying to strike any balance at all. . . . The majority would apparently reach the same result even if one could demonstrate at trial that the electoral advantage conferred by Amendment 73 upon challengers precisely counterbalances the electoral advantages conferred by federal law upon long-term members of Congress. (at 924)

The Supreme Court, Justice Thomas argues, was insensitive to the actual exigencies of political practice in the name of abstract principles and thus skewed the constitutional balance of federalism and representation. Heintz (1997, 684) writes: "By allowing members of Congress to use federal resources to keep themselves in office, and thus possibly keeping out the most capable women and men from these offices, the Court left the *states* at the mercy of the *federal* government" (emphasis in original).

Whereas the majority characterized any qualifications restriction as a step toward the destruction of the federal government, the dissent sees any resistance to such restrictions as an opening of the doors to criminals and the mentally infirm and the elimination of state autonomy. One could argue, however, that if the states want to allow their citizens to elect mentally infirm persons or convicted criminals, there is no reason why they should be forbidden from doing so. It is highly unlikely, of course, that such a thing might ever happen. The problem is that the majority and the dissent regard candidates on the ballot as individuals being elected by abstract collectives of people. They do not see candidates as the results of processes controlled and operated by the political parties. One would think, therefore, that if meaningful term limits reform ever comes about, it will come about within party regulations.

FORMAL VERSUS FUNCTIONAL FEDERALISM

The majority and the dissent in *Thornton* share a very formalistic understanding of federalism. They treat the separation and division of power as fixed and absolute. A more nuanced understanding might be the "functionalist" interpretation. This pragmatic approach to federalism insists only that it stay true to the anti-tyranny rationale at the heart of federalism (Sullivan 1995, 93). Federalism is not a finished doctrine but a pragmatic balance. Wellington has described the Supreme Court's all-or-nothing approach as "derived from some highly abstract propositions about American government, for example, federalism and democratic principles, reinforced by the problematic use of snippets of historically questionable evidence" (Wellington 1996, 841). Justice Stevens argued that any state-imposed restriction is a violation of federalism. In this view, all restrictions—whether against criminals, neophytes, or people with red hair—are equally invidious, and the federal government is fully immune from any such action. Justice Thomas, in contrast, would allow the states more or less untrammeled power to restrict the ballot.

A more functionalist argument would stress that the mixed powers of the federal government and the states, not some clear separation, might have followed the anti-entrenchment theory implied in the qualifications clause. Such an analysis would have assessed whether one power was unduly gutting another. It also would have explored whether the autonomy of Congress was being challenged (Sullivan 1995, 100; Klarman 1997, 509–13). Neither the majority nor the dissent, however, seems particularly concerned about how politics or federalism actually works. The justices appear to forget that the Constitution is not a sacred text with a fixed meaning but a compromise document designed to handle pragmatically some of the inherent contradictions of democracy.

Justice Kennedy has emerged as the swing vote on federalism issues and is the only member of the Supreme Court who operates with something akin to this functionalist understanding. Although functionalism is susceptible to accusations of vagueness and indeterminacy, it recognizes that federalism is an incomplete design. The functionalist view is that federalism is not a neat resolution of the problem of sovereignty but a mechanism for learning to live with divided sovereignty. The genius of the founders, according to Kennedy, was "to split the atom of sovereignty," creating a system stable enough to protect individual liberties and flexible enough to respond properly to the given exigencies of the day (*U.S Term Limits*, at 838).

Even Kennedy, however, does not fully understand the difficulties of federalism. Nagel writes: "An aspiration for control by legal prescription is what drives modern Constitutionalism and its derivative, modern nationalism. This aspiration is a profound part of our political culture . . . but it is shaky because in sober moments everyone knows that uncertainty and risk are elementary facts of political life that cannot be expunged by a written code or judicial review" (Nagel, 1996, 834).

In itself, this view is no criticism unless one can make the case for federalism. One must ask what the Supreme Court misses when it ventures into the realm of theory—and, more important, what this approach means for our actual politics. If federalism is still viable, how does the Court undermine it, and what difference does it make? I believe the Court's formalistic assumptions about political equality, derived from plebiscitary assumptions about democracy, subvert the traditional notion of pragmatic constitutionalism. In fact, the Court's stated concern with political equality necessarily diminishes the federalist experiment.

TOWARD AN ENRICHED (AND MORE REPRESENTATIVE) FEDERALISM

Observers of American culture have long lamented—inaccurately—that America is too much of an individualist society. The key insight of liberal politics was the free development of the self; liberal political institutions were designed to encourage such development and protect society from the negative consequences of such development gone awry. Thus, Madison could call government the greatest of all reflections on human nature (*Federalist 51*). Classical republicanism, with its emphasis on small communities, stressed the role of politics in the development of the citizen, and hence of the self. The boldness of the federalist experiment of "extending the sphere" of government built on the advantages of classical republicanism while negating its dangers—its tendency to dissolve into dissolution and strife. At the core of these ideas was the belief that human activity must always be contextualized locally, that virtue operated only in the realm of the concrete, and that citizenship demanded heavy obligations that had to be performed. The abstraction of the nation would prove to be a poor testing ground for the duties of citizenship; only in the immediate community could citizens prove themselves worthy and then move on to larger realms of responsibility.

The relation of the individual to the emerging nationalist government was explored most thoroughly by Alexis de Tocqueville. Tocqueville is often falsely assumed to be a critic of individualism; he actually criticizes privatism. In Tocqueville's analysis, individualism was already a dying idea in the Jacksonian period. Tocqueville believed that as people became more materialistic and more concerned with formal equality, the reality or thickness of social life would get pushed to the fringes—toward the self, on the one hand, and toward the national government on the other. The healthy middle—what social scientists call civil society—would be vacated. For Tocqueville, the situation was analogous to the Protestant epoch in which all the mediating institutions that grant vibrancy, balance, and order to the individual's relationship to God were eschewed in favor of leaving the soul naked in front of an all-powerful deity. Democratic despotism, Tocqueville claimed, was a thorough, widespread despotism that would "degrade men rather than torment them" (Tocqueville 1960, 691). Tocqueville saw America becoming a nation of undifferentiated persons "circling around in pursuit of the petty and banal pleasures with which they glut their souls." They would withdraw into themselves, and although they might "touch" their fellow citizens, "they feel nothing." They would exist only in and for themselves. Tocqueville wrote:

> Over this kind of men stands an immense, protective power which is alone responsible for securing their enjoyment and watching over their fate. That power is absolute, thoughtful of detail, orderly, provident and gentle. It would resemble parental authority if, fatherlike, it tried to prepare its charges for a man's life, but on the contrary, it only tries to keep them in perpetual childhood. . . . It provides for their security, manages their principle concerns, directs their industry, makes rules for their testaments, and divides their inheritances. Why should it not entirely relieve them from the trouble of thinking and all the cares of living? . . . Equality has prepared men for all this, predisposing them to endure it and often even regard it as beneficial. (692)

A strongly nationalized government, according to Tocqueville, will "cover the whole of social life with a network of petty, complicated rules that are both minute and uniform" (1960). Such rules will stifle creativity and individuality and ultimately attenuate the taste for freedom. This power does not destroy, but it prevents things from being born; it does not prohibit, but it does inhibit. It is, says Tocqueville, "not at all tyrannical, but it hinders, restrains, enervates, stifles, and stultifies so much that in the end each nation is no more than a flock of timid and hardworking animals with the government as its shepherd" (1960).

For Tocqueville, governing involved more than figuring out formal mechanisms of administration. It also meant learning how to fan the sacred fire of liberty to develop the self-responsibility of the citizen. The key was "the art of association," by which people would develop a taste for cooperation and the virtues necessary for democratic governance. Tocqueville regarded voluntary association as a way of linking the individual with political community so that self-interest would be transcended and freedom protected. A centralized government, he wrote, does not win "the concurrence of human wills. Men must walk forward in freedom, responsible for their acts" (92).

Federalism was the unique American invention designed to achieve this end. As such, it cannot be treated as an end in itself (the formalist approach) but must be adjudicated with an eye toward its animating principles. In *Federalist 45*, Madison noted that the powers of the federal government "are few and defined," whereas the power of the states "will extend to all objects which, in the ordinary course of affairs, concern the lives, liberties, and properties of the people, and the internal order, improvement, and prosperity of the State."

This discussion may seem far removed from the idea of Congressional term limits. The role of the Supreme Court is not to overturn what it considers bad policy, however.[7] Instead, its task is to decide whether something is constitutional in the sense that it is in keeping with our political traditions and principles. The main thing the Court should have considered was not a poorly balanced federalism, but whether the states and other forms of association can reasonably place restrictions on whom they choose to represent them. Instead of treating the American experiment as a simple relationship between the mass of people and the federal government, the Court should have paid attention to the vast array of mediating institutions that provide reason and direction to American politics. The members of the Court ought to have considered that people learn best how to be citizens when they operate within a narrow public realm and that part of the essence of constitutionalism is the desire of the people to place checks upon themselves. In this case, the Court missed its opportunity to be a good schoolmaster; it put away its book and took out its switch.

ENDNOTES

1. See *Time* magazine (August 18, 1997): "Municipal government has long been regarded as the great back-water of American democracy: a world of political patronage and special-interest jockeying in which policy discussions rarely move beyond synchronizing traffic lights. But a new breed of activist mayors, recently hailed by the *New Republic* as "the Pride of the Cities," has been turning city halls into hothouses of governmental innovation. They are challenging entrenched interests and butting heads with traditional allies in the pursuit of real reform: overhauling the school system in Chicago, reshaping labor-management relations in Philadelphia and privatizing municipal services all over."

2. Article I, section 2, states: "No Person shall be a Representative who shall not have attained to the Age of twenty-five Years, and been for seven years a Citizen of the United States, and who shall not, when elected, be an Inhabitant of that State in which he shall be chosen." The qualifications for Senators differ slightly (thirty years old, nine years as a citizen).

3. Justice Stevens employed some faulty analyses along the way: Because the nation pays the salaries of members of Congress, those representatives are employees of the nation and not the states; the delegation of power runs from the national government to the states, not the other way around.

4. Loveland (1997) suggested the use of this test, in a muddled mess of a piece whose argument seems to rest on two premises/prejudices: (1) Arkansas is a reactionary political backwater, and you can't trust anything people do down there, so the Court should strike down any amendment they pass; and (2) the Rehnquist Court's ultimate goal is to turn back abortion rights, and giving any quarter to the dissent on this issue is a step on that slippery slope. Indeed, Loveland thinks it "manifest absurdity" that the dissent and the majority would seek any authority in the words of the founders—men who "may indeed have been giants . . . within the political culture of their time" but, after all, "condoned slavery, . . . promoted genocidal wars against the Indian population," and did all other kinds of mean things that exclude them from having anything to say to our enlightened present.

   Although Loveland suggests that a rational basis test might come into play, he opts for the strict scrutiny test because he is afraid to allow the people of Arkansas to determine for themselves how they might be ruled. The problem with either of these tests, of course, is that they are rationalizations rather than tests. If a judge wants to strike down a law, he or she will use strict scrutiny; if the judge wants it to stand, she or he will employ the rational basis test. The conclusion comes before the rule.

5. For example, of the twenty-six law review articles I have read concerning this decision, not one mentions the role that political parties might play in the process. This omission is particularly curious given that term limits will obviously favor the "out" party. Only two articles touch on any topic that might be related to the role of representation. Elhauge, Lott, and Manning (1997) argue that the competitive pressures not to impose term limits are so great that it will not happen unless some sort of broad strategy is implemented. Thus, although these authors focus on collective action strategies, they nonetheless ignore the roles that political parties might play in the process; their notion of representation is candidate-driven. Likewise, Rotunda (1996) recommends that instead of dropping names from the ballot, states should require that candidates take a legally binding pledge that they will serve for limited terms——a strategy employed by the electoral college. Again, however, Rotunda fails to link this strategy to the potential role of political parties in determining whose name appears on the ballot. Rotunda, in fact, seems to take party labeling on the ballot as evidence of access restrictions (Rotunda 1996, 211). In fact, reading the literature, one might soon reach the conclusion that candidates do not run under any party label at all, so absent are political parties from the commentary.

6. Another spin on the issue, argued by Swan (1996), is that striking down term limits was in the best interests of the Supreme Court because it was a mechanism for placating Congress.
7. In this case, I am sympathetic to the Court: I think Congressional term limits are bad policy.

··· IV ···

The Court,
the Constitution, and
Election Law: Merging
Practice and Theory

The Supreme Court is sure to remain at the center of efforts to implement political reform. Given the public's skepticism toward parties and
politics, the inexorable push for greater direct input and more democracy
is likely to continue; this trend suggests that the Court will be drawn into
ongoing battles over reforms of the political process.

The constitutionality of other electoral practices are also live issues.
Campaign finance reform (though improbable) remains a possibility; such
reforms would draw an inevitable court challenge. The swirling controversy over soft money means that the constitutional status of political
parties continues to loom. The division on the Supreme Court with regard
to issues of federalism suggests that such issues will be hotly contested in
the future, especially in view of potential changes in the Court's makeup.
The 2000 census and upcoming elections likewise will give the Court
opportunity to clarify its redistricting jurisprudence.

In short, numerous practical political skirmishes are percolating.
Recent history suggests that the Court will continue to find itself in the
maelstrom of practical politics. The Court will have plenty of opportunity
to practice and apply the theories of representation explored in this
book—should it choose to.

Thus, the assessments offered herein are of ongoing topical importance. Part IV of this book attempts to put the wide variety of perspectives
in a broader frame of reference. The two final chapters aim to better
order the array of issues enveloping the Supreme Court and its work in

the realm of election law, in hopes of establishing clearer parameters for ongoing debate.

In chapter 12, Dan Lowenstein categorizes the Supreme Court's work in election law cases according to four possible "theories" that vie for the Court's jurisprudential attention. Lowenstein contends that none of the four theories—pluralism, progressivism, party government, or liberal rights theory—accurately captures Court doctrine as a whole. Instead, the Court selects from these alternative perspectives depending on the circumstances and issues it faces. Lowenstein applauds this approach, arguing that it would constitute an abuse of power if the Court were to go further and impose a single political theory.

The final chapter summarizes the arguments raised in the book within the context of the five themes identified in chapter 1. By fleshing out key points of consensus and divergence, it provides a platform for further dialogue that might edify and inform the Supreme Court's search for the answers to election law doctrine.

The Supreme Court Has No Theory
of Politics—And Be Thankful
for Small Favors

DANIEL H. LOWENSTEIN

As the title of this chapter suggests, I wish to show that the Supreme Court's decisions in election cases reflect no theory of electoral politics, and that this is a good thing. My hypothesis must be qualified, however, because the word *theory* is used in many ways. My claims are more true in some senses of the term than others.

AESTHETICS: THEORY AS RIGOR

Theory is used very loosely in academic circles—legal academic circles, at least—to describe written work that is *scholarly* in some sense. Work so described is often contrasted to *journalistic* or *descriptive* work. Because I believe this comparison is unfair to the best journalism and descriptive writing, I prefer to contrast theoretical work, in this sense, with work that is simply superficial.

Writing that is theoretical in the loose sense is characterized by comprehensive and rigorous analysis, conceptual depth, and intellectual integrity. *Theoretical* is almost a synonym for "good" academic writing—but not quite. Other qualities, such as excellent prose and exhaustive research, contribute to good academic writing but less so to the quality of being theoretical.

In this loose sense, great judges such as Holmes, Brandeis, Frankfurter, and Harlan have produced opinions that in various ways might be described as theoretical. Few observers would argue, however, that judicial decisions routinely are theoretical in this sense. In election law cases before the Supreme Court, only Justice Frankfurter's dissent in *Baker v.*

Carr, 369 U.S. 186 (1962) (an opinion with whose conclusion I disagree), seems to me to come close. Even if more of the Court's election law decisions were theoretical in this sense, that circumstance would not indicate that the Supreme Court as a whole has a theory of politics that underlies the decisions.

The proposition that the Supreme Court's political jurisprudence is nontheoretical in the loose sense is probably relatively noncontroversial. This is not to say, however, that the lack of theory in the loose sense is a good thing. The great judges were great precisely because they wrote *theoretical* opinions, and we are right to value them. Neither, however, is it an especially bad thing that most Court decisions are not theoretical. The value of greatness in judicial decisions, including the qualities that make an opinion theoretical, is akin to an aesthetic value. This is said by no means to denigrate that value. We learn from great judges on many levels, just as we learn from writers of great literature. Greatness can never be widespread, however, and members of the Court have many things to be concerned about besides the elegance of their opinions. We must be satisfied when we get good judgment and reasonably clear guidelines from the Court.

Readers may regard the argument in this section as obvious and trivial. It may be obvious, but there is reason for making it explicit. Theory—in the loose sense used in this section and, often, by legal academics—is like motherhood, baseball, and apple pie: a Good Thing. No one is against rigor, depth, and open-mindedness. Because theory is a Good Thing in one sense and because the different ways in which theory is used are rarely defined with clarity, there is a tendency for the benignity of theory in the loose sense to seep unseen and undeservedly into discussion of theory in the more limited or precise senses to which we now turn. By making the "good" meaning of theory explicit and differentiating it from the other meanings, I hope to minimize the seepage.

APPLICATION: ESTABLISHED THEORIES OF POLITICS

A second sense in which the Supreme Court might be said to have a theory of politics would be if it resolved cases by applying an established theory of politics that is present in the general culture. A *theory of politics*, in this sense, would be a cluster of ideas describing how the political process works—and how it should work. The ideas need not fit together with the mathematical precision that characterizes, say, a model in game theory or statistics, but they ought to have a general coherence.

I believe there are two opposing models that have been pervasive in American political thought and debate: pluralism and progressivism. Each of these models has an important cousin: *party government* in the case of pluralism and *liberal rights theory* in the case of progressivism.[1] If the election law decisions of the Supreme Court reflected any of these theories more or less consistently, we could fairly say that the Court had a theory of politics.

Before demonstrating that the Supreme Court has no theory in this sense, I must concede that it would be possible—at a slightly higher level of generality than that of the theories just mentioned—to describe an established theory of politics that *is* reflected in the Court's decisions. Certain basic principles of democracy are held more or less consensually—for example, that government should serve the interests of the public generally and that it should operate with the consent of the public; that elections are central mechanisms for government to secure the consent of the governed; that a large subset of the general public has the right to vote in elections; that political parties and officeholders who are defeated in elections hand over public office in a peaceful and orderly manner to the electoral victors; that the powers of officeholders are defined by law with fair clarity and that officeholders freely exercise those powers and those powers only; and that all members of the public have the right to speak on matters of public or governmental significance. These and similar ideas constitute a theory of democracy that is nearly universally held in our society.

Supreme Court decisions reflect these common principles, and in that sense the Court does have a theory of politics. A similar set of principles characteristic of fascism, communism, or monarchy would look quite different. The fact that the Court's decisions reflect a generalized belief in democracy, however, is unsurprising and does not help to predict or explain how cases are decided—not because cases would be decided similarly on fascist, communist, or monarchic principles but because cases are not brought or defended on those principles.

The theories of government that are of interest, then, are the four mentioned above. The most pervasive in our culture is *progressivism*.[2] Progressivism sees the basic unit in politics as the individual, who is conceived to be both rational and public spirited. Progressivists do not deny that individuals are sometimes uninterested in politics or self-interested. As an empirical matter, however, progressivists believe that people often have a public interest in politics, and as a normative matter they believe one of the main functions of education is to encourage and cultivate that interest. In the progressivist conception of democracy, candidates debate their sincerely held views on issues of public policy. The people listen to and participate in the debate, rationally consider all of the arguments, and vote accordingly. Representatives, once elected, continue the process in the legislature and in other public offices. That is, they study and debate the merits of each issue and act in accordance with what their reason tells them is in the public interest.

Progressivism's cousin, *liberal rights theory*, is like progressivism in that it takes the individual as the basic unit of analysis. Rights theorists, however, are less concerned than progressivists with reason and public-spiritedness. To the rights theorist, individuals may lead their lives—including their lives as citizens—as they wish. Within the boundaries of those rights, individuals may vote, speak, and otherwise act as they see fit even if their votes, utterances, or actions are irrational or self-interested.[3]

Pluralism rejects or marginalizes each of the three most basic assumptions of progressivism. Pluralists see groups instead of the individual as the basic unit of political analysis. Although pluralists have nothing against rationality, they do not expect most political conflicts to be resolved through rational deliberation. Instead, they expect resolution through a process of conflict and compromise that will reflect the relative power of interested groups. Similarly, pluralists have nothing against public-spiritedness. To the contrary, most pluralist theorists emphasize that for democracy to survive, there must be a substantial consensus within the society that certain ideas and principles reflect the public interest and should command support (Truman 1971; Sorauf 1957). Beyond that consensus, pluralism acknowledges that some groups may form for public-spirited or philanthropic reasons but assumes that groups typically will seek to promote the interests of their own members.

Most pluralists probably also believe in some form or other of *party government*. Whether they believe in this notion because they do not expect most voters to be highly public-spirited most of the time or simply because they have accepted the findings of voter behavioral research, pluralists do not rely on voters to be highly knowledgeable about public issues and candidates for office. Political parties provide a shorthand cue for voters and thereby permit a degree of accountability that is difficult to attain when voters have no easy way to know what candidates stand for or who is responsible for what public policies (Fiorina 1981). In addition, political parties—especially in a two-party system—provide an arena in which coalitions consisting of numerous and diverse interest groups may form. This dynamic helps to assure groups of some representation and encourages them to moderate their demands. For these and other reasons, party government theorists favor institutions that encourage voters and officeholders to think primarily in partisan terms.[4]

We must now consider whether the Supreme Court adheres to any of these theories. Rights theory raises distinct questions, which I consider in the following section. In the remainder of this section, I consider progressivism, pluralism, and party government theory.

The best indication that the Supreme Court is adhering to a political theory would be if its opinions contained ideas and arguments more or less explicitly tracking the theory. On at least a couple of occasions—the reapportionment cases and *Elrod v. Burns,* 427 U.S. 347 (1976)—debates between the justices *have* been cast in terms strikingly reflective of the progressivist, pluralist, and party government models.

Chief Justice Warren, writing for the majority in *Reynolds v. Sims,* 377 U. S. 533 (1964)—in which the Supreme Court ruled that districts for each chamber of each state legislature must be equally populated—cast his argument explicitly in individualist, progressivist terms:

> A predominant consideration in determining whether a State's legislative apportionment scheme constitutes an invidious discrimination violative of rights asserted under the Equal Protection Clause is that the rights allegedly impaired are individual and personal in nature. . . . While the result of a court decision in a state legislative apportionment controversy may be to require the restructuring of the geographical distribution of seats in a state legislature, the judicial focus must be concentrated upon ascertaining whether there has been any discrimination against certain of the State's citizens which constitutes an impermissible impairment of their constitutionally protected right to vote. . . . Legislators represent people, not trees or acres. Legislators are elected by voters, not farms or cities or economic interests. (*Reynolds v. Sims,* 377 U.S. at 561–62).

In sharp contrast to Warren's progressivist view, Justice Stewart's view in the reapportionment cases was grounded solidly on pluralist principles. Stewart agreed with the result in *Reynolds v. Sims* but dissented in the Colorado redistricting case decided the same day. In that dissent, Stewart wrote:

> Representative government is a process of accommodating group interests through democratic institutional arrangements. Its function is to channel the numerous opinions, interests, and abilities of the people of a State into the making of the State's public policy. Appropriate legislative apportionment, therefore, should ideally be designed to insure effective representation in the State's legislature, in cooperation with other organs of political power, of the various groups and interests making up the electorate. In practice, of course, this ideal is approximated in the particular apportionment system of any State by a realistic accommodation of the diverse and often conflicting political forces operating within the State. (*Lucas v. Colorado General Assembly*, 377 U.S. 713, at 749 (1964)

It would be an overstatement to say that the dispute between Chief Justice Warren and Justice Stewart was caused by their commitment to two distinct theories of politics that happened to dictate different results in some of the redistricting cases. Warren's emphasis on the individual nature of the rights at stake probably resulted more from doctrinal than from political theoretical concerns. The reapportionment cases were decided only two years after the Supreme Court had ruled, in *Baker v. Carr*, 369 U.S. 186 (1962), that redistricting controversies are justiciable—that is, that they can be decided by the federal courts. *Baker v. Carr* overruled *Colgrove v. Green*, 328 U.S. 549 (1946), which held that redistricting controversies were nonjusticiable. A plurality in *Colgrove* took the view that a challenge to a redistricting plan amounted to a claim that the system of representation violated Article IV, section 4, of the Constitution, which "guarantee[s] to every state in this union a republican form of government."

The Supreme Court has long held that claims brought under the guarantee clause are nonjusticiable. According to the Court in *Baker*, the fact that guarantee clause claims are nonjusticiable cannot preclude a plaintiff from challenging a districting plan under the equal protection clause. In *Reynolds*, Chief Justice Warren's emphasis on the individual voting rights at stake undoubtedly reflected a desire that the claim should "look like" an equal protection claim rather than a claim of denial of a republican form of government.

Whereas Chief Justice Warren's individualism in *Reynolds* was motivated at least in part by doctrinal rather than political theoretical concerns, Justice Stewart's pluralism was less than pure. Although his emphasis on the group nature of representation could have come out of a pluralist textbook, Stewart's conclusion was rather different: "[S]o long as a State's apportionment plan reasonably achieves, in the light of the State's own characteristics, effective and balanced representation of all the substantial interests, without sacrificing the principle of effective majority rule, that plan cannot be considered irrational." (*Lucas v. Colorado*, 377 U.S., at 751). On largely pluralist grounds, then, Stewart was proposing that federal judges should assess redistricting plans on the decidedly unpluralistic criterion of rationality.

Some pluralist writers have been critical of the Supreme Court's ruling in *Reynolds*. Although this criticism may not be surprising in light of Chief Justice Warren's progressivist reasoning, it is misplaced. These writers have viewed the Court in *Reynolds* as detaching the Madisonian system of countervailing groups and factions from redistricting.[5] Despite *Reynolds*'s progressivist foundation, however, there was no good reason to suppose a priori that the "one person, one vote" rule's constraint on redistricting would fundamentally alter the pluralist process of negotiation and compromise that characterizes legislative redistricting. Considered retrospectively, it certainly has not done so (Cain 1984). Stewart's approach—however well grounded in a pluralist conception of group-based politics—would have been a threat to a pluralist system of districting based on negotiation and compromise by requiring that the *content* of the outcome of such a process be rational. A pluralist would not expect the content to be rational in any sense other than that it is the outcome of a proper democratic process.

Despite these significant qualifications, the grounding of Chief Justice Warren's opinion in progressivist reasoning and of Justice Stewart's in directly opposed pluralist reasoning is impressive. A similar opposition occurred in *Elrod v. Burns*, in which the Supreme Court ruled that traditional patronage problems may violate the First Amendment. Here, Justice Powell grounded his dissenting opinion in party government theory. Justice Brennan's plurality opinion acknowledged the legitimacy of party government concerns but regarded them as outweighed by individualist claims based in progressivist and rights-based theory. Thus, Brennan wrote:

> The illuminating source to which we turn . . . is the system of government the First Amendment was intended to protect, a democratic system whose proper functioning is indispensably dependent on the unfettered judgment of each citizen on matters of political concern. . . . Parties are free to exist and their concomitant activities are free to continue. We require only that the rights of every citizen to believe as he will and to act and associate according to his beliefs be free to continue as well. (*Elrod v. Burns*, 427 U.S. 347, at 372 (1975)).

In contrast to Justice Brennan's emphasis of progressivist over partisan values, Justice Powell's dissent was equally explicit in its advocacy of party government:[6] "Patronage practices broadened the base of political participation by providing incentives to take part in the process, thereby increasing the volume of political discourse in society. Patronage also strengthened parties, and hence encouraged the development of institutional responsibility to the electorate on a permanent basis" (*Elrod*, at 379). If the distinct echoes of prevailing political theories that appeared in the opinions in the reapportionment cases and *Elrod v. Burns* were typical, it would be fair to conclude that theories of politics have played a major role in election law. If the progressivist view regularly prevailed, as in both these instances, it would be fair to conclude that the Court has a theory—namely, progressivism. The reapportionment cases and *Elrod* are not typical in this respect, however. No other instances come to mind in which differences among the justices tracked established political theories to such a degree.

Even absent frequent explicit debate in political theoretical terms, a theory of politics might be attributed to the Supreme Court by inductive reasoning if we could show that the results of election law cases consistently line up with what a particular theory would prescribe. This inquiry is complicated by the fact that theories tend to be rather Delphic in their prescriptions. Thus, as we have seen, the "one person, one vote" rule established by the reapportionment cases has not been nearly as detrimental to pluralist politics as many neo-Madisonians feared. *Tashjian v. Republican Party of Connecticut*, 479 U.S. 208 (1986), provides another example. In that case, the Court ruled that a party could open its primaries to independent voters despite a state statute calling for primaries that were closed to all but party members. Party government enthusiasts were divided between their support for greater autonomy for the parties and their support for closed primaries.

One of the major advantages of an election law jurisprudence that is guided by political theory is that only such jurisprudence supposedly leads to "principled" results because the theory—not the political preferences of individual judges—will determine the outcome of cases. In fact, theories typically do not dictate the outcomes of particular cases, which is one reason we need not regret the Court's lack of a theory. Indeed, anyone who reads much work by theoretically oriented constitutional law scholars will be struck by the remarkable consistency with which the theory favored by a particular scholar yields results in accord with the scholar's political ideology.

Even setting aside this difficulty, the Supreme Court's election law decisions do not line up consistently behind any of the established theories. In a few instances, the Court has engaged in astute analysis leading to results supporting party government. Perhaps the best example is *Storer v. Brown*, 415 U. S. 724 (1974), in which the Court upheld a California statute aimed at preventing "sore losers" in a primary from challenging the party's nominee in the general election. The Court has reached pro-party results in other instances as well, though with less articulate explanations—for example, when it upheld the constitutionality of partisan gerrymandering[7] and antifusion ballot laws (*Timmons v. Twin Cities Area New Party*, 520 U. S. 351 (1997)).

The Supreme Court has by no means taken a consistently pro-party stance, however. As we have seen, party or pluralist concerns were subordinated to progressivist ideas in the patronage cases and, to a lesser degree, in the reapportionment cases. Moreover, the Court's racial gerrymandering cases, though not defensible on progressivist grounds—or, indeed, on any grounds—constitute a significant threat to pluralist and party control of legislative districting in the states (Lowenstein 1998). Often, individual justices have taken positions in different cases that are hard to reconcile with a single theoretical perspective. Thus, Justice Powell articulated a strongly pro-party position in *Elrod v. Burns* but would have permitted judges to determine who should be seated as delegates to a party's national nominating convention in his dissenting opinion in *Democratic Party of the United States v. Wisconsin ex rel LaFollette*, 450 U. S. 107 (1981).

I shall not attempt an exhaustive cataloguing of the Supreme Court's election law decisions to categorize them in terms of their consistency with the established political theories. My sense is that such a canvass, if conducted, would show that the Court tends loosely to favor progressivist ideas—but with numerous exceptions and with occasional strains of pluralism and party government. This assessment hardly amounts to a judgment that the Court has a theory of politics. Instead, it suggests that the Court's thinking about politics is representative of the American political culture generally.

DOCTRINE: RIGHTS-BASED THEORY

In the previous section I identified four established theories of politics that might guide the Supreme Court's election law jurisprudence and attempted to show that three of these theories have not so guided the Court's decision. This analysis leaves what might be the most plausible candidate: the rights-based theory of liberalism.

Most constitutional election law cases arise under provisions of the Constitution that grant individual rights, especially the First Amendment and the equal protection clause.[8] Constitutional doctrine is the more or less detailed set of rules that the Court enunciates for the resolution of constitutional controversies in various areas. Especially in First Amendment jurisprudence, the Court has developed elaborate tests for different subject areas, in a process sometimes referred to as "definitional balancing" (Nimmer 1968). As described recently by one proponent of this approach, "the Court has done its free speech 'balancing' by creating relatively concrete doctrinal structures that help decide when a competing government interest 'outweighs' the free speech value" (Volokh 1997, 168).

If the Supreme Court, following the definitional balancing approach, had developed and more or less consistently adhered to a coherent set of doctrinal rules for deciding election law cases, it might be said to have applied liberal rights theory to election law. No body of doctrine explains more than a fraction of election law cases, however, and much of the doctrine that does exist scores low on the coherency scale.

Some followers of the Supreme Court's recent decisions may wish to put forward the "weighing of factors" test as a unified doctrine for constitutional election law. The Court initially propounded this test in *Anderson v. Celebrezze*, 460 U. S. 780 (1983), in which the justices struck down overly restrictive requirements in Ohio for presidential candidates to qualify for the ballot. In the first such ballot access case to be decided— *Williams v. Rhodes*, 393 U.S. 23 (1968)—the Court had applied "strict scrutiny." This standard can be satisfied only if the requirements are necessary to further a compelling state interest. In *Anderson*, the Court set forth a more flexible test:

> [S]tates have enacted comprehensive and sometimes complex election codes. Each provision of these schemes, whether it governs the registration and qualifications of voters, the selection and eligibility of candidates, or the voting process itself, inevitably affects—at least to some degree—the individual's right to vote and his right to associate with others for political ends. Nevertheless, the State's important regulatory interests are generally sufficient to justify reasonable, nondiscriminatory restrictions.
>
> Constitutional challenges to specific provisions of a State's election laws therefore cannot be resolved by any "litmus-paper test" that will separate valid from invalid restrictions. Instead, a court must resolve such a challenge by an analytical process that parallels its work in ordinary litigation. It must first consider the character and magnitude of the asserted injury to the rights protected by the First and Fourteenth Amendments that the plaintiff seeks to vindicate. It then must identify and evaluate the precise interests put forward by the State as justifications for the burden imposed by its rule. In passing judgment, the Court must not only determine the legitimacy and strength of each of those interests, it also must consider the extent to which those interests make it necessary to burden the plaintiff's rights. Only after weighing all these factors is the reviewing court in a position to decide whether the challenged provision is unconstitutional. The results of this evaluation will not be automatic; as we have recognized, there is "no substitute for the hard judgments that must be made." (*Anderson v. Celebrezze*, 460 U.S. 780, at 788–89 (1982)).

Although the discussion in the foregoing passage suggests that the approach enunciated would be broadly applicable to constitutional election law cases, *Anderson* had relatively little doctrinal influence for a considerable time, even in the limited area of ballot access. As late as the beginning of the 1990s, a commentator could persuasively argue that doctrine in the ballot access cases was confused and unsettled (Latz 1991). During the 1990s, however, the Supreme Court has relied on the flexible *Anderson* test to uphold Hawaii's denial of the opportunity for voters to cast write-in votes (*Burdick v. Takushi*, 504 U.S. 428 (1992)), to uphold Minnesota's anti-fusion law (*Timmons*), and to strike down various Colorado rules regulating the circulation of initiative petitions (*Buckley v. American Constitutional Law Foundation (ACLF)*, 119 S. Ct. 636 (1999)).

These decisions reveal that the Supreme Court has expanded the flexible *Anderson* test beyond the specific question of ballot access for minor parties and independent candidates. The use of the *Anderson* test in *Buckley v. ACLF* is particularly striking. That case was a sequel to *Meyer v. Grant*, 486 U.S. 414 (1988), in which the Court struck down a Colorado ban on the use of paid circulators for qualifying initiative petitions. In *Meyer v. Grant*, the Court had not only used the strict scrutiny test, it had given strict scrutiny what may have been its strongest formulation ever—saying that the state's burden of justification for its statute was "well-nigh insurmountable." Although *Anderson* predated *Meyer* by several years, *Meyer* ignored the *Anderson* test. In *ACLF*, the Court was faced with rules adopted in the wake of *Meyer* that attempted to regulate the qualification of initiatives for the ballot in ways comparable to, but not specifically addressed in, *Meyer*. Although the questions raised in *ACLF* were therefore similar to those in *Meyer*, the Court employed the flexible *Anderson* test in place of the strong form of strict scrutiny it used in *Meyer*.

In recent years, the Supreme Court clearly has expanded the scope of the *Anderson* test. Each of the foregoing cases in which the Court applied the test, however, involved a challenge to the state's control of its ballot. The test was broadly enough conceived to enable the state to prohibit write-in votes, prohibit a candidate from appearing on the ballot as the nominee of more than one party, and set the rules by which initiative proposals qualify for the ballot. In litigation in which parties have challenged the California "blanket primary" (a form of open primary), lower courts have applied the *Anderson* test to reject the parties' challenge (*California Democratic Party v. Jones*, 169 F. 3d 646 (1999)).

The Supreme Court used strict scrutiny in the 1980s when it reviewed regulation of parties' control of their nomination processes and internal affairs (*Eu v. San Francisco County Democratic Central Committee*, 489 U.S. 214 (1989)). If the Court accepts the California blanket primary case for review, the resulting decision may give some indication of how much further the *Anderson* test will be extended. The Court has continued to employ strict scrutiny, however, in reviewing matters such as regulation of speech near a polling place (*Burson v. Freeman*, 504 U.S. 191 (1992)). Hence, there is no indication that the *Anderson* test will be extended to major areas such as campaign finance regulation—much less areas of election law that arise under the equal protection clause, such as racial gerrymandering.

Even if the *Anderson* test were extended to cover all or most election law, it would not support the conclusion that the Supreme Court decides election cases by applying the political theory of rights-based liberalism. The reason is that in reality, the *Anderson* test is a sort of antidoctrine. It calls for judges to consider all of the factors that bear on a particular problem, giving each its due weight under the particular circumstances. Judges who have favored the concept of definitional balancing have done so precisely for the purpose of avoiding such case-by-case balancing.

In some areas of election law not affected by the *Anderson* test, definitional balancing holds sway. Two such issues of particular importance are racial gerrymandering and campaign finance. In each of these areas, the Supreme Court has developed a complex set of criteria for when strict scrutiny should be applied and what state interests might survive strict scrutiny. To qualify as applying a political theory, however, the Court must not simply have doctrinal rules; it must have doctrinal rules that cohere. The doctrine governing racial gerrymandering and campaign finance does not cohere.

In the racial gerrymandering cases, the Supreme Court has been hamstrung by the fact that in each case, the majority has consisted of only five justices—who happen not to agree on the nature of the racial gerrymandering cause of action. As I and others have demonstrated elsewhere, the result has been conceptual confusion (Lowenstein 1998; Briffault 1995).

In its campaign finance jurisprudence, the Supreme Court so far has managed to avoid actually reversing any of the doctrinal rules it has established since venturing into the field with *Buckley v. Valeo*, 424 U.S. 1 (1976). To do this, it has had to place more weight than can reasonably be borne on a series of dichotomies: contribution limits versus expenditure limits, regulation of candidate elections versus ballot proposition elections, and regulation of corporate financial activity versus regulation of others (Lowenstein 1992).

Furthermore, the Supreme Court has made inconsistent use of the concept of corruption, which it sees as the prime evil whose control may justify restrictions on campaign finance activity. Thus, the Court upheld a ban on corporate spending to support candidates by viewing corruption broadly enough to include the "corrosive effects" of using corporate treasuries, which contain money raised from business activity rather than by politically motivated contributions, to influence the outcome of elections (*Austin v. Michigan Chamber of Commerce*, 494 U.S. 652 (1990)). On the other hand, the Court struck down a prohibition on corporate spending in ballot measure elections by defining corruption more narrowly to include only improper influence over the decision making of public officials (*First National Bank of Boston v. Bellotti*, 435 U.S. 765 (1978)).

Certainly election law has been influenced by constitutional doctrine. The foregoing discussion demonstrates, however, that there is no body of doctrine nearly comprehensive or coherent enough to be described as a specific manifestation of a rights-based political theory that can be said to guide the Supreme Court. This is not bad news. In fact, when the Court is most guided by constitutional doctrine, it seems most likely to engage in a mechanical jurisprudence that often misconceives the nature of the problem. Examples, which I have elaborated elsewhere, are cases on associational rights of parties—in which the Court mistook what are often intraparty disputes for disputes between private associations and the state (Lowenstein 1993)—and *Meyer v. Grant*, in which the Court mistook a state's procedures for rationing its own ballot positions for a regulation of speech (Lowenstein and Stern 1989).

WEAK TEA: ACADEMIC THEORIES

A favorite pastime of some legal academics—especially those with an interest in constitutional law—is to make up their own theories that they propose the Supreme Court should adopt for the decision of cases. In constitutional law generally, and especially in First Amendment jurisprudence, various strains of moral philosophy are popular starting points. Election law, alas, has not been exempt from such efforts. Inventors of formulas for the resolution of all election law problems, however, more often rely on what they see as a "functional" approach rather than starting with some variant of Kantianism, utilitarianism, or the like. That is, these election law theorists announce that there is some central defect in the

American political system, then propose that it should be the Court's business in election law cases to provide the remedy.

The medium of choice for the promulgation of these academic theories is a law journal article of 50–100 pages. In such an article, the author laments the aimlessness of all prior approaches to the subject and announces the hitherto undiscovered key in the form of a moral principle or functional need. The author then summarily disposes of an extensive sampling of the specific controversies that have made up the field—usually in a few pages each at most and usually, as previously noted, in a fashion that just happens to coincide with the political preferences of the author of the theory.

These academic theories differ in their narrow focus from the more established theories described above. The established theories have been in existence for centuries and have guided thinking about the entire range of issues affecting the organization of a democratic government. Many of the people who have contributed to the development and articulation of the established theories have had extensive political experience. The academic theories spring from the minds of one or a few scholars—usually with little or no political experience—who look at the subject from a single angle. Not surprisingly, academic theories tend to be thin and ineffectual, rather like weak tea.[9]

Academic theorizing in election law tends to be influenced by constitutional law's most famous footnote. *United States v. Carolene Products Company*, 304 U.S. 144 (1938), was decided when the Supreme Court was withdrawing from its aggressive oversight of economic and social legislation that had characterized the constitutional jurisprudence of the first third of the twentieth century. In footnote 4, Chief Justice Stone mentioned the circumstances in which it might continue to exercise rigorous review. One such circumstance exists when the Court reviews "legislation which restricts those political processes which can ordinarily be expected to bring about repeal of undesirable legislation."

The idea of the "political processes" plank of footnote 4 is that judicial deference to the political branches on substantive matters is based largely on the assumption that the processes controlling them are indeed democratic, open, and impartial. Rigorous review of the political process therefore is regarded as a corollary of deferential review of substantive legislation. *Carolene Products*—for those who find its logic compelling—provides a respectable basis for espousing aggressive judicial review in election law. It also imposes the burden, however, of explaining what electoral practices and procedures "restrict" the political process in an objectionable way. I have criticized *Carolene Products* as a rationale for aggressive judicial review in election law on the ground that questions of electoral institutional design are just as political as "substantive" policy questions (Lowenstein, in press). Academic theorists of election law, however, see *Carolene Products* as an invitation to peddle their wares.

The most recent theorists to have answered the call are Michael Klarman, who offers "anti-entrenchment theory," and Sam Issacharoff and Rick Pildes, who offer a similar idea—describing what they are against as "partisan lockups" (Klarman 1997; Issacharoff and Pildes 1998). These scholars have made the remarkable discovery that politicians tend to act in their own self-interest. More remarkably still, politicians consider their self-interest even when they are legislating on the rules of the political process itself. It follows, these theorists declare, that undoing all traces of such self-interested legislation should be the overriding, if not the sole, guide to election law adjudication.

One happy by-product of this approach is that problems that had previously seemed quite complex are simplicity itself. For example, previous judges and scholars had faced seemingly perplexing problems when they tried to unravel issues such as term limits, malapportionment, partisan gerrymandering, extension of the franchise, ballot access, campaign finance regulation, minority vote dilution, and racial gerrymandering. Klarman finds thirty pages in the *Georgetown Law Journal* sufficient to dispose of all of them (Klarman 1997).

Klarman grounds his anti-entrenchment theory in majoritarianism. He offers various reasons one might favor the principle of majoritarianism, which is hardly a wild suggestion in the American political culture. To support his theory, however, he would need to show not simply that majoritarian is *a* value that should be served by judicial review but that it is the *only* value that ought to be so served. He makes no serious attempt to do so. Perhaps more important, Klarman says nothing about the complexities of majoritarianism. For example, he does not address the likelihood that on most questions of legislation and public policy—including legislation and public policy on electoral procedures—most people have no opinion. Even less does he consider the possible implications of these complexities in assessing the likelihood that majority opinions, when they do exist, will be translated into public policies.

Klarman does not appear to recognize that the central assumption of his theory—that self-interested legislation will necessarily be anti-majoritarian—requires defending. Yet, the proposition is not in the least self-evident, nor does he consider second-order effects. For example, without noticing the empirical evidence to the contrary, Klarman assumes that redistricting controlled by incumbent legislatures will have major anticompetitive effects (Jacobson 1990; Cover 1977; Cover and Mayhew 1977; Ferejohn 1977). He does not even consider, however, the stimulus that redistricting by the legislature provides to partisan competition in state legislative races. Even if he had, his failure to consider how institutions such as political parties may affect majority rule would have made it difficult for him to integrate such second-order effects into his theory.

Whereas Klarman's anti-entrenchment theory emphasizes the self-interested action of incumbents, Issacharoff and Pildes focus more on self-interested actions by political parties. Oddly, however, their primary concern is not, in David Mayhew's phrase, the "dishing" of the Republicans by the Democrats and of the Democrats by the Republicans (Mayhew 1971). Issacharoff and Pildes apparently believe that American democracy would be better served if we had a multiparty, proportional representation system of the sort used by most continental European democracies. Perhaps because they hold this belief, they view a variety of electoral procedures from the perspective of third parties and seemingly project that perspective onto Democratic and Republican politicians.

It is probably true that most major party politicians regard third parties as nuisances.[10] Issacharoff and Pildes are wrong to assume, however, that major party politicians hold this mildly hostile attitude because they regard third parties as a competitive threat to themselves. To the extent that major party politicians regard third parties as having any relevance at all to themselves, it is because of a correct perception that third parties on general election ballots occasionally affect the competition between the major parties. Indeed, major parties have been known to try to stimulate third-party candidacies in contested districts, in hopes of drawing votes away from the opposing major party.

Pildes and Issacharoff, however, are sure that major party politicians are preoccupied with working together to create bipartisan "partisan lockups" to fend off competition from third parties. They criticize the courts for being "politically unsophisticated" (Issacharoff and Pildes 1998). If that lack of sophistication simply means failing to believe that Democrats and Republicans are engaged together in such a conspiracy, however, the charge applies to virtually all political observers. In any event, the Issacharoff-Pildes view leads them to odd analyses of election law controversies.

One example is Issacharoff and Pildes's criticism of *Burdick v. Takushi Director of Elections in Hawaii*, 504 U.S. 428 (1992), in which the Supreme Court upheld Hawaii's prohibition of write-in votes in primaries and general elections. Issacharoff and Pildes regard it as euphemistic to speak of "the State" having banned write-in votes because "the State" is made up of incumbent Democrats who dominate Hawaii's politics (Issacharoff and Pildes 1998). This argument would be fair enough, except that Issacharoff and Pildes also point out that the ban dates to the nineteenth century, and they do not claim that the Democrats had controlled the state government continuously ever since.[11] In any event, even if it were true that the Democrats—or the Democrats and Republicans acting together in lockstep—were responsible for the ban on write-in votes, it would hardly follow that the ban has or is intended to have the effect of locking out third parties from electoral competition.

Issacharoff and Pildes's only argument that the ban does have that effect is based on a claim that other features of the electoral system in Hawaii prevent other parties from effectively challenging the dominant Democrats. The ban on write-ins, they argue, "is particularly significant because other avenues for opposition are so effectively closed off." (672). Even if one grants their empirical premise, their argument is a non sequitur. If all the roads that lead to a particular place are closed off, it does not follow that opening some other road will make it possible to get to that place. Issacharoff and Pildes do not explain why the availability of write-in voting in the great majority of states has had no discernible effect on the two-party system—or why, for that matter, write-in voting has *not* been banned in most states if banning write-in votes does squelch third-party competition and if major party politicians are as preoccupied with that competition as Issacharoff and Pildes assume.

There are three structural features of the American system that are probably most responsible for the stability of the two-party system. The most widely recognized is the single-member-district system for electing legislators. The tendency for this system to produce two dominant parties, in contrast with the tendency of proportional systems to produce multiparty systems, is so well known that it has a name: Duverger's Law (Duverger 1959). Duverger's Law, however, does not explain why the same two parties predominate throughout a federal system such as that of the United States. E. E. Schattschneider—who described Duverger's Law long before it acquired the name—explained this phenomenon by identifying the second structural feature (Schattschneider 1942). The presidential election system discourages regional parties, which would not necessarily be discouraged by the single-member-district system. Even these two structural features combined, however, do not explain why the same two parties have predominated since the 1850s. Indeed, prior to that time, in the relatively short period of sixty years the major opponents of the Democratic Party were, successively, Federalists, Whigs, and Republicans. The most probable explanation for the endurance of the Democrats and the Republicans since the Civil War period is the emergence of the direct primary, which permits new ideas and movements to compete within the major parties rather than having to oppose those parties (Lowenstein 1992).

Issacharoff and Pildes do not expect the Supreme Court to eliminate single-member districts, presidential elections, or direct primaries. It is not clear, therefore, what difference it would make if the Court were to subscribe to their theory of partisan lockups as the key to election law adjudication. If the Court accepted the theory and were truly sophisticated regarding the causes of Democratic and Republican predominance in American politics, they would simply deconstitutionalize election law and have done with it.

The more important point is that academic theories such as those of Klarman and of Issacharoff and Pildes inevitably are woefully insufficient as guides to adjudication. The deficiencies in the theories are not caused by deficiencies in the authors—who are first-rate scholars on the faculties of first-rate law schools, publishing their theories in first-rate law journals. The starting points for their theories are much too narrow, however. These authors' failure to make any serious inquiry into the nature of political competition in the United States is more indicative than idiosyncratic. Such an inquiry would inevitably reveal the complexity of the system and the vast areas of empirical uncertainty that exist. The magic bullet that is to instantly solve all problems would inevitably dissolve.

CONCLUSION

Some readers may imagine that the thinness and narrowness that characterizes the foregoing academic theories can be overcome. Certainly, the established theories considered in this chapter are much richer and more comprehensive. Some observers may therefore believe that it would be better for the Supreme Court—or at least individual justices—to adhere consistently to one of those theories.

Even the established theories, however, do not encompass enough. Pluralism and progressivism both appeal, at least in part, to most Americans who think about politics. There may be popular discontent with political parties, but a voter's party identification is still the best single predictor of his or her voting behavior, and most people who think seriously about democratic politics believe that political parties are indispensable. Moreover, although many observers would agree that the political rights of individuals must be defined in light of systemic requirements, few would discredit the notion that individuals have political rights. In short, the enrichment of one of the established theories would entail losing the element of truth that inheres in each of the others.

Even if members of the Supreme Court individually had political theories that they were willing and able to use as a guide for deciding election law cases, the problems of collective action would likely prevent the Court as a whole from having such a theory. The more important point, however, is that using any political theory as a guide is the wrong way to decide cases.

It is often said that the Constitution is intended not to embody one theory of society and government but to provide a structure within which people who hold differing views can compete in an orderly manner. The same notion applies to theories of politics. The Supreme Court should not select a political theory and impose it on the nation any more than it should impose an economic theory.

This argument does not imply that the Supreme Court should abandon its power of judicial review in election law cases. The Court has that power not because of any very impressive theoretical justification but because the history and tradition of our country gives it that power. The Court would abuse the power if it used it to impose a single political theory. We would probably benefit if all or most of the justices had political experience, an astute understanding of electoral politics, and a proper sense of humility about what they do not know, as some justices have had in the past. History—including contemporary history—suggests, however, that the republic will survive the exercise of judicial review in election law cases even by a Court whose members lack these attributes.

ENDNOTES

1. I do not include *public choice theory* or *civic republicanism*—each of which is a cousin of progressivism—because although they have been used by academics to generate interesting debates and insights, they are not pervasive in the general culture. Feminism has been influential in academic thought and the general culture, but as far as I am aware it has not developed a distinctive perspective on the central issues in election law. In any event, I doubt whether anyone would contend that the election law decisions of the Supreme Court reflect consistent adherence to public choice theory, civic republicanism, feminism, or any of the other theories that have been fashionable in law schools in recent years.

2. I use the term *progressivism* because the Progressive movement of the early twentieth century was especially imbued with the ideas to which I am referring. These ideas were widespread in American thought and debate long before the rise of the Progressives, however, and they continue to be so long after the decline of the Progressives. Therefore, I use the adjective *progressivist* rather than *progressive*.

3. Plainly, I am offering a general or composite picture, though one that I hope will be immediately recognizable. Progressivism and rights theory are so pervasive that it would be pointless to give particular references. Certainly, Thomas Jefferson was an early exponent of these ideas.

4. There is an immense literature on party government. A leading text is Beck and Sorauf (1992). The most prominent defense of party government by a legal scholar is Fitts (1988). For overviews of party government in the United States, see Epstein (1986) and Lowenstein (1992b).

5. See Bickel (1978) and Moeller (1984). Bruce Cain has recently written that many political scientists took an ambivalent view of *Reynolds*; they supported its "one person, one vote" rule on political grounds, though they were troubled by what Cain and the political scientists he is referring to regard as its antipluralist foundation (Cain, forthcoming).

6. In this respect, Justice Powell's opinion in *Elrod v. Burns* is much closer to the views of the great majority of political scientists who study American politics. There is therefore some irony in the fact that Powell accused Justice Brennan of basing his position on "the theoretical abstractions of a political science seminar."

7. The Supreme Court's partisan gerrymandering decision, *Davis v. Bandemer,* 478 U.S. 109 (1986), has received diverse interpretations. For an overview, see Lowenstein (1995).

8. There are occasional exceptions. For example, *U.S. Term Limits v. Thornton,* in which the Supreme Court declared state-enacted congressional term limits unconstitutional, was decided under the qualifications clauses.

9. I apologize to readers of this chapter who are fond of weak tea and are offended by having their favorite beverage used in such an unflattering metaphor.
10. At least, that has tended to be the view expressed by major party politicians with whom I have discussed the question.
11. According to the *Almanac of American Politics*, Hawaii tended to be Republican during the 1950s.

··· 13 ···

The Supreme Court as Architect of Election Law: Summing Up, Looking Ahead

David K. Ryden

This volume provides a variety of views and perspectives on the Supreme Court's election law jurisprudence. Less concerned about broad consensus or firm conclusions, it has sought to explore issues and themes that run throughout judicial resolution of representation law. In the process, we hope that these essays will generate a more holistic debate that is cognizant of the big picture and the interrelatedness of these issues. The introductory chapter highlighted five general themes that frame the election law decisions. Although not every chapter addressed all of these themes explicitly, they surfaced repeatedly. We now return to them.

THE COMPLEXITIES OF REPRESENTATION: IS THE COURT CLUELESS OR CLUED IN?

To what extent has the Supreme Court demonstrated a nuanced and sophisticated comprehension of the complexities and subtleties of political representation? Several contributors give the Court relatively high marks. To Paul Petterson, the Court's effort in *Morse v. Virginia Republican Party* to balance party autonomy and individual voting rights was a "healthy, thoughtful, and vigorous judicial debate" regarding questions of democracy and representation. Likewise, Cynthia Grant Bowman applauds the democratic theory and representational values made by the Court in the patronage cases. The prevailing majorities in those cases were firmly grounded in political philosophy, their assumptions regarding the democratic process much more reflective of the practical realities of politics. Bowman finds the dissenters, by comparison, doing political science, but doing it badly. In her view, they are *too* wedded to party theory, neglecting the empirical evidence that calls their theory into serious question. The rights on which patronage impinges—namely, free speech and the open exchange of political ideas and information—are critical to a healthy democratic system.

Other contributors, however, find serious fault with the Supreme Court's judicial understanding of representation. Howard Scarrow examines the Court's four-decade-long effort to constitutionally ensure "fair and effective representation" in the drawing of electoral districts and ultimately concludes that it has been a futile enterprise. The Court, in Scarrow's estimation, has proved itself incapable of grasping the multifaceted nature of political representation or of handling redistricting questions clearly, logically, or consistently. These shortcomings have weakened important goals of stability, fairness, and representativeness.

Nancy Maveety credits the earlier Burger Court with a relatively sophisticated grasp of the multiple forms of representation; its "communities of interest" balancing approach identified many of the groups that produce representation. The current Court compares unfavorably because it has strayed from the "communities of interest" doctrine. Indeed, Maveety finds the Court under Rehnquist unable even to agree on a definition of representation. Likewise, the conclusion that sound theorizing might be beyond the Court's reach is supported by the political fallout in several key areas. The minefields in which the Court has arguably pursued more theoretically grounded jurisprudential principles—racial redistricting and campaign financing—are as badly muddled doctrinally, if not more so, than any other and have had far-reaching, unintended practical consequences.

Brad Smith and Jeff Polet detect a lack of cognizance on the Supreme Court's part of the institutional or structural building blocks of representation: federalism, political parties, separation of powers, and enumerated powers. In justifying the use of initiatives, Smith decries the Court's neglect of structural representation through constitutional notions of enumerated powers and limited government. These constitutional constraints preserve the nexus between governmental action and the consent of the governed. When the government disregards them, Smith argues, the initiative process (here in the context of *Romer v. Evans*) offers a legitimate representative check. As a limited adjunct to legislative policymaking, ballot proposals ensure a representative system by correcting a government that has exceeded the limits on its authority.

Federalism is a second structural avenue to representation, balancing the tensions between the liberal and republican faces of our politics. Through federalism, government can recognize all political dimensions of society: individuals, groups, communities, states, and the nation and the public as a whole. Polet finds the Supreme Court's nationalistic understanding of federalism (on display in *U.S. Term Limits v. Thornton*) impoverished, diminishing states in favor of an undifferentiated American public. This view, according to Polet, fails to live up to the Madisonian vision of an enlarged republican government simultaneously mediating and representing all interests. It neglects the intermediate groups, interests, and associations that are an integral part of the representational equation. As the public in a mass democracy becomes diffused, representation is undecipherable. In short, representation (through parties, groups, and communities) is the victim of the Court's impoverished federalist structure.

The Supreme Court's manner of delivery also feeds the perception that its grasp on representation is weak indeed. If the Court is sensitive to the myriad of theoretical and practical implications of its decisions, its opinions clearly do not reflect that awareness. The opinions manifest a disturbing proclivity for easy conclusions unaccompanied by explanation, elaboration, or elucidation. *Timmons v. Twin Cities Area New Party* provides the starkest example; there, the Court made a foundational claim in favor of the two-party system with no serious attempt to support or explain it. One need not disagree with the outcome to be troubled by the Court's failure or refusal to at least acknowledge the larger issues involved. The Court's view of representation appears uninformed, even naive, when it treats complex issues as if they were self-evident.

DEMOCRATIC DILEMMAS: INDIVIDUALS AND COLLECTIVES IN REPRESENTATION JURISPRUDENCE

The Supreme Court's difficulties in getting its conceptual arms around political representation are inextricably linked to the central paradox of the constitutional arrangement as a whole—what Mike Fitts and others have called the countermajoritarian difficulty. How is the Court to reconcile individual rights with the reality of the significance played by groups and the need ultimately to reflect the will of the majority? Laws passed via the ballot (as in *Romer v. Evans* and *U.S. Term Limits v. Thornton*) hinge on how the Court balances exercises in direct democracy with the rights of individuals and minority groups. The patronage disputes and *Morse v. Virginia Republican Party* pit the individual rights of free speech, association, and participation against limitations on those rights in the name of effective group behavior—in these instances, party control and governance. The tension is evident in how the right of association is cast: Is the right only held by the individual, or does it inure to the group or party apart from its members? Unfortunately, these diverse contexts lead to a common conclusion: The Court struggles mightily to strike the appropriate balance between individual and collective dimensions of politics.

The Supreme Court's doctrinal focus clearly has shifted since it became more active in electoral issues earlier in this century. The Warren Court tended to reduce questions to a simple matter of individual rights, whereas the Burger Court was fairly aggressive in its cultivation of a group-conscious jurisprudence. The Rehnquist Court has back-peddled from those rules—studiously avoiding a more theoretically coherent alternative.

Thus, the Supreme Court's leap into the redistricting thicket produced a simplistic, individualistic notion of fair representation as defined by the efficacy of the individual vote. This one-dimensional focus on equal voting weight and "one person, one vote" ignored the existence of group interests that are essential to a truly representative electoral system.

Nancy Maveety and Howard Scarrow detail the Burger Court's gradual incorporation of collective interests, followed by the Rehnquist Court's retrenchment. Maveety attributes to the Burger Court a "communities of interest" doctrine that is more cognizant of collective political interests and activity. This doctrine revealed a relatively sophisticated judicial grasp of the complexities of representation. The Rehnquist Court, however, has not hewn to the Burger Court's interest-balancing, classic pluralist understanding of political representation. To Maveety, this failure to replicate the Burger Court analysis by itself does not necessarily spell philosophical incoherence. Rather, it may mark a new focus on the *type* of activity used to secure representation: Is it voluntary and uncoordinated or expressive (and therefore constitutionally protected) group action, or is it institutionalized group action (and hence unprotected)?

Scarrow is less charitable in his assessment of the Burger Court and the Rehnquist Court. The Burger Court's redistricting jurisprudence laid down group markers—from territorial community considerations flowing from supposedly neutral geographic traditional standards (contiguousness, compactness, and political subdivision boundaries) to demographic considerations implicated by race-based districting. Scarrow characterizes those judicial group representation efforts as superficial; he argues that they exhibit a thin, descriptive definition of group representation that is limited to race and ethnicity. The Burger Court's treatment of groups was undermined by its neglect of partisan representation, as evidenced by its refusal to counter blatant partisan gerrymandering. More recently, the Rehnquist Court has retreated from race-conscious descriptive redistricting, but it remains theoretically adrift as issues of partisan representation remain unaddressed.

My analysis of the Supreme Court's campaign finance jurisprudence parallels Scarrow's. The Court began with a one-dimensional individualism in *Buckley v. Valeo* before moving to a group-centered scheme of campaign funding regulation. Although the Court has since backed off that largely unsuccessful neopluralist effort, it has neither embraced a party-conscious constitutional approach nor developed other doctrinal solutions to the tension between individual and group rights.

Ultimately, the Supreme Court has ducked the hard questions of practical pluralism: Who deserves recognition in our system of representation? What interests are to be acknowledged and facilitated in the creation of electoral districts and in determining the control of schools, in setting the parameters on financing campaigns, in determining the respective rights of major and lesser parties? The Court suffers from a dual propensity—either to avoid these hard questions or to capitulate by subordinating group considerations to individual rights. In *Board of Education of Kiryas Joel Village School District v. Grumet*, the Court sidestepped the only real answer to the redistricting puzzle it faced—what makes good and bad districting. What groups deserve recognition? What representation flows from the system of districting with respect to individuals, groups, or the whole? Elsewhere, individual rights trump collective considerations. The speech rights of individuals win out over the partisan resort to patronage; individual participatory rights prevail over party control over nominating procedures. In sum, the Court is plagued by an inability to delineate clearly how groups fit into theories or structures of representation.

CONSTITUTIONAL TREATMENT OF POLITICAL PARTIES AND PARTY STRUCTURES

Any analysis of the individualistic and collective faces of representation is incomplete without a consideration of political parties. Because political parties are one form of collective behavior, the constitutional issues overlap considerably. Political parties also provide a theoretical response to tensions between individuals, groups, and the interests of the whole. Political parties are an important functional means of alleviating the countermajoritarian dilemma.

The Model of "Responsible Party" Governance

The Supreme Court's constitutional handling of political parties can be assessed from several reference points. One benchmark for evaluating the Court's party jurisprudence is the "responsible party" model of politics. In this view, party systems are a structural and organizational tool for satisfying crucial representative functions; they institutionalize the mobilization of public opinion, the channeling of that opinion, compromise, and the discernment of majority sentiment. In the process, political parties produce a system that simultaneously heeds the individual, the group, and the whole. Representation comes through coalitional parties offering competing agendas and programs that are pursued with some degree of party unity.

In *Morse v. Virginia Republican Party*, for example, the "responsible party" school would be willing to narrow the individual right to participate in the convention so that the party could more clearly define itself and its agenda. The Supreme Court rejected that argument, siding instead with the individual.

The patronage cases mark the clearest rejection of the party government argument. Although the majorities expressed concern that patronage would impede two-party politics by entrenching one party in power, that conclusion is not the same as accepting the value of vigorous, intellectually defined political parties. The majorities seemed intuitively skeptical of strong party assertions, subordinating any need for strong and coherent political parties to the individual speech right of government employees. The Court did little to seriously engage or rebut the dissenters' party-based rationale of the earlier cases; neither did it make an effort to examine the relevant empirical and social science methodology, as Bowman does so ably in her article. The cases display a striking absence of cognizance of party systems as channels of representation. Patronage may be an anachronism rightly discarded, but the Court could have provided a far more thoughtful and reasoned account of associational realities and their effects.

More generally, the Supreme Court has failed to grasp the relation of political parties to other interest groups. The responsible party model regards parties not only as an avenue for group input but also as moderating and assimilating influences because they work to submerge specific group interests within larger party goals and platforms. The Court, however, seems to share the public perception of political parties as just another interest group. Thus, political parties are of no more import than groups—and possibly less so—in determining what interests are acknowledged in districting. In the campaign finance realm, political parties and groups are treated as interchangeable in their influence and corrupting potential. The "responsible party" model, in contrast, would constitutionally accept elevated party financing in hopes of controlling and muffling interest group money and influence.

The Supreme Court has been less than consistent in its handling of political parties in the electoral process. Howard Scarrow interprets the Court's refusal to address partisan gerrymandering as evidence of a lack of appreciation for party systems. Yet the Court has reached pro-party results in several cases, though it did not explicitly invoke a "party government" rationale to justify those decisions. The antifusion decision in *Timmons v. Twin Cities Area New Party* was sympathetic—at least to the two major parties. The Court's deference to the two-party system at least tacitly recognized the role of political parties in stabilizing the electoral system. Likewise, the decision in *Colorado Republican Federal Campaign Committee v. FEC* worked decisively to the benefit of the parties, immediately boosting their influence in campaigns. Moreover, there is a critical mass of justices who appear amenable to "responsible party" reasoning. Four justices would have jettisoned all campaign financing restrictions on political parties, presumably because of the functional attributes of partisan organizations. Given the controversy surrounding soft money, the Court may well have an opportunity to revisit this issue.

One objection to raising political parties to constitutional prominence is the difficulty of squaring "responsible party" arguments with the Constitution itself. Cynthia Bowman finds it significant that political parties are not mentioned in the Constitution and argues that party-building arguments run counter to the constitutional structure of limited government. In this view, political parties attempt an end run around the systems of dispersion and separation of powers, federalism, and checks and balances. Party proponents reply that this objection loses its force in an era of broad, active, central power. The only alternative to strong political parties is purely self-interested, candidate-centered, interest group-dominated politics. The price is the loss of constitutional values of responsiveness, representativeness, public control, and accountability.

Even some analysts who accept the unique benefits of political parties in service of representation reject the idea that political parties should be written into constitutional law. For Michael Fitts, it is precisely how political parties accomplish their tasks that makes them problematic in the realm of constitutional law. Political parties perform their functions informally and flexibly, adjusting to their political environment and circumstances. Constitutionalizing them might only rigidify political parties and debilitate their ability to do these tasks. Nor is it clear what party theory, forms of party competition, structures, or systems best facilitate the desired functions. The ambiguity and variance in party qualities and how they carry out their functions make it difficult to integrate them into legal or constitutional doctrine.

The Three Dimensions of Political Parties

We can also appraise judicial treatment of parties with respect to traditional analysis by party scholars. Students of political parties identify three dimensions of parties, distinguished by the function being performed. The *party in government* refers to governing capacity of political parties; government actions reflect the partisan makeup of the legislative and executive branches. Political parties determine the policy agenda, manage the legislative process, and dominate the ranks of the executive branch and administrative offices. They make governance possible. The *party in the electorate* refers to the standing of political parties among voters: who the electorate aligns itself with and votes for. The electoral dimension is the bond or connection that the political parties are able to maintain with the voting public. These bonds are badly frayed and are far looser and more fluid than they once were. Finally, the *party organization* refers to party activists who stand between the party electorate and are the party government; they work to mobilize and enlarge the party presence in the electorate so that it might translate into success at the voting booth, majority status in government, and control of the machinery of power. The party organization includes candidates running for office, party activists who recruit them, fundraisers, contributors, volunteers, consultants, admakers, and a host of others who conduct the array of electioneering activities on the national, state, and local levels.

Clearly, political parties are not a uniform, monolithic institution. Alternative functions and dimensions affect and determine how we assess political parties. One would hope, then, that the Supreme Court's treatment of political parties constitutionally would reflect or acknowledge which of these functions is under consideration. If the party in the electorate is at issue, one would hope the constitutional rule would promote electoral results that are representative in proportion and character to the party in the electorate. If party organizational activity is under scrutiny, as in *Morse v. Virginia Republican Party*, that function is more akin to a public function and is thus subject to regulatory action. If party government is implicated, as in patronage disputes, then issues regarding the need for party discipline, loyalty, and cohesiveness come into play.

The Supreme Court's cursory treatment of political parties reveals no cognizance of these functional distinctions. If the Court is aware of these distinctions or takes them into account, there is little evidence in its decisions. The Court has not judicially acknowledged the three party dimensions—at least explicitly. Is a thoughtful constitutional reckoning of political parties possible without taking these facets into account? The Court may be unable to truly determine the constitutional connotations of these party distinctions. Familiarity with the literature on political parties, however, might enable the Court to discern which dimension is at stake and which representative party functions are involved. This knowledge might better inform the Court's quest to constitutionally place these entities that sprung up outside the Constitution itself.

Competing Visions of Hierarchical versus Progressive Parties

The third approach to analyzing the judicial treatment of political parties is along the hierarchy/progressivism spectrum. This approach puts the Supreme Court's treatment of political parties within the framework of the other political perspectives vying for the Court's favor. Of the four theories raised by Dan Lowenstein, two are hierarchical (republican and partisan) and two are individualistic (progressivism and rights theory). No clear philosophical position marks the Court's cases. The Court's ruling in *Colorado Republican Federal Campaign Committee v. FEC* was decidedly hierarchical and antiprogressive. It has altered the balance of power and access in electoral politics—not between parties and political action committees (PACs) but in favor of parties and PACs at the expense of individuals. The hierarchy of party bosses and big city machines has been replaced by national party organizations, fed by large soft money donations of businesses, unions, and the wealthy.

The ruling in *Timmons v. Twin Cities Area New Party*, by entrenching the two-party system, also reflects a judicial bias toward a hierarchical party system. Legal barriers that suppress new and minor party challenges limit voter options and candidate alternatives. They preserve the dominant party organizations at the expense of individual voters' choices, stifling change and insulating political parties from—and making them less responsive to—public choice. This endorsement of the two-party system means more of the fuzzy, flexible, nonideological parties that characterize our politics.

In *Morse v. Virginia Republican Party* and the patronage cases, the Supreme Court leaned in the opposite direction, focusing on participation at the expense of hierarchical party control over party activity. In both instances, the progressive preference for broad and inclusive participatory rights prevailed over the idea that political parties can impose restrictions to repel interlopers who might taint the associational well. Thus, the hierarchy-versus-progressivism debate leads to no clear or consistent conclusion.

In sum, the constitutional status of political parties will probably remain difficult to categorize or predict. Perhaps the most that pro-party advocates can hope for is judicial neutrality toward political parties—a recognition by the Supreme Court that it is incapable of discerning when to bolster political parties and when to rein them in—and a laissez-faire, hands-off approach. The Court's removal of oppressive antiparty laws and its avoidance of explicitly pro-party positions might leave political parties with the freedom to perform and the burden of responsibility for the tasks attributed to them in theory.

THE COURT'S RELATION TO POLITICAL REFORM

The Supreme Court's relation to the implementation of political reform is an important subtext in this book. Is the Court an agent of change? Is it an impediment? Should it be either? These are far-reaching questions; we can touch on them only briefly here. The conflicting hierarchical and progressive visions of party systems parallel those times when the Court is amenable to reform. *Morse v. Virginia Republican Party* and the patronage decisions, which expanded individual participatory rights at the expense of political parties, were reform minded. The Court also has extinguished serious reform movements, however. The barriers it has thrown up to reform are traceable to its substantive doctrine and to its cautious style of collective judicial decision making.

Implicit in Brad Smith's and Jeff Polet's essays are hints of elitism: The Supreme Court preempts exercises in direct democracy that it considers ill-advised or unwise, paternalistically substituting its judgment of what is sound policy for that of the public. The Court's abrogation of the initiatives in *U.S. Term Limits v. Thornton* and *Romer v. Evans* is defended as necessary to preserve the integrity of representative democracy against the encroachment of direct democracy and its concomitant dangers to the rights of individuals and minorities. To Smith, this is a double foul; periodic exercises in direct democracy in fact safeguard representative democracy in an era in which the Court and Congress routinely ignore the textual confines of government.

In *U.S. Term Limits v. Thornton*, the Supreme Court effectively countermanded overwhelmingly popular majority sentiment even though there was no danger to minority rights from a majority storming the initiative process. Indeed, the Court in *Thornton* thwarted reform on two planes. On the surface, the ban on term limits nullified a widespread populist movement; it obstructed the most genuine of reforms—a grassroots expression of the will of the people. On a deeper level, the Court's version of federalism is a more pervasive and problematic barrier to reform. Election reforms are most likely to come from the states, which have constitutional authority over elections. The skewed federalism of *Thornton,* however, clouds the ideal of states as laboratories of change, experimentation, and innovation. It squelches reform that otherwise might bubble up from the states in more democratic, *representative* form. (Of course, self-interested, popularly elected *state* representatives also pursue legislative entrenchment. The more the justices defer to states in federalism issues, the more state legislators can practice self-serving incumbency protection.)

Reform issues also raise important questions of whether the Supreme Court ought to be attuned to the whispers (or, as in *U.S. Term Limits v. Thornton*, the thundering) of public opinion. Does the Court subvert its legitimacy or pervert the Constitution when—as in *Thornton* and *Timmons v. Twin Cities Area New Party*—it counteracts clear expressions of public sentiment? Normally, public opinion would not play an explicit role in judicial decision making. Does that description hold true, however, when the issues involved—term limits, campaign finance, minor party rights—pertain to the electability of the actors who are implementing them? In the face of bald conflicts of interest, should the Court exhibit less deference to legislative behavior? The Court acts as an institutional guardian of representative values because popularly elected officeholders cannot be trusted to make anything but self-interested decisions with regard to the workings of the electoral process. In other words, the latter inevitably will pursue paths that perpetuate their hold on power and preserve the status quo.

In *Timmons v. Twin Cities Area New Party*, the Supreme Court arguably abandoned that role; it acquiesced to a legislature dominated by entrenched major parties whose rule making redounds to their benefit. This ruling comes at a time when the public is less bound to the major parties than ever and is increasingly open to alternative partisan voices and choices. Judicial deference to legislative edict is understandable, especially when the constitutional text or framers' intentions are ambiguous. Instincts of self-preservation and power make legislators dubious caretakers of representative government, however. The practical impact of the adjudicatory principle of yielding to the legislature in this context is potentially devastating. Too often, the Court is consigned by default to the role of accomplice to incumbent officeholders and legislative entrenchment. Instead of more aggressively protecting the representativeness of the system, the Court becomes a major obstacle to legitimate, democratic reform.

THE NATURE OF THE COURT AND ITS DECISION-MAKING STYLE

In this section, I consider general impressions that characterize the Supreme Court's decision-making style. One such observation is that the Court tends to render decisions without regard for the implications for democratic theory. This tendency is attributable to the Court's neglect of important outside sources and larger bodies of information. In general, the Court disregards the relevant political science literature. (The judicial inattention to literature on political parties has already been noted.) Doug Amy's discussion of party systems reveals the Court's disinterest in the comparative perspective. Multiparty arrangements remind us of an entire democratic world of experiences upon which we might draw. Yet the Court rarely considers other democratic experiments.

Nor does the Supreme Court consult pertinent empirical or social science evidence. Cynthia Bowman's essay on patronage is illustrative; she makes extensive use of social science data to support the constitutional narrowing of patronage. The Court, in contrast, made no use of such data. Bowman did what the Court should, but does not, do. Similarly, the issues in *Timmons v. Twin Cities Area New Party* clamor for the application of social science methods and an appraisal of their constitutional implications. Yet the Court is indifferent to the wealth of empirical material and commentary on multiparty electoral systems and their effect on representation. As a result, the decision strikes one as simplistic and ignorant of the complex theoretical issues regarding party systems.

Brad Smith's exploration of *Romer v. Evans* makes the same point. In nullifying Colorado's Amendment 2, the Supreme Court logically reasoned that initiatives imperil the interests of unpopular minorities and individuals. Smith plumbs the empirical evidence and social science literature, however, to show that plebiscites in fact present no greater systematic danger to minorities than does the legislative process. The Court ignored that body of material.

The Supreme Court is not wholly to blame for such oversights. It is constrained by the particulars of the case before it, including the substance and caliber of the written and oral arguments. The Court's social science is likely to be only as good as that of the lawyers submitting it. The Court is further constrained by its reactive nature: It cannot make law except from cases that find their way onto its docket.

Contributors who are more sympathetic to the Supreme Court's representation jurisprudence (Fitts, Petterson, Bowman, Lowenstein) contend that the justices are correct not to strain for some coherent theory of politics. They view the Court's task as more limited: to narrowly answer only the issues necessary to resolve the specific dispute before it. This view limits the Court's ability to weave a more comprehensive, encompassing constitutional theory that reflects political realities. That limited role has been circumscribed even further by the current Court, however, and the judicial philosophies that characterize its decision making. The Rehnquist Court is tentative and cautious to a fault. Unlike the Warren and Burger Courts, this Court is so pragmatic, fact-specific, and narrow in its decisions that it cannot be considered (or will not consider itself) a generator of any cohesive philosophical framework.

Variances in the assessments of the Supreme Court's work in this area may be attributable to differences in the perspectives of legal practitioners/

academics and political scientists. At the risk of caricaturing the respective disciplines, lawyers and political scientists judge these issues—and the Court's role in resolving them—differently. For lawyers and judges, the Court's task is to decide the particular dispute before it in a way that establishes sound precedent and provides sufficient guidance for lower courts. Political scientists are more theory-oriented and big-picture-conscious; they want clearer explanations and understandings of political behavior that contribute to a more efficient, well-ordered, representative system.

These contrasting goals lead to different emphases. The legal mind-set seeks workable adjudicatory standards, fair processes, and "bright line" principles. Although this approach is useful in guiding lower court decision making, it does not allow for the nuances and subtleties of representation. For judges and lawyers schooled in the language of rights and constantly conditioned to issues of equality, representation presents a conceptual minefield that is better left alone. Political scientists consider the Supreme Court's task to be broader. They are hard-pressed to understand why the Court would not consult bodies of evidence that might edify its constitutional framework. The areas of oversight outlined above—theory, empiricism, comparative politics—are all major areas of study within the discipline. For political scientists who feel they have something to contribute to the quest for a well-ordered electoral system, these ways of explaining political behavior should be thoroughly explored.

Hence, the Supreme Court's distrust of party-conscious doctrine or overt theorizing is indicative of the values that lawyers bring to the table. Lawyers' and judges' concern for equal participation and political rights helps explain their inbred skepticism for political collectivities generally and political parties in particular. They carry with them the vision of political parties as antidemocratic, hierarchical machines that are antithetical to the participatory rights of individuals. Political scientists are likely to regard political parties as serving effective representative democracy. They will have a much more favorable view of organized associational political behavior, especially by partisan organizations.

Constitutional interpretation is linked to political theory, however. To say that the Supreme Court merely resolves isolated cases ignores its function as interpreter of the written expression of the people's consent. The Constitution and its amendments presume particular political values and perspectives—namely, those of their framers and of the people who ratified them. To interpret the Constitution, the Court must likewise try to discern and apply those values. It is specious to think that the Court can decide cases affecting the electoral system without reflecting some set of values and theoretical assumptions, consciously or otherwise. If this resort to political presuppositions is unavoidable, it is preferable that it be done explicitly and straightforwardly.

Consider Stephen Gottlieb's analysis of the Court's efforts in *Board of Education of Kiryas Joel Village School District v. Grumet*. Gottlieb exhaustively details the Court's labored search for a magical standard— legislative motives, governmental neutrality, consistency, delegation of control—that would lend clarity to the task of creating school districts. In the end, the search proves futile; the inherently political exercise of redistricting cannot be governed by a nicely packaged, neutral test. The Court must make some determinations, Gottlieb argues, about what constitutes good and bad redistricting. That determination requires that the Court offer some substantive definition of representation. Instead, the Court sweeps under the rug the fundamental conflict underlying the redistricting dispute—namely, the tension between the competing values of integration and assimilation. On one hand, we expect representation to embody common identity and the interests of the whole. We also value enough segregation, however, to allow for cultivation of group identity and distinct cultural practices and values. Although the Court might not want to definitively resolve this debate, it should at least articulate or identify what the fight is really about.

ADVANCING THE DEBATE: WHERE TO FROM HERE?

The Supreme Court's authority in formulating election law continues to expand. Only four decades ago, it routinely declined to intervene in a host of political questions; now it habitually thrusts itself into the political and electoral arena. The Court reshapes practical politics in dramatic ways, often inadvertently. The judicial gloss applied to the Voting Rights Act in *Thornburg v. Gingles* had a stark impact on the drawing of electoral district lines and the kind of representation those districts produced. It led to the abandonment of multimember, at-large electoral districts in hundreds of jurisdictions across the country. The Court's focus on "racial bloc voting" produced the widespread creation of majority-minority districts in single-member districts as well. That trend added large numbers of black representatives to Congress; it also made it easier to elect Republicans in adjoining districts. The Court had a remarkable effect in aiding

African Americans in their quest for *descriptive representation*; this bene-fit came at the expense of the *partisan representation* they were likely to realize through the Democratic Party.

Given the Supreme Court's expanded authority and the ramifications of its rulings, the Court delivers its decisions incongruously. Regardless of whether the Court is sufficiently attuned to the theoretical and practical implications of its decisions, its opinions do not reflect that awareness. It exhibits a disturbing propensity to pronounce easy conclusions without explanation, elaboration, or elucidation. *Colorado Republican Federal Campaign Committee v. FEC* altered the campaign financing landscape virtually overnight. If the Court knew that its decision would clear the way for the precipitous escalation of soft money spending and party influence, however, it gave no such indication. Its sanction of the two-party system in *Timmons v. Twin Cities Area New Party* lacked a serious attempt to support such a fundamental conclusion. One need not disagree with the outcomes of those cases to be troubled by the Court's failure or refusal to acknowledge the larger issues involved.

What, then, is the answer for this problematic area of constitutional law? For some contributors, the Supreme Court's involvement is pre-sumptuous, smacking of "judicial activism." Given the Court's inability to render clear and thoughtful decisions, the Court and the political process might be better off if matters were left to the elected branches (or independent entities, as some commentators have suggested). For others, the Court is doing as well as can be expected. Dan Lowenstein applauds the Court's refusal to engage in excessive theorizing, commending it for not preempting the competition between alternative visions of politics. Similarly, Mike Fitts concludes that the Court need do little to improve its doctrinal approach to political parties. Even if the Court were more philosophically aware with respect to political parties, its decisions still would largely turn on technical, fact-specific issues; technical considera-tions are far more consequential than some "functional parties" approach to constitutional law. Fitts lauds the Court's deference to the political forces at work; he preaches judicial caution with respect to parties and political judgments.

For still other contributors, the Supreme Court has no choice but to be more activist. Given the importance of these questions and the legis-lative conflicts of interest, the Court cannot sit on its hands. Although it cannot avoid theorizing, it must invoke sounder theory (see chapters by Jeff Polet and David Ryden). Political representation presents a daunting theoretical challenge, however; it weaves together multiple concepts, players, and behaviors. The complex network of representational modes, means, and outcomes mandates explicit acknowledgment of the importance of group voices, as well as group disparities that muffle or exclude some voices. Hence, representation theory demands structures that simultaneously enhance individual effectiveness, facilitate group politics, and alleviate group inequities.

In this context, Lowenstein is correct in concluding that the Supreme Court is right not to have settled on a single view or theory of representation. Not only could we not count on the Court to make the right choice (it surely has lots of company here), but the competition between the contrasting theories—progressivism, party government, pluralism, liberal rights theory—is the essence of politics. Yet the Court's wisdom in not adopting a grand theory of representation does not imply that its mediating of the competing visions has been wise. An informed conceptualization of representation is necessary to decide the cases at hand. An awareness of the multifaceted patterns of representation would position the Court to at least isolate the dimensions at issue in any given context.

Unfortunately, the Supreme Court is too skewed in the direction of liberal rights theory. Its tendency is to rely on rights as the rule and to practically limit those rights to individuals. Even the right of association is individually bound—belonging not to the party or group but to its individual adherents as a means of amplifying their voices. This approach does not do justice to the collective dimensions of association, especially with respect to political parties. Political parties are far more than the sum of the individuals they comprise, and they do much more than engage in speech. They recruit and support candidates, register voters, and develop programs—all of which advance representation. Party association in elections leads to power in government; party government affects policy and procures benefits for constituents. Thus, the institutional activities of political parties enlarge and augment individual political effectiveness and warrant extension of associational rights to political parties and groups. Constitutional recognition of the individual right, which ignores its corporate manifestation, is a thin right indeed.

Pursuing representation through narrowly conceived rights only rigidifies and ossifies the contradictions in representation theory. Representation is about *conflicts of interests*. As E. E. Schattschneider remarked, representative politics requires a means of generating conflict and widening its scope. Only by maximizing the host of interests to which legislators must respond are the complex demands of representation met. This concept of representation requires institutional means of producing conflict, constraining it, and translating it into representative action. This conclusion brings us full circle to the organizational prerequisites of representative democracy—namely, party organizations. Conflicts of interests are engendered and ultimately resolved—and representation advanced—through the subsystems of multidimensional political parties. In the process, political parties mediate, balance, and serve the other three theories (albeit far from perfectly). Political parties are singularly constituted to weave together the patchwork of representational threads and cloths.

Many readers will disagree adamantly with this position; indeed, I suspect that most of the contributors to this volume would reject it. That is as it should be. Let the debate advance—perhaps even into the courtroom and conference chambers of the Supreme Court.

References

Ackerman, Bruce A. 1991. *We the People*. Cambridge: Harvard University Press.

———. 1995. "Crediting The Voters: A New Beginning for Campaign Finance." In *The American Prospect Reader in American Politics*, edited by Walter Burnham. Chatham, N.J.: Chatham House.

Aldrich, John H. 1995. *Why Parties? The Origin and Transformation of Political Parties in America*. Chicago: University of Chicago Press.

Alexander, Herbert E. 1992. *Financing Politics: Money, Elections, & Political Reform*. 4th ed. Washington, D.C.: Congressional Quarterly Press.

Allswang, John M. 1986. *Bosses, Machines and Urban Voters*. Rev. ed. Baltimore: Johns Hopkins University Press.

Amy, Douglas. 1998. "The Fusion Decision and the Spectre of Multiparty Democracy." Paper presented at annual meeting of the American Political Science Association, Boston, September 3–6.

Aoki, K. 1997. "Direct Democracy, Racial Group Agency, Local Government Law, and Residential Racial Segregation: Some Reflections on Radical and Plural Democracy." *California Western Law Review* 33:185–204.

Argersinger, Peter H. 1980. "A Place on the Ballot: Fusion Politics and Antifusion Laws." *American History Review* 85:287–306.

Bailey, Douglas. 1995. "Tech Speak." *Boston Globe*, 19 May, 41.

Baker, C. Edwin. 1998. "Campaign Expenditures and Free Speech." *Harvard Civil Rights and Civil Liberties Law Review* 33:1.

Baker, L. A. 1991. "Direct Democracy and Discrimination: A Public Choice Perspective." *Chicago Kent Law Review* 67:707–76.

Balkin, J. M. 1997. "The Constitution of Status." *Yale Law Journal* 106: 2313–74.

Barnett, R. E. 1995. "Guns, Militias, and Oklahoma City." *Tennessee Law Review* 62:443–59.

Barone, Michael, and Grant Ujifusa. 1997. *The Almanac of American Politics 1998*. Washington, D.C.: National Journal.

Baugh, Joyce A., Christopher E. Smith, and Thomas R. Hensley. 1995. "The First Term Performance of Justice Breyer." *Judiciature* 79:74.

Beck, Paul Allen, and Frank J. Sorauf. 1992. *Party Politics in America.* 7th ed. New York: Harper Collins.

Becker, Gary. 1983. "A Theory of Competition Among Pressure Groups for Political Influence." *Quarterly Journal of Economics* 98:37.

Bell, D. A., Jr. 1978. "The Referendum: Democracy's Barrier to Racial Equality." *Washington Law Review* 54:1–29.

Bickel, Alexander 1962. *The Least Dangerous Branch: The Supreme Court at the Bar of Politics.* Indianapolis: Bobbs-Merrill.

———. 1978. *The Supreme Court and the Idea of Progress.* New York: Harper & Row.

Birch, A. H. 1971. *Representation.* New York: Praeger.

Blaise, Andre, and R. K. Carty. 1990. "Does Proportional Representation Foster Voter Turnout?" *European Journal of Political Research* 18: 167–81.

Bogdanor, Vernon. 1984. *What Is Proportional Representation?* London: Martin Robertson.

Bowman, Cynthia Grant. 1991. "'We Don't Want Anybody Sent': The Death of Patronage Hiring in Chicago." *Northwestern University Law Review* 86:57–95.

———. 1996. "The Law of Patronage at a Crossroads." *Journal of Law and Politics* 12:34–36.

Brest, Paul. 1981. "The Fundamental Rights Controversy: The Essential Contradictions in Normative Constitutional Scholarship." *Yale Law Journal* 90:1062.

Briffault, Richard. 1985. "Distrust of Democracy." *Texas Law Review* 63: 1347–75.

———. 1995. "Race and Representation After *Miller v. Johnson.*" *University of Chicago Legal Forum* 1995:23.

———. 1996. "Campaign Finance, the Parties and The Court: A Comment on *Colorado Republican Federal Campaign Committee v. Federal Elections Commission.*" Paper prepared for 1996 Annual meeting of the American Political Science Association, San Francisco.

Brinkley, Alan, Nelson W. Polsby, and Kathleen M. Sullivan. 1997. *New Federalist Papers: Essays in Defense of the Constitution.* New York: W. W. Norton and Co.

Burke, C. C. 1993. "Fencing Out Politically Unpopular Groups From the Normal Political Processes: The Equal Protection Concerns of Colorado Amendment Two." *Indiana Law Journal* 69:275–98.

Burke, Edmund. [1790] 1955. *Reflections on the Revolution in France*. Reprint, Indianapolis: Liberal Arts Press.

Bybee, Keith J. 1998. *Mistaken Identity: The Supreme Court and the Politics of Minority Representation*. Princeton: N.J.: Princeton University Press.

Cain, Bruce E. 1984. *The Reapportionment Puzzle*. Berkeley: University of California Press.

———. 1995. *Moralism and Realism in Campaign Finance Reform*. University of Chicago, Legal Forum 1995:111.

———.1999 "Election Law as a Field: A Political Scientist's Perspective." *Loyola of Los Angeles Law Review* 32:1105.

Cantor, Dan. 1996. *Rehnquist, Scalia and the New Party: Our Day at the Supreme Court* [http://www.newparty.org/fusion7.html]. December 4.

Cassidy, Suzanne. 1995. "Quest for Board Seats Becomes Holy War; Christian Coalition at Heart of CD Schools Debate." *Sunday Patriot News* Harrisburg, Penn., 14 May, B3.

Charlow, R. 1994. "Judicial Review, Equal Protection and the Problem With Plebiscites." *Cornell Law Review* 79:527–630.

Choper, Jesse H. 1982. "Defining 'Religion' in the First Amendment." *U. Illinois Law Review* 579.

Claude, Richard. 1970. *The Supreme Court and the Electoral Process*. Baltimore: Johns Hopkins University Press.

Cohen, Adam. "City Boosters." *Time*, 18 August, 20.

Congressional Globe. 1866. 39th Congress.

Congressional Quarterly. 1991. "Voting Rights Act, Law Suits Result in Many Delays." *Congressional Quarterly* 49 (November 9):3323–25.

Connolly, Lincoln. 1996. "Mowing Down a Grass Roots Movement but Protecting the Crabgrass: Congressional Term Limits are Unconstitutional." *University of Miami Law Review* 50:661.

Cover, Albert D. 1977. "One Good Term Deserves Another: The Advantage of Incumbency in Congressional Elections." *American Journal of Political Science* 21:523.

Cover, Albert D., and David R. Mayhew. 1977. "Congressional Dynamics and the Decline of Competitive Congressional Elections." In *Congress Reconsidered*, edited by Lawrence C. Dodd and Bruce I. Oppenheimer. Washington, D.C.: Congressional Quarterly Press.

Cox, Archibald. 1966. "Constitutional Adjudication and The Promotion of Human Rights." *Harvard Law Review* 80:91.

Cronin, T. E. 1989. *Direct Democracy: The Politics of Initiative, Referendum and Recall*. Cambridge, Mass.: Harvard University Press.

Dahl, Robert. 1956. *A Preface to Democratic Theory*. Chicago: University of Chicago Press.

————. 1982. *Dilemmas of Pluralist Democracy: Autonomy v. Control*. New Haven, Conn.: Yale University Press.

Dailey, J. D., and P. Farley. 1996. "Colorado's Amendment 2: A Result in Search of a Reason." *Harvard Journal of Law & Public Policy* 20: 215–68.

Davidson, Chandler, and Bernard Grofman. 1994. *Quiet Revolution in the South*. Princeton, N.J.: Princeton University Press.

de Grazia, Alfred. 1951. *Public and Republic: Political Representation in America*. New York: Alfred A. Knopf.

Dixon, Robert. 1968. *Democratic Representation*. New York: Oxford University Press.

Downs, Anthony. 1957. *An Economic Theory of Democracy*. New York: Harper-Collins.

Duncan, R. F., and G. L. Young. 1995. "Homosexual Rights and Citizen Initiatives: Is Constitutionalism Unconstitutional?" *Notre Dame Journal of Law, Ethics & Public Policy* 9:93–135.

Duverger, Maurice. 1954. *Political Parties: Their Organization and Activity in the Modern State*. New York: Wiley.

————. 1959. *Political Parties*. 2nd ed. New York: Wiley.

Dworkin, Ronald. 1996. "The Curse of Money." *New York Review of Books* 19.

Elhauge, Einer, John R. Lott, Jr., and Richard L. Manning. 1997. "How Term Limits Enhance The Expression of Democratic Preferences." *Supreme Court Economic Review* 5:59.

Elliott, Ward E. Y. 1974. *The Rise of Guardian Democracy: The Supreme Court's Role in Voting Rights Disputes, 1845–1969*. Cambridge, Mass.: Harvard University Press

Ely, John H. 1980. *Democracy and Distrust: A Theory of Judicial Review*. Cambridge, Mass.: Harvard University Press.

Epstein, Edwin M. 1980. "Business and Labor Under the Federal Election Campaign Act of 1971." In *Parties, Interest Groups, and Campaign Finance Laws*, edited by Michael Malbin. Washington, D.C.: American Enterprise Institute.

Epstein, Lee, and Jack Knight. 1997. *The Choices Justices Make*. Washington, D.C.: Congressional Quarterly Press.

Epstein, Leon. 1986. *Political Parties in the American Mold*. Madison: University of Wisconsin Press.

Epstein, Richard A. 1992. *Forbidden Grounds: The Case Against Employment Discrimination Laws*. Cambridge, Mass.: Harvard University Press.

———. 1995. *Simple Rules for a Complex World*. Cambridge, Mass.: Harvard University Press.

Erie, Steven P. 1988. *Rainbow's End: Irish-Americans and the Dilemmas of Urban Machine Politics, 1840–1985*. Berkeley: University of California Press.

Eulau, Heinz, and Kenneth Prewitt. 1973. *Labyrinths of Democracy: Adaptations, Linkages, Representation, and Policies in Urban Politics*. Indianapolis: Bobbs-Merrill.

Eule, J. N. 1990. "Judicial Review of Direct Democracy." *Yale Law Journal* 99:1503–90.

———. 1991. "Representative Government: The People's Choice." *Chicago Kent Law Review* 67:777–90.

Farrand, Max, ed. 1966. *The Records of the Federal Convention of 1787*. New Haven, Conn.: Yale University Press.

Felton, E. 1993. *The Ruling Class: Inside the Imperial Congress*. Washington, D.C.: Heritage Foundation.

Ferejohn, John A. 1977. "On the Decline of Competition in Congressional Elections." *American Political Science Review* 71:166.

Fiorina, Morris P. 1981. *Retrospective Voting in American National Elections*. New Haven, Conn.: Yale University Press.

Fiss, Owen. 1996. *The Irony of Free Speech*. Cambridge, Mass.: Harvard University Press.

Fitts, Michael. 1988. "The Vices of Virtue: A Political Party Perspective on Civic Virtue Reforms of the Legislative Process." *University of Pennsylvania Law Review* 136:1537.

———. 1990. "Can Ignorance Be Bliss? Information as a Positive Influence in Political Institutions." *Michigan Law Review* 88:917.

———. 1996. "The Paradox of Power in The Modern State: Why A Unitary Centralized Presidency May Not Exhibit Effective or Legitimate Leadership." *University of Pennsylvania Law Review* 144:827.

Foley, Edward. 1994. "Equal Dollars-Per-Voter: A Constitutional Principle of Campaign Finance." *Colorado Law Review* 94:1204.

Freedman, Anne. 1994. *Patronage: An American Tradition*. Chicago: Nelson-Hall.

Frug, Gerald. 1993. "Decentering Decentralization." *University of Chicago Law Review* 60:253.

Garrett, E. 1997. "Who Directs Direct Democracy?" *University of Chicago Law School Roundtable* 4:17–36.

Gerstmann, E. 1999. *The Constitutional Underclass: Gays, Lesbians, and the Failure of Class Based Equal Protection*. Chicago: University of Chicago Press.

Gibson, Ray, and Hanke Gratteau. 1992. "Helping Their Cronies Is The Least Politicians Can Do." *Chicago Tribune*, 29 December, 1.

Gillette, C. P. 1988. "Plebiscites, Participation, and Collective Action in Local Government Law." *Michigan Law Review* 86:930–88.

Gora, Joel M. 1998. "Dollars and Sense: In Praise of A Landmark Case." Paper presented at Conference on Parties, Politics, and the Law, University of Akron, Akron, Ohio, September 25.

Gottlieb, Stephen E. 1982. "Rebuilding the Right of Association: The Right to Hold a Convention as a Test Case." *Hofstra Law Review* 11:191–247.

———. 1986. "Reformulating the Motive/Effects Debate in Constitutional Adjudication." *Wayne Law Review* 33:97.

———. 1987. "In the Name of Patriotism: The Constitutionality of 'Bending' History in Public Secondary Schools." *New York University Law Review* 62:497.

———. 1988. "Fashioning A Test for Gerrymandering." *Journal of Legislation* 15:144.

Grady, Robert. 1993. *Restoring Real Representation*. Chicago: University of Illinois Press.

Gratteau, Hanke, and Ray Gibson. 1992. "Contracts Are State's Cookie Jar." *Chicago Tribune*, 27 December, 1.

Green, Paul M. 1984. "The 1983 Chicago Democratic Mayoral Primary: Some New Players—Same Old Rules." In *The Making of the Mayor: Chicago 1983*, edited by Melvin G. Holli and Paul M. Green. Grand Rapids, Mich.: William B. Eerdmans.

Greenhouse, Linda. 1996. "Supreme Court Debates State Bans on Multiparty Candidates." *New York Times*, 5 December.

Grimshaw, William J. 1982. "The Daley Legacy: A Declining Politics of Party, Race, and Public Unions." In *After Daley: Chicago Politics in Transition*, edited by Samuel K. Gove and Louis H. Masotti. Urbana, Ill.: University of Illinois Press, 57–87.

———. 1992. *Bitter Fruit: Black Politics and the Chicago Machine, 1931–1991*. Chicago: University of Chicago Press.

Grofman, Bernard, and Chandler Davidson, eds. 1992. *Controversies in Minority Voting: The Voting Rights Act in Perspective*. Washington, D.C.: Brookings Institution.

Grofman, Bernard, Lisa Handley, and Richard Niemi. 1992. *Minority Representation and the Quest for Voting Equality*. New York: Cambridge University Press.

Guinier, Lani. 1991. "No Two Seats: The Elusive Quest for Political Equality." *Virginia Law Review* 77:1413–1514.

———. 1994. *The Tyranny of the Majority: Fundamental Fairness in Representative Democracy*. New York: The Free Press.

———. 1995. "The Representation of Minority Interests." In *Classifying by Race*, edited by Paul Peterson. Princeton, N.J.: Princeton University Press.

Gunn, P. F. 1981. "Initiatives and Referendums: Direct Democracy and Minority Interests." *Urban Law Annual* 22:135–59.

Hamilton, Alexander, James Madison, and John Jay. [1787], 1961. *The Federalist Papers*, edited by Clinton Rossiter. New York: Mentor.

Hamilton, M. A. 1997. "Perspective on Direct Democracy: The People: The Least Accountable Branch." *University of Chicago Law School Roundtable* 1997:1–16.

Hasen, Richard. 1993. "An Enriched Economic Model of Political Patronage and Campaign Contributions: Reformulating Supreme Court Jurisprudence." *Cardozo Law Review* 14:1311–41.

———. 1996. "Clipping Coupons for Democracy: An Egalitarian Public Choice Defense of Campaign Finance Vouchers." *California Law Review* 84:1.

———. 1998. "Entrenching the Duopoly: Why the Supreme Court Should Not Allow the States to Protect the Democrats and Republicans from Political Competition." In *The Supreme Court Review 1997*, edited by Dennis Hutchinson, David A. Strauss, and Geoffrey R. Stone. Chicago: University of Chicago Press, 331–71.

Heintz, Julie. 1997. "Why Can't a Chicken Vote for Colonel Sanders? *U.S. Term Limits, Inc. v. Thornton* and the Constitutionality of Term Limits." *Pepperdine Law Review* 24:649.

Impoco, Jim. 1995. "Separating Church and School; Second Thoughts in Vista." *U.S. News & World Report*, 24 April, 30.

Issacharoff, Samuel, and Richard H. Pildes. 1998. "Politics as Markets: Partisan Lockups of the Democratic Process." *Stanford Law Review* 50:643.

Issacharoff, Samuel, Pamela Karlan, and Richard Pildes. 1998. *The Law of Democracy: Legal Structure of the Political Process*. Westbury, N.Y.: Foundation Press.

Jackson, Brooks. 1988. *Honest Graft: Big Money and the American Political Process*. New York: Alfred A. Knopf.

Jackson, J. S. 1997. "Persons of Equal Worth: *Romer v. Evans* and the Politics of Equal Protection." *UCLA Law Review* 45:453–501.

Jacobson, Gary C. 1990. *The Electoral Origins of Divided Government: Competition in U.S. House Elections, 1946–1988*. Boulder, Colo.: Westview Press.

Jessup, David. 1980. "Can Political Influence Be Democratized? A Labor Perspective." In *Parties, Interest Groups, and Campaign Finance Laws*, edited by Michael Malbin. Washington, D.C.: American Enterprise Institute.

Keiser, Richard A. 1989. "Black Political Incorporation or Subordination?: Political Competitiveness and Leadership Formation Prior to the Election of Black Mayors." Unpublished Ph.D. dissertation, University of California at Berkeley.

Kemp, Kathleen A., and Robert L. Lineberry. 1982. "The Last of the Great Urban Machines and the Last of the Great Urban Mayors?" In *After Daley: Chicago Politics in Transition*, edited by Samuel K. Gove and Louis H. Masotti. Urbana, Ill.: University of Illinois Press.

Key, V. O. 1949. *Southern Politics in State and Nation*. New York: Alfred A. Knopf.

King, Gary, John Bruce, and Andrew Gelman. 1995. "Racial Fairness in Legislative Districting." In *Classifying by Race*, edited by Paul Peterson. Princeton, N.J.: Princeton University Press.

Kirschner, William R. 1995. "Fusion and the Associational Right of Parties." *Columbia Law Review* 95:683–723.

Klarman, Michael. 1991. "The Puzzling Resistance to Political Process Theory." *Virginia Law Review* 77:747.

———. 1997. "Majoritarian Judicial Review: The Entrenchment Problem." *Georgetown Law Journal* 85:491.

Kleppner, Paul. 1985. *Chicago Divided: The Making of a Black Mayor*. De Kalb, Ill.: Northern Illinois University Press.

Knauss, Peter R. 1972. *Chicago: A One-Party State*. Champaign, Ill.: Stipes Publishing Co.

Kolbert, Elizabeth. 1989. "Town Wants a Hassidic Public School District." *New York Times*, 21 July, A1.

Latz, Martin E. 1991. "The Constitutionality of State-Passed Congressional Term Limits." *Akron Law Review* 25:155.

Lawson, Kay. 1997. "The Case for a Multiparty System." In *Multiparty Politics in America,* edited by Paul S. Herrnson and John C. Green. New York: Rowan and Littlefield.

Leong, R. 1997. "Ballot Initiatives and Identifiable Minorities: A Textual Call to Congress." *Rutgers Law Journal* 28:677–708.

Lijphart, Arend. 1984. *Democracies: Patterns of Majoritarian and Consensus Government in Twenty-One Countries.* New Haven, Conn.: Yale University Press.

———. 1991. "Constitutional Choices for New Democracies." *Journal of Democracy* 2:72–84.

Lively, D. E., P. A. Haddon, D. E. Roberts, and R. L. Weaver. 1996. *Constitutional Law: Cases, History and Dialogues.* Cincinnati: Anderson Publishing.

Loveland, Ian. 1997. "Liberals Lost in the Political Thicket? *U.S. Term Limits, Inc. v. Thornton.*" *Anglo-American Law Review* 26:1.

Lowenstein, Daniel H. 1982. "Campaign Spending and Ballot Propositions: Recent Experience, Public Choice Theory, and the First Amendment." *UCLA Law Review* 29:505–641.

———. 1992a. "A Patternless Mosaic: Campaign Finance and the First Amendment After *Austin.*" *Capital University Law Review* 21: 381.

———. 1992b. "American Political Parties." In *Developments in American Politics,* edited by Gillian Peel, Christopher J. Bailey, and Bruce Cain. London: Macmillan.

———. 1993. "Associational Rights of Major Political Parties: A Skeptical Inquiry." *Texas Law Review* 71:1741.

———. 1995. *Election Law: Cases and Materials.* Durham, N.C.: Carolina Academic Press.

———. 1998. "You Don't Have to Be Liberal to Hate the Racial Gerrymandering Cases." *Stanford Law Review* 50:779.

———. In press. "Political Reform Is Political." In *This Old House: Remodel or Rebuild?,* edited by Joe Zimmerman and Wilma Rule. Westport, Conn: Praeger.

Lowenstein, Daniel H., and Jonathan Steinberg. 1985. "The Quest for Legislative Districting in the Public Interest: Elusive or Illusory?" *UCLA Law Review* 33:1.

Lowenstein, Daniel H., and Robert M. Stern. 1989. "The First Amendment and Paid Initiative Circulators: A Dissenting View and a Proposal." *Hastings Constitutional Law Quarterly* 17:175.

Lowi, Theodore. 1979. *The End of Liberalism: The Second Republic of the United States*. New York: W. W. Norton.

———. 1992. "The Party Crasher." *New York Times*, 23 August.

———. 1996. "A Ticket to Democracy." *New York Times,* 28 December.

———. 1997. "Presidency-Congress: What the Two Party Duopoly has Done to American Separation of Powers." *Case Western Law Review* 47:219.

Lublin, David. 1997. *The Paradox of Representation: Racial Gerrymandering and Minority Interests in Congress*. Princeton, N.J.: Princeton University Press.

MacDonald, Forrest. 1985. *Novus Ordo Seclorum: The Intellectual Origins of the Constitution*. Lawrence: Kansas University Press.

Macey, Jonathan. 1990. "The Role of the Democratic and Republican Parties as Organizers of Shadow Interest Groups." *Michigan Law Review* 89:1.

———. 1994. "Chief Justice Rehnquist, Interest Group Theory, and the Founders' Design." *Rutgers Law Journal* 25:577–96.

Magleby, D. B. 1984. *Direct Legislation: Voting on Ballot Propositions in the United States*. Baltimore: Johns Hopkins University Press.

Magleby, David, and Marianne Holt. 1999. "The Long Shadow of Soft Money and Issue Advocacy Ads." *Campaigns and Elections*, May, 22–27.

Malbin, Michael J. 1980. *Parties, Interest Groups, and Campaign Finance Laws*. Washington, D.C.: American Enterprise Institute.

Maltese, John. 1997. "Bound by Law: the Pragmatism of David Souter." Paper presented at annual meeting of the Midwest Political Science Association, Chicago, April 10–12.

Mansnerus, Laura. 1993. "At the Bar." *New York Times*, 3 September, A17.

Martin, Susan Lorde. 1989. "A Decade of *Branti* Decisions: A Government Official's Guide to Patronage Dismissals." *American University Law Review* 39:11–58.

Maveety, Nancy. 1991. *Representation Rights and the Burger Years*. Ann Arbor: University of Michigan Press.

———. 1996. *Justice Sandra Day O'Connor: Strategist on the Supreme Court* Lanham, Md.: Rowman and Littlefield.

May, Larry. 1987. *The Morality of Groups: Collective Responsibility, Group-Based Harm, and Corporate Rights*. Notre Dame, Ind.: University of Notre Dame Press.

Mayhew, David. 1971. "Congressional Representation: Theory and Practice in Drawing the Districts." In *Re-apportionment in the 1970s*, edited by Nelson Polsby. Berkeley: University of California Press.

McClay, Wilfred. 1996. "The Soul of Man Under Federalism." *First Things*, June/July: 64.

McConnell, Grant. 1966. *Private Power and American Democracy*. New York: Alfred A. Knopf.

McDonald, Laughlin. 1992. "The 1982 Amendments of Section 2 and Minority Representation." In *Controversies in Minority Voting*, edited by Bernard Grofman and Chandler Davidson. Washington, D.C.: Brookings Institution.

McDonald, Michael D., and Richard L. Engstrom. 1990. "Detecting Gerrymandering." In *Political Gerrymandering and the Courts*, edited by Bernard Grofman. New York: Agathon Press.

Merton, Robert. 1949. *Social Theory and Social Structure*. Glencoe, Ill.: The Free Press.

Miniter, Richard. 1992. "Running Against the Computer: Stephen Solarz and the Technician-Designed Congressional District." *Washington Post*, 20 September, C5.

Moeller, John. 1984. "The Supreme Court's Quest for Fair Politics." *Constitutional Commentary* 1:203.

Murphy, Walter F. 1964. *Elements of Judicial Strategy*. Chicago: University of Chicago Press.

Nagel, Robert F. 1996. "The Term Limits Dissent: What Nerve," *Arizona Law Review* 38:843–57.

Neuberger, Christine. 1995. "*Seventeen* Back on the Rack at Stafford Middle School but Parents Can Notify Library to Keep it Away from Child." *Richmond Times-Dispatch*, 26 April, B1.

New York State Legislative Task Force on Demographic Research and Reapportionment. 1992. *Co-Chairmen's Proposed 1992 Assembly and State Senate District Boundaries*. January 21.

Niemi, Richard G. 1990. "The Swing Ratio as a Measure of Partisan Gerrymandering." In *Political Gerrymandering and the Courts*, edited by Bernard Grofman. New York: Agathon Press.

Niemi, Richard G., and John Wolkerson. 1990. "Compactness and the 1980s Districts in the Indiana State House: Evidence of Political Gerrymandering?" In *Political Gerrymandering and the Courts*, edited by Bernard Grofman. New York: Agathon Press.

Nimmer, Melville. 1968. "The Right to Speak from *Times* to *Time*: First Amendment Theory Applied to Libel and Misapplied to Privacy." *California Law Review* 56:935.

Olson, Mancur. 1965. *The Logic of Collective Action*. Cambridge, Mass.: Harvard University Press.

"Party, PACs, and Campaign Finance: Preserving First Amendment Parity." 1997. *Harvard Law Review* 110:1573.

Persily, N. A. 1997. "The Peculiar Geography of Direct Democracy: Why the Initiative, Referendum, and Recall Developed in the American West." *Michigan Law & Policy Review* 2:11–41.

Peterson, Paul E. 1995. "A Politically Correct Solution to Racial Classification." In *Classifying by Race*, edited by Paul Peterson. Princeton, N.J.: Princeton University Press.

Petterson, Paul R. 1998. "The Meaning of *Morse*." Paper presented to annual meeting of the American Political Science Association, Boston, September 3–6.

Phillips, Anne. 1997. "Why Worry About Multiculturalism?" *Dissent* 57 (Winter).

Pildes, Richard. 1995. "The Politics of Race." *Harvard Law Review* 108:1359.

Pildes, Richard, and Richard Niemi. 1993. "Expressive Harms, 'Bizarre Districts,' and Voting Rights: Evaluating Election-District Appearances After *Shaw v. Reno*." *Michigan Law Review* 92:483.

Pitkin, Hannah. 1967. *The Concept of Representation*. Berkeley: University of California Press.

Pomper, Gerald. 1980. "The Contribution of Political Parties to American Democracy." In *Party Renewal in America*, edited by Gerald Pomper. New York: Praeger.

Posner, Eric. 1996. "The Regulation of Groups: The Influence of Legal and Nonlegal Sanctions on Collective Action." *University of Chicago Law Review* 63:133.

Preston, Michael B. 1984. "The Resurgence of Black Voting in Chicago: 1955–1983." In *The Making of the Mayor: Chicago 1983*, edited by Melvin G. Holli and Paul M. Green. Grand Rapids, Mich.: William B. Eerdmans.

Richards, Neil. 1996. "*U.S Term Limits v. Thornton* and Competing Notions of Federalism." *Journal of Law and Politics* 12:521.

Riker, W. H. 1991. "Comment on Baker, 'Direct Democracy and Discrimination: A Public Choice Perspective.'" *Chicago Kent Law Review* 67: 791–94.

Robinson, C. 1997. "Texas Two Step: Preferences, No—Affirmative Action, Yes." *Houston Chronicle*, 16 November.

Rogers, C. A., and D. L. Faigman. 1996. "'And to the Republic for Which It Stands': Guaranteeing a Republican Form of Government." *Hastings Constitutional Law Quarterly* 23:1057–72.

Rosenkranz, Joshua. 1999. "Campaign Finance Reform and the Constitution: What's Hot in the Courts." *Extensions*, Spring: 13–17.

Rotunda, Ronald. 1996. "The Aftermath of *Thornton*." *Constitutional Commentary* 13:201.

Royko, Michael. 1971. *Boss: Richard J. Daley of Chicago*. New York: Dutton.

Rush, Mark. 1993. "Voters' Rights and The Legal Status of American Political Parties." *Journal of Politics* 9:487.

———. 1994. "In Search of a Coherent Theory of Voting Rights: Challenges to the Supreme Court's Vision of Fair and Effective Representation." *Review of Politics* 56:503.

Ryden, David. 1996. *Representation in Crisis: The Constitution, Interest Groups, and Political Parties*. Albany: State University of New York Press.

Sabato, Larry J. 1988. *The Party's Just Begun: Shaping Political Parties for America's Future*. New York: Scott, Foresman.

Schacter, J. S. 1995. "The Pursuit of 'Popular Intent': Interpretive Dilemmas in Direct Democracy." *Yale Law Journal* 105:107–76.

———. 1997. "*Romer v. Evans* and Democracy's Domain." *Vanderbilt Law Review* 50:361–410.

Schattschneider, E. E. [1942], 1977. *Party Government*. Westport, Conn.: Greenwood Press.

———. 1960. *The Semi-Sovereign People*. New York: Holt, Rinehart, and Winston.

Schneider, Bryan A. 1992. "Comment: Do Not Go Gentle Into That Good Night: The Unquiet Death of Political Patronage." *Wisconsin Law Review* 1992:511–46.

Schuck, Peter. 1987. "The Thickest Thicket: Partisan Gerrymandering and Judicial Regulation of Politics." *Colorado Law Review* 87:1325.

Schwartz, Bernard. 1996. "Term Limits, Commerce, and the Rehnquist Court." *Tulsa Law Journal* 31:521.

Seidle, F. L. 1994. "The Canadian Electoral System and Proposal for Reform." In *Canadian Parties in Transition*, edited by A. B. Tanguay and A. G. Gagnon. Scarborough, Ontario: Nelson Canada.

Smith, Bradley. 1996. "Faulty Assumptions and Undemocratic Consequences of Campaign Finance Reform." *Yale Law Journal* 105:1049.

Sorauf, Frank. 1957. "The Public Interest Reconsidered." *Journal of Politics* 19:616.

————. 1960. "The Silent Revolution in Patronage." *Public Administration Review* 20:28–34.

Sullivan, Kathleen. 1995. "Dueling Sovereignties: *U.S. Term Limits, Inc. v. Thornton.*" *Harvard Law Review* 109:98.

Sunstein, Cass. 1995. *Democracy and the Problem of Free Speech*. New York: Free Press.

Swan, George. 1996. "The Political Economy of Congressional Term Limits: *U.S. Term Limits, Inc. v. Thornton.*" *Alabama Law Review* 47:755.

Taagepera, Rein, and Matthew Shugart. 1989. *Seats and Votes: The Effects and Determinants of Electoral Systems*. New Haven, Conn.: Yale University Press.

Tedford, D. 1997. "Judge Criticizes Study on Affirmative Action: Warning May Signal Death Knell for City Program." *Houston Chronicle*, 15 November.

Thernstrom, Abigail. 1987. *Whose Votes Count? Affirmative Action And Minority Voting Rights*. Cambridge, Mass.: Harvard University Press.

Tocqueville, Alexis de. 1960. *Democracy in America*. Translated by George Lawrence. New York: Harper.

Tolchin, Martin, and Susan Tolchin. 1971. *To The Victor: Political Patronage from the Clubhouse to the White House*. New York: Vintage Books.

Trachtenberg, Jeffrey A. 1995. "CD Flap Embroils Apple." *Wall Street Journal*, 20 February, C1.

Tribe, Laurence 1980. "The Puzzling Persistence of Process Based Constitutional Theories." *Yale Law Journal* 89:1063.

Truman, David B. 1971. *The Governmental Process*. 2nd ed. New York: Alfred A. Knopf.

Tymkovich, T., J. D. Dailey, and P. Farley. 1997. "A Tale of Three Theories: Reason and Prejudice in the Battle Over Amendment 2." *University of Colorado Law Review* 68:287–333.

United States Senate. 1992. Committee on the Judiciary. *Report* No. 97-417. 97th Cong., 2nd Session, 25 May.

Volokh, Eugene. 1997. "Freedom of Speech, Shielding Children, and Transcending Balancing." *Supreme Court Review* 141:168.

Wall Street Journal. 1992. 4 February, A14.

Waters, M. Dane. 1998. *Initiative and Referendum Institute–1998 Pre-Election Synopsis* [http://www.iandrinstitute.org/98pre.htm].

Weisberg, Robert. 1978. "Collective v. Dyadic Representation in Congress." *American Political Science Review* 72:535–47.

Wellington, Harry. 1996. "Term Limits: History, Democracy and Constitutional Interpretation." *New York Law School Law Review* 40:833.

Wertheimer, Fred. 1980. "Commentary." In *Parties, Interest Groups, and Campaign Finance Laws*, edited by Michael Malbin. Washington, D.C.: American Enterprise Institute.

Westen, Peter. 1990. *Speaking of Equality*. Princeton, N.J.: Princeton University Press.

Weyrich, Paul M. 1980. "The New Right: PACs and Coalitional Politics." In *Parties, Interest Groups, and Campaign Finance Laws*, edited by Michael Malbin. Washington, D.C.: American Enterprise Institute.

Wilson, Bradford, and Ken Masugi. 1998. *The Supreme Court and American Constitutionalism*. Lanham, Md.: Rowman and Littlefield.

Wilson, James Q. 1961. "The Economy of Patronage." *Journal of Political Economy* 69:369–80.

Wolfinger, Raymond E. 1972. "Why Political Machines Have Not Withered Away and Other Revisionist Thoughts." *Journal of Politics* 34:365–98.

Wood, Gordon. 1969. *Representation in the American Revolution*. Charlottesville: University Press of Virginia.

Young, Iris Marion. 1990. *Justice and the Politics of Difference*. Princeton, N.J.: Princeton University Press.

Zywicki, Todd. 1994. "Federal Judicial Review of State Ballot Access Regulations: Escape From the Political Thicket." *Thurgood Marshall Law Review* 20:87.

Table of Cases

301

Index

activity representation vs. group representation, in Rehnquist Court, 21–22, 33–36

Adams, Terry v., 98, 112

Adarand Constructors, Inc. v. Pena, 84

affirmative action programs, 23, 205–6

African Americans: Chicago's patronage politics, 134, 136–37; white primaries, 98–99, 111–12. *See also* race-based districting; Voting Rights Act (1965)

Agostini v. Felton, 64

AIPAC (American Israel Public Affairs Committee), 27, 31, 36

Akins, FEC v., 27, 31, 36

Alabama, NAACP v., 113

Allen v. State Board, 56n5

Allwright, Smith v., 112

Ambach v. Norwick, 83

Amendment 2 (Colorado's initiative). *See* plebiscites, and minority group interests; *Romer v. Evans*

American Constitutional Law Foundation (ACLF), Buckley v. See Buckley v. American

Constitutional Law Foundation (ACLF)

American Independent Party, 114

American Israel Public Affairs Committee (AIPAC), 27, 31, 36

Amish communities, education rulings, 77

Anderson, John, 114

Anderson v. Celebrezze, 114, 118, 119, 147, 254–57

antidiscrimination laws, and rational basis standard, 211–13

anti-entrenchment theory, 260–61

Apple Computer, Inc., 86n12

Arizonans for Official English v. Arizona, 196

Arkansas, term limit initiative. *See U.S. Term Limits v. Thornton*

Arlington Heights v. Metropolitan Housing Dev. Corp., 86n7

Armenia, xi

Arsenault, Joseph G., 85n1

Arthur, King (anecdote), 221

Article I, U.S. Constitution, 227, 240n2

Aspen, Colorado, 212

associational rights. *See* cam-